Dear Reader:

The book you are about to read is the latest bestseller from the St. Martin's True Crime Library, the imprint *The New York Times* calls "the leader in true crime!" Each month, we offer you a fascinating account of the latest, most sensational crime that has captured the national attention. St. Martin's is the publisher of bestselling true crime author and crime journalist Kieran Crowley, who explores the dark, deadly links between a prominent Manhattan surgeon and the disappearance of his wife fifteen years earlier in THE SURGEON'S WIFE. Suzy Spencer's BREAKING POINT guides readers through the tortuous twists and turns in the case of Andrea Yates, the Houston mother who drowned her five young children in the family's bathtub. In Edgar Award-nominated DARK DREAMS, legendary FBI profiler Roy Hazelwood and bestselling crime author Stephen G. Michaud shine light on the inner workings of America's most violent and depraved murderers. In the book you now hold, TO HAVE AND TO KILL, acclaimed author John Glatt takes you along for the ride as he discovers the truth behind a suitcase filled with body parts.

St. Martin's True Crime Library gives you the stories behind the headlines. Our authors take you right to the scene of the crime and into the minds of the most notorious murderers to show you what really makes them tick. St. Martin's True Crime Library paperbacks are better than the most terrifying thriller, because it's all true! The next time you want a crackling good read, make sure it's got the St. Martin's True Crime Library logo on the spine—you'll be up all night!

D1096857

Charles E. Spicer, Jr.
Executive Editor, St. Martin's True Crime Library

Other True Crime Titles from
JOHN GLATT

Secrets in the Cellar

Forgive Me, Father

The Doctor's Wife

One Deadly Night

Depraved

Cries in the Desert

For I Have Sinned

Evil Twins

Cradle of Death

Blind Passion

Deadly American Beauty

Never Leave Me

Twisted

Available from St. Martin's True Crime Library

To Have

and

To Kill

*Nurse Melanie McGuire, an Illicit Affair, and
the Gruesome Murder of Her Husband*

John Glatt

St. Martin's Paperbacks

TO HAVE AND TO KILL

Copyright © 2008 by John Glatt.

Cover photos of Melanie and William McGuire © Jon and Sue Rice.
Cover photo of background © Getty Images.

All rights reserved.

For information address St. Martin's Press, 175 Fifth Avenue, New York, NY 10010.

ISBN: 978-1-250-02587-6

Printed in the United States of America

St. Martin's Paperbacks edition / December 2008

St. Martin's Paperbacks are published by St. Martin's Press, 175 Fifth Avenue, New York, NY 10010.

P1

To My Wife, Gail

A widow's peak is a descending V-shaped point in the middle of the hairline. The term comes from English folklore, where it was believed that this hair formation was a sign of a woman who would outlive her husband.

CONTENTS

ACKNOWLEDGMENTS

To explore the strange, distorted world of Melanie McGuire is like going through the looking glass—nothing is quite what it seems. And to this day many of the people who loved her are still trying to make sense of what she did.

On the one hand there's the highly respected fertility nurse, beloved by her fellow doctors and patients. And on the other is the convicted murderess, who a jury believed drugged and then shot her husband, Bill, the father of her children, dead, before cutting him into three pieces and throwing them into the Chesapeake Bay in matching designer suitcases.

"The depravity of this murder simply shocks the conscience of this court," Middlesex Superior Court Judge Frederick De Vesa declared, as he gave Melanie McGuire the maximum penalty. "One who callously destroys a family to accomplish her own selfish ends must face the most severe consequences that the law can provide."

The beautiful nurse seemed to have everything, with a loving husband and two beautiful children. But when she fell madly in love with her dashing boss Dr. Bradley Miller, the seeds of murder were planted.

I attended every day of Melanie McGuire's seven-week trial that played out like a Greek tragedy. And McGuire played her part to perfection. As she was out on bail at the time, she mingled freely with television producers and reporters all vying for her story.

I will never forget that beautiful spring day when the jury delivered its verdict, and how Melanie McGuire literally crumpled in front of our eyes. She and her parents had always vehemently protested her innocence. And they were certainly not expecting a guilty verdict, which will keep her behind bars for the rest of her life unless her upcoming appeal is successful.

During my exhaustive research for this book, I was helped by many of the main players in the case, some who wish to remain anonymous. Unfortunately, after some consideration, Melanie McGuire and her parents, Linda and Michael Cappararo, declined to be interviewed.

But I owe a huge debt of gratitude to Bill McGuire's family and friends, who freely spoke to me to set the record straight after the distorted way the defense portrayed him at trial.

I am most of all indebted to Bill McGuire's devoted older sister, Cindy Ligosh, who spent many hours talking to me over a two-year period. She is an amazing woman, who is now caring for his two young boys while seeking full custody. I was also helped by Bill's other sister Nancy Taylor, who shared her memories of him growing up. And gratitude also to Michael Cappararo Jr. for sharing his revealing memories of Melanie as a child.

Great thanks to his best friends, Jon and Sue Rice, who were instrumental in identifying Bill's dismembered body after it washed up near their home in Chesapeake, Virginia. And thanks for their hospitality during my visit to Virginia Beach. I also spent a delightful evening in a New York hotel with his other close friends, James and Lisa Carmichael, and their daughter, Chelsea.

Invaluable help also came from the former Assistant Attorney General of New Jersey, Patti Prezioso, and New Jersey State Police Detective Sergeant First Class David Dalrymple, who patiently guided me through the twists and turns of this complicated case and how they jointly led the investigation.

I would also like to thank: Beth Dunton, Chris Hinkle, Laura Ligosh, Detective Ray Pickell, Rick Malwitz, Jim O'Neill, Ken Serrano, Detective John Pizzuro, Kathy Chang, Susan Marcinczyk, Avi Cohen, Liza Finlay, Peter Aseltine,

Gail Faille, Detective William Scull, Denise Hacker, Grace Wong, Patti Sapone, Anthony Sclafani, Jaychandra Tandava, Lori Thomas, Selene Trevizas and Joe Tacopina.

As always thanks to my editor at St. Martin's Press, Charles Spicer, who first suggested to write this book, and his assistant Yaniv Soha, lawyer Michael K. Cantwell, super-agent Peter "The Lion" Miller, and Adrienne Rosado of PMA Literary and Film Management.

And not forgetting Jerome and Emily Freund, Debbie, Douglas and Taylor Baldwin, GKBC, Roger Hitts, Gertrude Gurcher, Danny and Allie Trachtenberg, Cari Pokrassa, Benny and Kim Sporano and Benny Jr., Virginia Randall, Don, Doug and Carol MacLeod and Annette Witheridge.

PART ONE

Virginia Beach

PROLOGUE

Wednesday, May 5, 2004

It was a welcome day off for Chris Henkle, who had a long-standing arrangement to go fishing with his friend Dee Connors. Early May is the start of the spring trophy fishing season in the Chesapeake Bay, with rock fish, striped bass and perch, and the burly Virginia Beach fireman rose at the crack of dawn.

At 5:45 a.m. he arrived at Connors' house, finding him already waiting outside with his young son Sam and daughter Claire, excited to be going on their first fishing trip. After loading Connors' twenty-one-foot fishing boat on a trailer, they made the short drive to the City Marina by Vista Circle.

But as they launched the small boat into the choppy waters, it started raining.

"It wasn't as nice as we hoped for," remembered Henkle. "The seas were kicking up a little bit, the wind was blowing and it was kinda chilly."

Around 7:30 a.m., Henkle took the wheel, heading out towards the 17.6-mile Chesapeake Bay Bridge-Tunnel, linking Virginia Beach to the Eastern Shore of Virginia—the Chesapeake Bay on one side and the Atlantic Ocean on the other.

Acclaimed as one of the seven engineering wonders of the modern world, the Bridge-Tunnel is composed of twelve miles of elevated roadway, two bridges, two mile-long tunnels and four artificial islands. It shaves 95 miles off the journey north from Virginia Beach to Delaware and beyond.

As the busy rush hour traffic hummed 75 feet above, Henkle followed the Bridge-Tunnel on the Chesapeake Bay side. By now it was raining hard and rough-going, as they passed the first island, where the bridge dramatically plunges into a mile-long tunnel, connecting to the next bridge at Island 2.

Eventually the wind dropped and the waters became calmer, as they sailed past Islands 3 and 4 to Fisherman Island, a private wildlife refuge at the tip of the Eastern Shore.

"We dropped anchor," remembered Henkle. "Fishing wasn't real good that day, but we caught a couple of little mud sharks, some little spot and flounder. The kids were having a blast."

By 10:00 a.m. the rain had stopped and it was warming up, so they turned back towards the four artificial islands, where the fishing was good.

As they passed Island 4, the two men were talking at the back of the boat, while 12-year-old Sam and his little sister played up front.

"Hey," said Connors suddenly. "You just passed a suitcase floating in the water. Turn around. Let's check it out."

So Henkle cut off the engine and turned around, where a medium-sized dark green suitcase was gently bobbing in the water. As he pulled alongside it, Connors and his son grabbed the expandable handle to pull it aboard. But it was too heavy.

Then Henkle came over and together they finally hauled it onboard.

"It's pirates' treasure," screamed Sam excitedly, unzipping the unlocked suitcase, which opened easily. Then the little boy folded back the soft cover to discover its contents, securely wrapped in thick black plastic trash bags.

"I was nervous and looking around," said Henkle. "Did we pick up something we shouldn't have? Is whoever dropped it still here to make sure it sunk?"

But before Henkle could tell him to zip it back up, Sam ripped open the soaking plastic bags, revealing two pale hairy legs, severed from the knees down.

The little boy screamed, recoiling in horror as Henkle

pulled him to the side of the boat. For several minutes they all just stared at the human legs without saying a word, as the terrible realization of what they had found dawned on them.

"I knew it was foul play," said Henkle. "Then I really started looking over my shoulder. Those legs looked very, very fresh. They didn't have an odor."

After closing the bag, he nervously dialed 911 on his cell phone. Although they were far closer to the Eastern Shore, the Virginia Beach police dispatcher answered.

"She thought I was kidding," he said. "I said, 'No. No. No. I need someone to come here and pick this thing up.'"

The dispatcher told him to go to Island 4, where the Bridge-Tunnel police would meet him.

Blood was leaking out of the suitcase, so the two men placed it at the back of the boat. Then they headed towards Island 4.

When, after half an hour of circling it, there was still no sign of police, Henkle dialed 911 again. The dispatcher apologized for the delay, telling them to proceed to Island 2, promising that a police boat was already on its way.

When the same thing happened at Island 2, Henkle became angry.

"It was more than an hour after we had found the case," he remembered, "and I'm really not happy. The boy was traumatized. I told him, 'There's no reason to get upset and nothing in there is going to hurt you. It's something really bad, and you don't need to worry about it.'"

Finally, Henkle dialed 911 a third time, announcing that they were returning to the Virginia Beach marina.

"There was starting to be a mess," said Henkle. "The deck of the boat had turned pink. Blood was seeping out and I was worried."

It was around noon, about two hours after they had found the suitcase, as they approached the Lesner Bridge, that a Virginia Beach Special Operations Marine Patrol police boat came alongside. Then Henkle and Connors picked up the suitcase and threw it onto the police boat, telling the two officers to look inside.

ONE

The Suitcases

When Master Officer John Runge of Virginia Beach's Marine Patrol Unit first received a report of a suitcase containing human legs, he didn't know what to think. It was one of the first hot days of the year and the veteran ex-naval officer, whose crack unit patrols the Chesapeake Bay area around Virginia Beach, was looking forward to a quiet shift.

"The water was calm and it was hot outside," he remembered. "Murder was the last thing on my mind."

After placing the suitcase on the front bow of his patrol boat, Officer Runge told Chris Henkle and Dee Connors to go to the City Marina to be interviewed. Then he put on a pair of gloves and unfastened the zipper.

"There were black-colored trash bags in the suitcase," he said. "Once I peeled [them] back I saw a pair of human legs from the knees down. Then I zipped it back, called my superior and asked for a homicide detective to meet me."

At 12.30 p.m., Virginia Beach Homicide Detective Janine Hall had just finished testifying in court when her pager went off. She was then told to go the marina by Vista Circle to check out a possible murder.

The former U.S. Air Force officer, who had worked the tough Virginia Beach beat for four years, arrived at the Marina at 1:06 p.m., where she was joined by Steve Stockman, a senior technician at the Virginia Beach Police Department Forensics Unit.

"I walked to the dock," she recalled. "I saw John Runge on one of our police boats [with] a closed dark green carry-on case."

She then paged Virginia Beach Medical Examiner Dr. Turner Gray, who arrived at the marina within minutes. A police launch took the three of them over to join Runge on the police boat.

As Stockman photographed the suitcase from all angles, Dr. Gray donned a pair of medical gloves and carefully opened it.

"I observed a large black plastic bag with yellow drawstrings," Detective Hall would later testify. "Dr. Gray opened the garbage bags and I [saw] two legs. There was no decomposition or decay. They were cut off around the knee area and there was a blue paper towel in there."

Then Dr. Gray closed the suitcase, placing it in a large clear plastic bag, and brought it to his office in Norfolk, Virginia, for autopsy.

Several hours later, Dr. Wendy Gunther, the assistant chief medical examiner for Virginia Beach, carefully removed the legs from the black trash bags. She then laid them out on a surgical table in an autopsy bay.

"This was very unusual," said the round-faced bespectacled pathologist, who has performed more than 3,000 autopsies in her long career. "I have never before received a pair of legs from the knees down."

Although it was impossible to tell gender from lower legs, it was obvious they were male from the hairy muscular calves.

"You could tell they were right and left," she said. "They looked like they'd been sawed off, and they also looked fresh. They had no smell . . . like the legs of people who come from the hospital the day before. The right leg was cut through the knee, exposing the tibia. It looked like a saw mark, cutting through the cartilage, and the muscle looked kind of fresh."

She also noted there was no blood where the knees had been severed, as though someone had started to cut and suddenly stopped. There was little else she could do, except taking blood and hairs for DNA analysis.

Then Detective Hall brought the medium-sized Kenneth

Cole Reaction suitcase back to the Virginia Beach police head-quarters, to be forensically examined the following day.

Later that evening, she briefed her colleague Detective Doug Zebley, who was to head up the homicide investigation. Early the next morning, he drove to the medical examiner's office in Norfolk, Virginia, to meet Dr. Gunther.

"At that point my investigation was focused on who could these [legs] belong to," said Investigator Zebley, "since this was all I had at the time."

Then, after taking X-rays of the lower legs to a radiologist, for information about height, weight and age, Zebley went to the Virginia Beach P.D. Forensics Unit, to examine the suitcase.

"It was a carry-on bag with an expandable handle and wheels," he said. "Something that you would carry onto an airplane."

Inside the case Zebley discovered a Marshalls price tag, faxing the UPC code to the store's head office, to see where it had been purchased.

Then the Virginia Beach Police Department's Forensic Unit supervisor, Beth Dunton, who works crime-scene investigations, and her senior technician, Steve Stockman, began testing for trace evidence.

"When I first saw the legs, it looked almost surreal," said Dunton. "I thought to myself, 'This is the start of something that's going to be very, very bad.'"

The attractive blonde forensics expert noted that the bag was in fairly good condition, with only a little dampness, and there were no apparent traces of blood or biological fluids. But the two black plastic trash bags, which had contained the legs, were covered in a slimy wet film.

First they hung the bags in a six-foot-tall cyanoacrylate fuming chamber, where the fumes given off by heated super-glue attach themselves to fingerprints, rendering them easily visible. Then Dunton sprayed the bags with MBD, a fluorescent dye, to enhance the results. But there were no signs of any fingerprints.

At the bottom on the suitcase she found two blue paper towels and a piece of blue painter's tape with a hair attached to it.

These were also tested in the fuming chamber with negative results, the hair being sent to a Norfolk laboratory for analysis.

With the lucrative summer vacation season just weeks away, Beth Dunton and her team were under tremendous pressure to come up with results fast, because Virginia Beach officials were horrified at the negative impact that the discovery of human body parts could have on tourist dollars.

On Thursday, May 6, *The Virginian Pilot* broke the story, running a brief report of the suitcase, without revealing that two legs had been found:

A fisherman Wednesday found a suitcase containing human remains floating in the Chesapeake Bay. A preliminary investigation showed the remains to be that of a white male. Detectives are reviewing missing persons' reports and are seeking the public's help in identifying the man. Anyone with information is asked to call Crime Solvers.

For the next few days detectives and forensic experts could do little but sit tight, until the results of the DNA tests came in.

"Now we were anxiously waiting for the rest of the body," explained Dr. Gunther.

Four days later, on Monday, May 10, a young female graduate student was picking up litter on the Fisherman Island bird sanctuary when she spotted a large dark green suitcase lying on the sandy beach. Initially, she didn't pay it much attention, but the following day, when it was still there, she took a closer look.

It was midday, with temperatures in the high seventies, as she bent down and began to unzip the side. She had just opened it a few inches when the overpowering odor of rotting flesh first hit her. Then she glimpsed a human shoulder and screamed, running down the beach to call the police.

Beth Dunton was about to leave for work when she heard that a second suitcase had been found. She immediately jumped in her car, driving to the Chesapeake Bay Bridge-Tunnel Toll Plaza. There she met Medical Examiner Dr. Turner Gray and Virginia Beach Homicide Detectives Doug Zebley, Ray Pickell and Brian Seabold.

After paying the $12 toll, they drove in a convoy almost the entire length of the Bridge-Tunnel to Fisherman Island, nestled under the tunnel off the Eastern Shore and off-limits to the public.

"We met in the parking lot area," remembered Dunton. "And we all went over to the suitcase. From the smell, we knew we had another body part in there."

The large thirty-inch Kenneth Cole Reaction suitcase was lying face down in the sand with both zippers open, revealing the end of a black plastic trash bag. It was in far worse condition than the earlier suitcase, and waterlogged, with a lot of sand in it. It had probably been on the beach for several hot days before being discovered.

After Dunton photographed it from all angles, she and Dr. Gray placed the case, weighing between 70 and 80 pounds, into a black body bag, before putting it in a tin tub.

"We loaded it into my truck," said Dunton. "And we immediately brought it to a controlled, sterile environment."

On arrival at the medical examiner's office in Norfolk, the case was put on an autopsy table and more photographs were taken. Then, with Beth Dunton and Detectives Pickell and Seabold observing, Dr. Gray unzipped the top flap of the suitcase and folded it back, revealing black plastic trash bags inside.

"It smelled like decomposing flesh, rotten fish and the actual sea or bay water," recalled Beth Dunton.

The contents of this suitcase had been carefully packaged in four separate trash bags, two large industrial-sized ones and two small kitchen-type ones, with yellow drawstrings.

"We were doing it in a step-by-step procedure," explained Dunton. "Unzip it—photograph it. Start to remove the bags away from the torso—photograph it. So each step we took to remove the torso from the suitcase was documented."

It took a few minutes for Dr. Gray to carefully prise the trash bags apart and open them.

"It revealed the torso of a white male, his head and arms still attached," said Beth Dunton.

The torso was lying on its back in the suitcase, the right arm up over the shoulder. The left arm was under the chest across the belly, with three fingers curled. His first finger and thumb were in a cocked position, as if pointing a gun.

One of the kitchen-type bags had been raised over his head, while another went from the severed part up. The two bags met in the middle of his chest. Then two larger trash bags had been placed over them, from either end.

"The head was attached," she said. "You didn't have to look hard to see the bullet hole in his forehead, and then there was one on his back. They stood out. His eyes were closed, and let's hope that he was asleep."

A heavily bloodstained blanket had been wrapped around the back of the head to the ears, bunching up around the chin without covering the face. When Dunton removed it, she immediately recognized it as hospital linen, noting a tag reading "Property of HCSC." She later made a Google search, discovering that it had come from an Allentown, Pennsylvania–based medical supply company.

The head and torso were in the early stages of decomposition. The skin was discolored with gray-green marbling, and pale white, green and red spots. There was also skin slippage, and some hair had fallen off.

The hands had washerwoman's syndrome—severe wrinkling from the effects of being in the water so long. But there was little sign of any blood or other biological fluids.

"This was one of the most brutal crimes I have seen," said Dunton, who had worked seventeen years in CSI forensics. "The fact that somebody can dismember another human being like a piece of meat is just very disturbing."

Dr. Turner Gray carefully maneuvered the head and torso out of the trash bags and onto a gurney. All the internal organs were visible, near the jagged cut-line at the waist.

"The insides were coming out onto the gurney," remembered Detective Ray Pickell. "But I don't remember seeing a lot of blood on the body itself. There was decomposition, but no blood that was pooling or spilling out onto the gurney."

Then the torso was placed in a freezer, until it could be

autopsied the next day. Beth Dunton placed the suitcase, trash bags and blanket in a biohazard bag, for testing back in her laboratory at Virginia Beach police headquarters.

On arrival, she first placed the trash bags and blanket in a drying chamber, before processing for fingerprints and trace evidence. Then she searched the suitcase, finding a 5.5-pound Weider weight in one of the front small zipper pockets, as well as Marshalls store tags.

"I guess people watch television and think they can easily weigh down a body with a weight," she said. "But you have to have four times the body weight to actually weigh down somebody successfully."

Then, after taking more photographs, she examined the suitcase under luminescent fluorescent lights for blood, finding none. The trash bags were then fume-tested in the superglue chamber, but again there were no fingerprints.

She then sent the blood-stained blanket for forensic analysis, before logging the five trash bags and Weider weight into the property evidence room.

That night, lead investigator Detective Doug Zebley took account of the new evidence from the second suitcase.

"At least this gave me something," he would later recount. "And now I could find out who this man was. I noted he had short hair, and with our high military population, that was the direction we went in first."

TWO

Breakthrough

The next morning Dr. Wendy Gunther performed an autopsy on the head and torso, observed by Detective Ray Pickell and Beth Dunton, who documented it with photographs.

"I saw the body of a white man beginning to decompose," Dr. Gunther would later testify. "He was between thirty and forty and looked healthy, muscular and not overweight. The scalp hair was brown and about half an inch long. It was beginning to slide off."

She first X-rayed the body, immediately seeing two bullets, one in the chest and the other lower down in the belly, where the guts were hanging out. But she quickly decided that neither of these bullets had been fatal.

She then examined the face and nose with her hands, finding that they were not fractured. She noted the whites of the eyes were very pale, and there was no sign of petechiae—minute hemorrhages in the blood vessels that indicate strangulation. The chest appeared normal and muscular, and the teeth were natural.

"I saw the entry and exit gunshot wounds on the head," she later testified. "Both of the bullets that killed him seemed to have entered and exited the body."

She then sawed through the top of the skull, carefully removing it to reveal the brain, which was dark red and coated with old blood.

"[The bullet] enters on the left side of his forehead [and]

goes through his skull," she explained. "Right through the frontal bone. And it goes through his parietal bone on the opposite side and through his brain . . . leaving little pieces of lead wipe."

But the brain was so badly decomposed that it liquefied and fell apart when Dr. Gunther tried to remove it from the skull.

"We had a pan there waiting to catch it," she said. "So we were able to weigh it. I took my knife and made cuts through it. And I could see the bloody decomposed rot, where the bullet must have passed through. And it goes in a straight line from where the bullet goes in and goes out. But if you asked me what fine structure of his brain it went through, I don't know, because he's starting to rot. Going bad."

Then she turned her attention to the lower chest and abdomen, where there was another fatal gunshot wound. This bullet had entered the abdomen, just below the edge of his ribs, three-and-three-quarter inches left of midline. It had probably traveled through the lung before exiting out of the back, and has never been recovered.

It was impossible to determine if he had been shot three or four times, as the bullet could have been a short return, partially exiting the body and then falling back—something highly unusual, but not impossible.

"It was very frustrating," explained Dr. Gunther. "The bullet went right through his lung and leaves [the] back, after shattering his fifth rib."

She described this exit wound as being like "a big halo of blood," proving that the victim had been alive when shot.

The doctor then retrieved the two bullets still embedded in the body. The first, removed from the chest cavity area, was in pristine condition. But getting the second bullet proved far more difficult, for as the torso was lifted onto a gurney and rolled onto the stomach, the guts spilled out all over the place.

"Everything started shifting," explained Dunton. "The second bullet was found loose on the gurney, close to the waist area. A lot of the insides came out, and the bullet was under that."

This bullet was covered in green fibers, like ones used in furniture upholstery.

"There was another piece of fiber wrapped around the head," said Dunton. "Then I collected DNA of the torso to see if all the body parts matched up."

Dr. Gunther also took just 1,100 ccs of blood from the body cavity, leading her to believe that the unfortunate victim had been bled out before being dismembered.

"[The cause of death] was that he was shot through the head and chest," said Dr. Gunther. "That was the only part of the case that was easy."

Heavy media coverage after the discovery of the second suitcase led to the Virginia Beach Marine Patrol being deluged with sightings of more.

"Every single lead and report had to be looked at and investigated," said Beth Dunton. "I traveled across that Chesapeake Bay Bridge I don't know how many times."

Everyone knew there had to be another suitcase out there somewhere, with the remaining body parts, plunging the popular tourist destination into a grisly real-life whodunnit.

"So you've got the mayor looking closely at developments," said Dunton. "The city council and those at the highest levels. 'Hey what's going on with this? What can you tell me?' And you say, 'Nothing much.' It's coming right on the heels of our big summer tourist season. The pressure is there."

On Sunday, May 16, Carl and Linda Stevens found the third and final Kenneth Cole Reaction suitcase, floating off the Bridge-Tunnel's second island, where it was drifting in the current. By now the recreational boaters knew enough to immediately call police without touching it. And this time the Virginia Beach Marine Patrol tied the suitcase to the back of their patrol boat, dragging it back to the marina.

It was Beth Dunton's day off when she learned the news.

"At that point everyone pretty well knew," she said.

She immediately drove to City Marina, meeting Detective Zebley and Dr. Gray. Then they went to the dock area, where the new suitcase had been placed under a yellow safety blanket.

The CSI specialist first removed the blanket, immediately

recognizing a small twenty-six-inch Kenneth Cole suitcase, matching the other two. It was lying flat on its back, with two marine patrol ropes still attached.

The smallest of the three, it was full of water and extremely heavy. "This was probably the most potent of all the suitcases," Dunton said. "Again it was a strong odor of decomposing flesh, rotten fish and that nasty bay water." After photographing it, she put it in a white body bag, placing it in the same metal tub as the first one.

At the medical examiner's office in Norfolk, it was placed on a gurney in an autopsy bay. Then Dr. Gray opened it, revealing more black trash bags covered in slimy, oily film.

"You knew that this was probably going to be the least pleasant of them all," said Dunton. "You've got a body part that's opened at both ends. It had been out there the longest, so the rate of decomposition, decay and slippage was going to be much greater than the other two."

Dr. Gray found it extremely difficult to find the trash bags' openings. So, cautious not to destroy any trace evidence, he decided to remove the trash bags from the suitcase with the body part still inside, giving him more space to work in. Only when the bag and its grisly contents were placed on a gurney did he find the opening.

He then carefully pried it apart, discovering a smaller plastic kitchen bag, with yellow drawstrings, inside.

"We parted that," said Dunton. "And that is when we discovered the midsection of a white male. It had been severed at the waist and above both the left and right knee."

The midsection, still wearing a bloodstained pair of Fruit of the Loom men's briefs, was in far worse condition than the others.

"[There] was more decomposition," said Dunton. "The skin had a greenish tint to it. There was much more skin slippage, especially around the wounds where it had been severed."

The mid-torso had three cuts—one through the waist, and the others above where the left and right knees would have been.

"At each cut site," said Beth Dunton, "there was exposed tissue and bone."

After leaving the midsection behind at the medical examiner's office for autopsy, Dunton put the trash bags back in the suitcase, which was placed in a biohazard bag.

Later that day, back in her laboratory, she examined the suitcase under luminol and tested with superglue. Once again there were no fingerprints.

Then she searched the case, opening the inside flap to find a reordering form for the suitcase. In an exterior flap was another small Marshalls tag, which also tested negative for fingerprints. But she did find three strands of hair in the soiled briefs, which were sent off for testing.

On Monday morning, Dr. Wendy Gunther performed her third and final autopsy.

"This one was below the belly button to above the knees," she explained. "It was also badly decomposed and the connective tissue was exposed. The bladder was still intact. The testicles were normal."

She then removed the bones from the flesh, so they could be examined by a tool mark expert, to determine what instrument had been used to dismember the body.

A few hours later Dr. David Barron of the Virginia Department of Forensic Science received blood and urine samples from the torso for routine tests for ethanol/alcohol, cocaine and opiates. He found a trace amount of ethanol, but no cocaine or opiates, before returning the samples to the chief medical examiner.

That night, Beth Dunton worked late in her laboratory. "What in the world has this man done to deserve this?" she asked herself. "Who could have hated him so much? Who is this individual? Let's put a name to him. Let's contact his family members," so he could at least have a decent funeral. "Let's take care of him the best we can and find out who did this."

On Wednesday, May 19, Detective Ray Pickell replaced Doug Zebley as lead detective. So far investigators had not been able to match any DNA, hair or blood samples taken from the victim. All inquiries to the local military bases had proved fruitless.

Virginia Beach police spokesman Don Rimer told *The Virginian Pilot* that police had "exhausted" all missing person reports in the Hampton Roads area, covering Virginia Beach, Chesapeake, Norfolk and outlying areas. He pointed out that there were thousands of missing persons in North America every year.

Soon after being assigned the case, 43-year-old Detective Pickell asked a police sketch artist to prepare a drawing of the head from photographs.

"Hopefully we could develop some phone calls to identify who the victim was," said Pickell. "I provided her with several photographs of the victim, which I dropped off in her office."

Two days later, Detective Pickell released the pencil sketch to the media, and waited to see what would happen next.

THREE

The Sketch

On Friday May 21, the suitcase victim sketch led off the early morning news on all four TV network affiliates.

At 8:25 a.m. Susan Rice, a Chesapeake mother of three, was dressing for work when it appeared on her bedroom TV set. She froze as she instantly recognized the bloated face as belonging to Bill McGuire, her husband Jon's best friend and the best man at their wedding.

Three weeks earlier, the computer analyst had disappeared from his apartment in Woodbridge, New Jersey, just hours after closing on a half-million-dollar house. After receiving a call from McGuire's anxious sister Cindy Ligosh, the Rices had become increasingly concerned for his safety.

When Jon Rice had telephoned Bill's wife Melanie, she'd told a strange story. The beautiful fertility nurse had described how Bill had attacked her in front of their little son, just hours after they signed contract for the new house. He had stuffed a dryer sheet in her mouth, and, fearing for her life, she had taken the little boy into the bathroom and locked the door. Then, she told Jon, Bill had stormed out, shouting that she would be the reason their two young sons would never see him again.

Since that alarming conversation, the Rices had called Bill's cell phones repeatedly, leaving dozens of messages. They had become more and more worried, going as far as phoning around casinos in Atlantic City, where he liked to gamble.

Like everyone else in Virginia Beach, they had closely followed the sensational suitcase murder story. The previous Sunday night, they had seen a TV news report about the third suitcase washing up in the Chesapeake Bay. Jon had even remarked how "strange" it would be if it turned out to be Bill, instantly dismissing the idea as too far-fetched.

But now as Sue scrutinized the police sketch, she instinctively knew it was their best friend, the godfather to their youngest son Austin.

"It was him," she said. "I was shaky and I got sick."

After composing herself, she called Bill's older sister Cindy Ligosh, to see if he was still missing, without mentioning the sketch. Cindy said he was.

Then Sue went online, comparing a recent photograph of Bill with the police sketch now posted on a local television news site.

"I put the two together," she explained. "The sketch was very bloated, but that's what happens to a body in water. So I'm thinking, 'If it were shrunken in the hairline?' Suddenly it was like 9/11 all over again. It was just too close."

She then telephoned the Virginia Beach Crime Solvers hotline, saying she believed the sketch to be William McGuire from Woodbridge, New Jersey, missing since the end of April. The operator told her to e-mail a photograph of Bill, saying a detective would be in touch.

But by late afternoon when no one had called, Sue phoned Crime Solvers again, and was told all the detectives had left for the weekend.

When her husband Jon returned home at 5:30 p.m., she showed him the sketch, saying she thought it was Bill. He then called Virginia Beach Homicide, and was put straight through to Detective Ray Pickell, who spent the next forty-five minutes on the phone with Jon.

After the call, Detective Pickell ran a computer check on William McGuire. "He had been charged with [a felony offense]," said Pickell, "and been fingerprinted in our city," in the early 1980s, while in the Navy and stationed at Norfolk.

The detective then requested fingerprints from the suitcase victim, so they could be compared with those on record for McGuire.

At 9.30 p.m., Detective Pickell telephoned the Rices, asking them to come straight down to police headquarters to view photographs. When they arrived at Building 11, Princess Anne Road, twenty minutes later, there were several TV crews outside, covering the "Suitcase Murder" story.

"We walked though," said Sue Rice. "They had no idea who we were."

The lean mustached detective met them at the front desk, bringing them into a small room in the detectives' bureau. He then seated them around a table and started showing them black-and-white photographs of the body, while asking more questions about their friend.

"Then he showed us the colored ones," remembered Sue. "He had to prepare us, because there was the slippage. The body was bloated, so you had to use your imagination."

With her hands, Sue masked out the hairline and the bloating, to get a better idea of the features.

"It's so weird," she explained. "You have to look at the eyes, the nose, the mouth—and by [using my hands to block parts of the face] that was Bill. He had long eyelashes. That was still there. He had this little red mark. That was still there. The nose, the mouth, the crooked teeth—that was Bill."

But one close-up picture of the head was particularly disturbing, showing the fatal bullet wound to the temple. To try to spare them, the detective discreetly placed his hand over the gaping hole.

"There was this ugly, ugly dark thing on the temple that Detective Pickell kept hiding," said Sue. "I kept trying to pull it over because it gave that other side of Bill."

As they viewed the gruesome pictures, Jon Rice became more and more emotional, at one point bursting into tears.

"I didn't want it to be Bill," he remembered. "Anything but that."

Finally, Detective Pickell asked, on a percentage scale of one to a hundred, how likely they thought that this was Bill McGuire. Jon Rice said he was only 60 percent certain, while his wife said 85 percent.

"I felt he was in denial," said Detective Pickell. "He just didn't want to believe it was his friend. It was actually Mrs. Rice that gave me the nod that she believed it was him."

After the Rices left police headquarters, Pickell phoned Woodbridge Police Department. He was put through to Detective Sergeant Joseph Joraskie, who was working the night shift.

"I explained a little about the case," remembered Pickell, "and asked him if he could do some intel work on the name William McGuire."

At around midnight, Detective Joraskie called back, saying he had run a computer check, discovering that McGuire's wife Melanie had filed a temporary restraining order on April 30, alleging violence. But she had never reported him missing.

"That was suspicious," said Detective Pickell. "She'd filed a restraining order against him, and now we've got his body."

The next day, Detective Pickell received confirmation that the suitcase victim's fingerprints matched William McGuire's. When he informed Woodbridge police, Detective Joraskie offered to personally give Melanie McGuire the official death notification.

"I asked him not to," said Detective Pickell, "because I had every intention of getting into my car the next day to make it in person. That's the most crucial point. And I wanted to see her reaction, when I presented her [with] the news of the death of her husband. Because I did not believe Melanie McGuire was a grieving widow."

PART TWO

A Marriage Made in Hell

FOUR

Lolita

Melanie Lyn Slate was born on October 18, 1972, in Ridgewood, New Jersey, to Bob and Linda Slate. When she was still an infant, her father walked out on the family, moving to California. Four years later he died of liver cancer, leaving his tiny daughter feeling confused and abandoned.

Now a single mother, Linda Slate moved into a house in Oradell, New Jersey, with her parents Ann and William Moritz and two sisters, Debbie and Jan, who all helped bring up her baby daughter. She found a job working as a secretary in a large midtown Manhattan computer company, commuting to and from New Jersey.

Linda then embarked on a passionate love affair with her married boss, Michael Cappararo, who often stayed overnight at the Slates' Oradell home. A year into the affair, Cappararo started bringing along his young son Michael Jr. as a cover.

"It was a very big secret," remembered Michael Jr., then in the fifth grade. "My father always told me she was just a friend, but as I got older I realized what was going on. But I was instructed to keep this a secret."

Michael Jr. and Melanie, who was four years younger, would be left to play together for hours, while their respective parents spent time alone.

"I grew up with Melanie," explained Michael Jr. "She could always get you to do whatever she wanted. She always got her own way [and] could talk people into anything."

In 1978, Linda moved Melanie, now 6 years old, and her grandparents into an affluent apartment complex in Perth Amboy, New Jersey. Melanie soon made friends with the other kids in the complex.

"I met Melanie when we were six years old," remembered Selene Rodriguez, whose family lived next door. "She was a timid little girl."

The two soon became inseparable. "She was like my sister," said Selene. "We always visited at her house."

Melanie enrolled in a public school in Woodbridge and was a model student, always getting high grades with minimum work. She was smarter than her other classmates, possessing a natural academic ability and a photographic memory.

"She was every mother's dream," said Linda Slate. "A good girl. Never got into trouble. Happy. Wonderful student."

Over the next several years, Michael Jr. found himself becoming increasingly conflicted about having to keep his father's affair secret from his mother, who had no idea.

"I was a little kid and I was part of it," he explained. "I didn't know right from wrong."

When his parents eventually separated, putting the family home up for sale, Michael Jr. finally told his mother about Linda Slate.

"He was blaming it all on her," he explained. "My mother was very upset, that's why I had to open my mouth and tell her."

When his divorce came through, Michael Cappararo Sr. went to live with Linda and her family in a house on Allaire Avenue, an affluent neighborhood in Middletown, New Jersey. Michael Jr. moved in with them, where he bonded with Melanie.

"She was a smart girl," he recalled. "She and her mom were very close—she was a mama's girl."

Now 10 years old, Melanie did not get on with the new man in her mother's life, who was a strict disciplinarian. And when she rebelled, there were angry arguments.

"She got a little out of control," remembered Michael Jr. "There were a few heated battles. My father was very, very strict, and they really did not get along."

Always a manipulative child, Melanie became adept at getting her own way by playing her mother off against Michael Cappararo.

"If my father told her 'No' for something," said Michael Jr., "she would go to her mother, who would tell her 'Yes.' Or she would try to get me to talk to my father for her, so she could go out or something. But I wasn't getting involved in that."

There was also friction between Michael Jr. and Linda, who felt that his father treated him better than Melanie.

Things got calmer in 1982, when Linda became pregnant with Michael Sr.'s baby, giving birth to a boy they named Christopher. But it would be several years before they finally married and legitimized him.

Soon after they moved, Melanie had entered Middletown High School South, proving an exceptional student, always at the top of her class.

"Everything came to her very easily," said Selene, who had now moved to Brooklyn with her parents, staying in close touch. "She was very smart and always an overachiever when it came to school."

Every weekend Michael Cappararo Sr., now working as a service manager for Time Warner, took the family to Atlantic City. He and Linda would leave the children alone in a hotel room for hours at a time, while they played high-stakes blackjack or poker.

"It was boring," remembered Michael Jr. "He'd just leave us to roam around, whatever, or give us money to go to the game room or the pool."

While the adults spent the day at Caesars or the Playboy casino (then renamed the Atlantis Casino), Michael and Melanie watched TV movies or walked up and down the Boardwalk, until their parents had finished. According to Michael, his father was such a heavy gambler, several casinos provided free limousines and hotel suites, something that he liked to brag about.

"They used to take me too," said Selene Rodriguez. "We went to restaurants on the Boardwalk and I really liked going there."

Now in her early teens, Melanie was becoming more self-confident, with her own set of friends. And she had an innate talent for selecting weaker characters, who looked to her for emotional support.

The petite girl was blossoming into a stunning beauty, with nut brown eyes set wide apart in a pixyish face. Wherever she went, she turned heads, openly flirting with the boys at her school, upsetting several female classmates.

In 1985, Michael Cappararo Sr. took Linda and the kids to vacation in Aruba with the family of a close friend. During the Mexican trip, 13-year-old Melanie lost her virginity to an older boy.

"She was fooling around with him," remembers Michael Jr., who was there when it happened. "She was thirteen at the time and he was nineteen. We would go out every night to bars and the casino. I think that's where she picked up gambling."

After Aruba, Melanie embarked on a series of affairs at Middletown High South.

"She was very promiscuous," said her stepbrother. "She had a lot of boyfriends, and she also had affairs while she was with them. They were kind of weak and fairly timid, and she got what she wanted from them—dinners, meals, any kind of gifts."

One day Melanie boasted to Michael Jr. that she was having affairs with two of her high school teachers, who were both married.

Reportedly, her stepfather found out about one of the affairs, threatening to go to the school principal if the teacher didn't stop seeing his daughter.

"She was kind of proud of it," said Michael Jr. "Because I made a joke about it, saying, 'So that's how you're getting good grades.' And she just smiled."

But whatever the reason for Melanie's high grades, she had an excellent academic reputation at school, always setting herself tough goals and working hard to achieve them.

In addition to her demanding schedule, she also worked part-time as a check-out girl at a Chapel Hill A&P supermarket, as well as a TCBY store in Red Bank.

Every summer, the family summered in Wildwood, New Jersey, where Michael Cappararo Sr. had rented an efficiency apartment.

During the trips, Melanie and Michael Jr. would walk the Boardwalk and piers, going target shooting on the rifle range. Melanie and her mother would spend hours together, reading the latest true crime magazines, and watching TV cop shows.

"I always thought Melanie was going to be a cop," said Michael Jr. "They were always into these detective magazines."

On their rare weekends in Middletown, Melanie and Michael Jr. would take day trips together, or hang out at their backyard pool with friends.

"We went to different parties together," he said. "We didn't have a lot of low time."

According to Michael, Melanie was an incorrigible gossip, making many enemies at school. But she was highly articulate, using her razor-sharp wit as an effective weapon against any adversary.

"She didn't get along with girls that much," he said. "If she didn't like you, she could be very cold. Even if she did like you, she would still talk about you behind your back. She'd be your best friend one day and the next she'd be out with somebody else, talking behind your back."

Melanie also had a vicious temper, which could flare up at the least perceived slight.

"If you made her mad," explained Michael Jr., "you could see the rage in her. There were a couple of fistfights, and I've seen her hit people."

In her final two years at Middletown High School South, Melanie was active in the school theatrical society, taking leading roles in several school productions, including Neil Simon's *Brighton Beach Memoirs.*

Her lengthy entry in the school's 1989 junior yearbook lists her as a member of the National Honor Society and treasurer of the Spanish Club, as well as being in the school chorus.

Melanie's high school friend R. Armen McOmber often acted in plays with her, remembering her fondly.

"She was a good person, a good student," said McOmber. "She was very bright."

But in addition to her academic accomplishments, "she was a partier," says her stepbrother, who sometimes accompanied her to heavy metal music concerts, and clubbing in Manhattan. "Lots of boyfriends."

Whenever Michael Cappararo tried to rein her in, she became more rebellious than ever. There would be terrible arguments.

"She'd walk out and slam the door," said Michael Jr. "She'd talk back."

But soon Melanie would come to an understanding with Michael Cappararo, gradually accepting him as her very own father.

In 1990, Melanie Slate graduated in the top 5 percent of her class. She now set her sights on a career, enrolling in Rutgers University for a double major in Math and Psychology.

She moved into the red-brick Hagemann Hall dormitory, going home most weekends. She immediately applied herself to university life, joining several societies and groups, being appointed the student manager of the Brower Commons dining hall.

Her enigmatic beauty also attracted the attention of the male students, with whom she started several long-term relationships.

Late one night in the fall of 1992, Melanie was studying in the basement lounge when she struck up a conversation with a young male student. Anthony Scalfani had attempted suicide the previous April, after breaking up with his girlfriend. Despondent, he had driven his car at high speed off the end of a ramp by his dormitory, fracturing his neck and breaking a shoulder. After a long recuperation, he had returned to Rutgers, feeling desperately alone and suicidal. Then he met Melanie Slate.

"We began talking," remembered Sclafani. "She was friendly and very nice."

The nervous student immediately felt comfortable with Melanie, telling her about his suicide attempt.

"I had essentially given up on people," he said. "So without Melanie taking the time and just talking to me about the events, I really don't think I would have made it."

Over the next few weeks they met every night in the dormitory basement, with Melanie offering advice and guidance.

"We would talk for hours about my experiences and feelings toward my ex-girlfriend," explained Sclafani. "Melanie would always calm me down and keep [me] from doing ridiculous things. She was the only one who seemed like she wanted to help. There was nothing in it for her."

Before long, Sclafani fell in love with Melanie, eventually plucking up the courage to kiss her. But she gently pushed him away, saying she was not the right girl for him.

"She just said, 'Look, this isn't what's best for you now,'" he remembered. "She was a stronger person than I was at the time. A lot more adult."

From then on, she would always give him a hug at the end of their emotional talks.

"Nothing would mean more to me than the embrace we shared at the end of each night," he would later explain.

Soon afterwards, Melanie began dating one of his friends and he found a girlfriend. But Sclafani would always carry a torch for Melanie, as so many other young men would over the next few years.

"Melanie's a very bright girl," says Selene. "But when it came to men, she wasn't that bright at all. Her choices in men weren't the best. She dated this guy Mark that I actually set her up with. He wasn't such a nice guy, but she stayed with him for a little while."

Her stepbrother Michael believes she was far too selfish to ever be truly in love.

"She's a very self-centered person," he said. "Everything always had to be about her, and it had to be her way. If a boyfriend wanted to go to the movies and she wanted to go to a club, they'd have to go to the club, otherwise there would be a big fight."

In the spring of 1994, Melanie, now 22, graduated from Rutgers with a baccalaureate degree in Statistics and Psychology.

But instead of pursuing those, she decided, out of nowhere, to become a nurse.

That summer, Melanie found a job as a waitress in a seafood restaurant in Edison. She had now moved back with her mother and stepfather and had been dating a young man named Brian Gerber for about a year. At night, after the restaurant closed, the staff often socialized with waiters and kitchen staff from other local restaurants. And one night Gerber introduced her to his new roommate, William McGuire, who was working at the Red Lobster.

Within days she had ditched Gerber, falling madly in love with his handsome waiter friend.

FIVE

Bill McGuire

William Theodore McGuire was born on September 21, 1964, in River Edge, New Jersey. The youngest of Bill and Ruth McGuire's three children, he would always be the baby of the family.

His father worked for *The New York Times* as a pressman, and his mother was a homemaker. The McGuires were a hard-working blue-collar family, living in the Bronx, and although the *Times* did not pay well on the line, the union benefits were generous.

Their first child, Cindy, had been born in 1955, followed five years later by another daughter, Nancy.

Soon after Nancy was born, Bill McGuire Sr. moved the family to a larger apartment in River Edge. By the time little Billy, as the family always called him, was born, Nancy had just begun kindergarten.

"Then my mother kept me home," she remembered. "So I spent a lot of time playing with Billy. And he was so cute."

As an infant, Bill was adventurous and would always be trying to escape from his wooden playpen.

"My mother figured out he was opening up the bottom and crawling out underneath," said Nancy. "So she sawed off the legs. There was something about Billy where you couldn't lock him up. I had to watch him when she turned her back."

Although a good-natured child, Billy was naturally mischievous. When he was 4 years old he crawled out of his room, climbing up a kitchen cabinet and taking a jar of St. Joseph's orange baby aspirin. Then he went outside into the street, handing out the pills to his friends.

"Everybody but Billy took some," remembered Nancy. "When the other parents found out, they took them to get their stomachs pumped. After that we reversed the lock on his door."

In 1968, Bill and Ruth McGuire divorced and the three children moved out with their mother, into a two-story house in East Paterson. Over the next few years, the troubled couple would remarry and then divorce several times.

Ruth was forced to get a night job to support them, while 13-year-old Cindy looked after her younger siblings.

"I was like a mom to Billy," remembered Cindy. "When we came home from school [our mother] had already left for work, and we went to bed before she got home. She worked six days a week, and on the seventh she worked at home."

Ruth McGuire was a strict disciplinarian, and there was much tension in the house. In 1974, Nancy could not take living there anymore, later accusing her father of molesting her.

"I asked to go into a foster home," she explained, "because I didn't want to run away."

Billy McGuire was now going to the Reverend George A. Brown Elementary School in Sparta, New Jersey. The strict Catholic school incorporated the Gospels into all subjects, installing in students the desire to live by their faith.

The boy did just enough academically to get by at the school. But he was a born leader, always arranging games for his many friends and teasing them mercilessly if they did not perform well.

When Bill was twelve, his sister Cindy left home and married a pharmacist named Bill Ligosh, leaving her little brother alone with his mother. Soon afterwards Ruth moved to Clifton, New Jersey, where she enrolled Bill in Clifton High School.

"He was a 'B' student," said Cindy. "But he always had friends."

Bill found it difficult living at home with just his mother

and no father figure. "It was hard for him," said Cindy. "He was her entire focus, and there was no buffer."

At 15, Bill McGuire ran away from home, turning up without warning on his sister Cindy's doorstep in Vernon Township, New Jersey. After consulting their mother, it was agreed Billy should move in with them permanently. They welcomed him into their family, where he became close to their baby daughter Laura, who he would often babysit.

Cindy and her husband Bill tried to be the parents the troubled teenager had never had. He loved the stability of being in a real family, something he had yearned for all his life.

"I looked at Bill as a son," said Cindy. "For I more or less performed the functions of a mother."

Cindy enrolled him in Vernon Township High School in the middle of his junior year. He soon made friends with a classmate named Lenny Polsky.

Not everything went smoothly in the new school. Bill showed no interest in extracurricular activities, and often cut classes. "He had a rocky relationship with his mom," said Polsky. "He was just a rebel. He was a hothead."

Soon after coming to Vernon High, Billy, who had adopted a fashionable David Cassidy look, asked a classmate, Lisa DeVosa, out on a date. When she turned him down, as he had just broken up with someone else, he merely smiled, as if he knew she would come around.

Finally, she did become his girlfriend.

"He was fun," she remembered. "He was very smart [and] we always had a good time together."

At his new home, Billy looked up to his "Uncle" Bill as a father figure, deciding to follow in his footsteps and become a pharmacist.

"He was studying for the SATs," said Cindy. "At one point my husband was working with him and they practiced together. So Bill took the SATs and got a perfect score."

Bill Ligosh was fanatical about working out with free weights and a punching bag, and introduced his brother-in-law to the sport. This would become a passion for the rest of his life.

To make extra money, he got an after-school job in a local restaurant, working his way up from busboy to waiter.

Although the 15-year-old was as thin as a rail, he loved eating large dinners, never putting on any weight. Cindy always insisted that her brother clean up after himself, and keep his room tidy. Later he would tell stories of how she made him clean with a toothbrush.

"I was real prissy," admitted Cindy. "I was wall-to-wall carpet [cleaning], vacuuming three times a day, and don't leave prints on the rug. He was good around the house, clean and neat."

One day, just before his 16th birthday, Cindy came home to find a strange car in front of the house. Billy told her he had gotten a "great deal" on the car, promising he would not drive it until he got his official permit.

A couple of weeks later, Cindy returned to find that the car had disappeared, with no sign of her brother.

"I just flipped out," she said. "He got home just before midnight. He had taken three friends to Jones Beach, and none of them had a license. So we got into a big fight, and I lost my temper and I threw him out."

Bill McGuire packed up all his belongings and left. It would be years before he spoke to his older sister again.

A few hours later, he turned up at his sister Nancy's apartment in Montclair, New Jersey. He begged her to let him move in, suggesting that they find a bigger apartment. But she told him it was impossible, as she could hardly afford rent now.

"I couldn't just pick up and leave and be his parent," she explained.

Then Nancy phoned his Vernon High School coach, who agreed to let Bill come and live with his family, until somewhere more permanent could be found. Nancy drove her brother there and left him.

"He wanted family," said Nancy. "I would have done anything in the world for him. He didn't understand financially I couldn't just break a lease and move."

After a brief stay with the school coach, Bill McGuire moved in with his best friend Lenny Polsky's family in Vernon.

"He had a lot of issues," explained Lenny's sister Marci, who also attended Vernon Township High School. "My mom invited him to live with us."

Before long, 12-year-old Marci developed a big crush on her brother's handsome friend. But Bill, who was still dating Lisa DeVosa, barely noticed her.

"My sister was mesmerized by him," remembered Lenny Polsky. "He could sweet-talk people that way."

On June 16, 1982, Bill McGuire graduated from Vernon High School, not even getting a mention in the senior yearbook. He worked in various restaurants for the next five months.

But in early December, he went to the U.S. Navy recruiting station in Newark, enlisting for four years' service. A week later he said good-bye to his girlfriend Lisa and the Polsky family, heading off to California for his first assignment. He promised Lisa that he would keep in touch, and one day they would be together.

He had no idea little Marci Polsky was desperately in love with him, devastated that he was leaving her behind.

SIX

Serving His Country

Bill McGuire did his boot camp at the U.S. Naval Base Coronado in San Diego, before transferring to Vallejo for basic training. Now a handsome 20-year-old, standing 5 feet, 10 inches and weighing a trim 185 pounds, the new recruit loved his new life as a sailor.

He began general training in "A" school, which orients raw naval recruits. One morning, another new recruit named Jon Rice, then 23, was lining up for the routine march to class when he first encountered Bill, cracking jokes for a group of sailors.

"I just wrote him off as some punk, a jerk," remembered Rice. "But I guess I was kind of envious of the attention he was getting."

A few months later, after being promoted to third class petty officers, they found themselves in the same class in "C" school, doing specialized training as computer techs. They soon became friends, working the lonely midnight–to–7:00 a.m. shift.

"We played volleyball in the middle of the night to get our blood going," remembered Rice. "We enjoyed the same sense of humor and fought to be the class clown."

Over the next year they became close, doing much of their training together. And although naval wages were meager, Rice soon noticed how Bill McGuire always dressed well, driving a Camaro and indulging in expensive wines and top-of-the-line stereo equipment.

"Bill had to have the best of everything," said Rice. "He was going for that image."

McGuire eventually admitted that he financed his luxurious lifestyle by forging fake IDs and opening up checking accounts in false names and writing bad checks.

"Once, he asked me if I wanted anything," remembered Rice. "But I was a little too chicken for that. But he never got caught."

On occasion, Bill smoked marijuana, though he was always careful of the U.S. Navy's random drug-testing program.

In early 1984, Bill McGuire was-transferred to Norfolk, Virginia, to serve on the USS *America* aircraft carrier. He had now passed all his exams in "C" school and would spend much of the next three years traveling the world aboard the giant warship. Also on board was Jon Rice, who had flunked out of "C" school and been transferred a few months earlier when it was in Spain.

Launched on February 1, 1964—the year Bill McGuire was born—the Kitty Hawk class supercarrier had a crew of 5,500 men. Fully loaded, it weighed 83,573 tons and carried seventy-five aircraft.

When McGuire first joined the battleship, there was a sea/shore rotation of thirty-eight months on the boat, followed by forty-two months ashore. He was placed in S8 Division as a data systems tech, handling all data processing and responsible for maintaining the battleship's sophisticated computer equipment. In time he would be promoted to a supervisor.

Not everyone appreciated Bill McGuire's cocky sense of humor, especially when they were the butt of his jokes.

"When I first met him I thought, 'Aaaaagh, what's wrong with this guy?'" said Jim Carmichael, who was posted to the USS *America* that summer. "Bill was so completely full of it . . . but first impressions can be faulty."

McGuire loved to mess with people, teasing one of his shipmates so mercilessly, he finally stormed out of the shop in tears.

"Bill had basically no upper lip," said Carmichael. "It's not really pronounced, and it curls up at the very end. The result of that is that he looks like he's got that smart aleck look on his face all the time. And it caused him untold problems through his early life."

Even Jon Rice sometimes found it hard to take his best friend's wacky humor.

One night, Bill started deriding Jon's ears and laughing. Despite Rice's pleas to stop, Bill refused. Finally Jon had enough and wrestled him to the floor.

"It was a joke to Bill," remembered Carmichael, who was also there. "But it wasn't a joke to Jon."

Before long, though, they had made up, becoming closer than ever.

"Bill could be very aggravating," said Rice. "We got up and pushed each other around, and that was the end of it."

In June 1985, Bill arranged for Lisa DeVosa to fly to Norfolk to see him on a weekend leave. Jon Rice's new girlfriend Sue, whom he had met in Michigan that February, also flew in.

"The first time I met Bill, he was with Lisa," remembered Sue. "So he was preoccupied with her. I immediately liked him. Bill had that dry sense of humor, and Jon played off of it."

A few months later, Bill McGuire visited Lisa in Vernon, New Jersey, but by then their relationship was over. While there he asked Marci Polsky out on a date, and they became romantically involved, staying in touch when he returned to the USS *America*.

On Friday, August 23, Jon Rice became engaged to Sue, who moved to Norfolk to prepare for the wedding. The following day, the USS *America* left for a six-week NATO exercise in Norwegian waters, nicknamed "Ocean Safari."

This was Bill McGuire's first real taste of life at sea, and he loved the excitement and adventure. But like all the other sailors, he also had to learn patience.

"You wait in line for absolutely everything," said Jim Carmichael. "Showers, going to the bathroom, eating."

There was a lot of downtime, with little to do except the

required maintenance checks to see if all the equipment was working. The sailors worked twelve-hour shifts and Third Petty Officer McGuire and his friends spent their time watching MTV videotapes.

On March 10, 1986, the USS *America* left Norfolk for the Mediterranean for a six-month mission, joining the 6th Fleet for the escalating Libyan crisis. Tensions had been growing since the hijacking of a TWA airliner in Beirut the previous July, followed by bombing attacks of American Airline offices in Rome and Vienna.

Libyan leader Muammar Qaddafi had been implicated, and President Ronald Reagan broke off all diplomatic relations with Libya, ordering the Joint Chiefs of Staff to explore military options.

On March 10, Petty Officers McGuire, Rice and Carmichael were aboard the USS *America* when it arrived in the Gulf of Sidra, to participate in the third phase of Operation Attain Document. Two weeks later, on March 23, the USS *America* crossed Qaddafi's infamous "Line of Death," as Libya fired Soviet-made surface-to-air missiles at American warplanes during the exercise.

"Together we crossed the Line of Death," remembered Jon Rice. "And we did it in the middle of the night . . . they kept launching the jets. We had to go over and bomb Muammar Qaddafi, and Bill was right there with us."

After the operation, the USS *America* sailed into Naples, where it would be based over the summer. For the next few months, Bill McGuire and his friends made several trips to Rome and London.

"Our home away from home was Naples," remembered Rice. "That was where we pulled into port all the time, and from there we'd catch a ferry to Rome."

On one memorable trip, McGuire, Rice and Carmichael went to the Leaning Tower of Pisa, before going to London.

Photographs show the smiling young American sailors sightseeing in London at St. Paul's Cathedral and Trafalgar Square. These would be some of the happiest days of Bill McGuire's life, and he would boast about his European exploits for years to come.

In September, the USS *America* arrived back in Norfolk, and Jon Rice married Sue, settling down in naval married quarters near the base. One night Rice happened to mention how much more money he would be making, thanks to generous naval marriage benefits.

"I told Bill my paycheck basically doubled by getting married," said Rice. "He was like, 'Oh. OK.' And off he ran."

Soon after the conversation, McGuire called Marci Polsky back in New Jersey, proposing marriage. She had just graduated Vernon Township High School, so he suggested she move to Virginia, marry him and go to college. The love-struck young girl immediately accepted, and started preparing to move South.

"Bill was always trying to figure out the angle," Rice explained. "And that's one of the main reasons he got married."

Marci arrived in Norfolk in October, and they secretly married in a civil ceremony settling down in a one-bedroom apartment on Greenbrier Parkway, Chesapeake.

"It was a paper wedding," said Jim Carmichael. "She was just young and foolish. Their relationship reminded me more of a brother and a sister, than of a husband and wife."

Jon and Sue Rice first met Marci at a Navy picnic.

"Bill introduced her to us as his wife," said Sue Rice. "We were very, very shocked."

The Rices remember Marci as young and insecure, totally dependent on her new husband.

"She was like a deer in the headlights anytime she was around him," said Jon Rice. "She was in awe."

Soon after arriving, Marci enrolled in Virginia Wesleyan College, and tried to become a housewife. But she had few cooking skills, something Bill would constantly tease her about.

"He made fun of her," said Jon, "and she would take it to heart. I mean, he wouldn't mean anything by it, but it would hurt her feelings."

Whenever the USS *America* was docked in Norfolk, the two married couples would socialize together, going out for dinner, or shooting pool in Smackwater Jack's Bar in Virginia Beach.

Jim Carmichael also spent much time at the McGuires' apartment, often staying the night.

But by the summer—less than nine months into their marriage—Bill admitted that he had never really loved Marci, and had made a terrible mistake.

"He absolutely told me they simply were not compatible," said Carmichael. "He wanted someone he could interact with on a more intellectual level. Marci isn't stupid, but she wasn't that person. Unfortunately she loved Bill to death."

Just before Christmas 1987, Bill McGuire, now 23, telephoned his sister Cindy Ligosh out of the blue, wishing her a happy holiday. It was the first time they had spoken in the six years since she had thrown him out, but they immediately reconnected.

"In my family, we hold grudges," said Cindy. "But once you make up, you don't have to say anything."

Bill invited Cindy to come to Norfolk and meet his new wife. And the next summer she came for three days, with her two children, Laura, now 7, and 3-year-old Max.

"It was the first time I got to see him in his uniform," remembered Cindy. "He was adorable, and looked just like Tom Cruise."

But when she met Marci, Cindy couldn't understand why he had married her.

"She had no personality and no intelligence. Nothing," said Cindy. "She was a shock to everyone."

Bill McGuire had little respect for authority, playing fast and loose with the rules during his six years' service with the U.S. Navy. On one occasion he was arrested by Norfolk police for a minor felony involving checks. After being fingerprinted, he was allowed to go home without being charged.

Bill loved fast sports cars, having replaced his Camaro with a Triumph TR7. One night he was out driving with Jim Carmichael, when he was pulled over by a state trooper for not wearing a seat belt. Bill strongly denied the charge, claiming it would have been impossible to see whether he was wearing a belt or not.

After a few minutes of arguing, the trooper wrote out a ticket and handed it to him.

"Is that it?" asked McGuire, winking at Carmichael. "Is that the best you can do? You must be a rookie. A real cop could have written me a lot more tickets than that."

So the policeman obliged, writing him several more tickets.

On another occasion with Carmichael, Bill decided not to stop for any red lights that night, and was soon chased down by a state trooper, ending up in court on a reckless driving charge.

"This was kind of silly," said Carmichael. "But that's the kind of guy Bill was—he was so larger than life."

In late 1990, Bill McGuire left the Navy, after getting an associate's degree from Tidewater Community College. His best friend Jon Rice had been discharged a few months earlier, moving to South Carolina with Sue.

Then Bill and Marci moved to Edison, New Jersey, where he enrolled at Rutgers University to study Pharmacy. They moved into a cheap apartment, both finding jobs in local restaurants to support themselves.

But their marriage was disintegrating and Bill was now looking for a way out.

In early 1992, Bill McGuire brought Marci to his ten-year Vernon Township High School reunion. But soon afterwards, he walked out on her, telling Jim Carmichael that he had stayed in the marriage until Marci could look after herself.

Marci was heartbroken and didn't see it coming. For the next two years she would try to get him back.

After the separation, Bill McGuire moved into a townhouse in Woodbridge, New Jersey, with Brian Gerber and another roommate. He started dating again, but Marci always seemed to be in the picture.

"She was still trying to mend that relationship," said Jim Carmichael. "Trying to bridge that gap."

For the next two years Bill studied hard, working nights in restaurants around the Edison area. He also started going to Atlantic City to play the casinos, something he'd first gotten a taste of in Virginia Beach. He started rolling the dice at the Trump Taj Mahal, becoming a rated player for the first time in 1994.

Then in the summer of 1994, Brian Gerber introduced McGuire to his girlfriend Melanie Slate, and sparks flew.

SEVEN

A Perfect Match

Bill McGuire and Melanie Slate had much in common, sharing the same sarcastic humor and a love of the good life. Although the 21-year-old student nurse was eight years younger than Bill, they were on the same wavelength. Where Bill had always considered Marci dull and slow, he viewed Melanie as his beautiful intellectual equal.

"She was adorable," remembered Cindy. "Smart, witty and cute. She was more Billy's type, and completely his equal. They liked to fool around, and they were madly in love with each other."

Soon after meeting Bill, Melanie told her best friend Selene Rodriguez that she was in love.

"She actually fell head-over-heels for Bill," remembered Selene. "They got each other's humor. Melanie's very sarcastic in her way, and so was he. And they understood each other."

But when Marci, still legally married to Bill, heard about the new girlfriend, she turned up at Melanie's apartment without warning.

"She actually came and found me," Melanie later related, "and said, 'He's going to make you think you're crazy. I'm telling you right now that is what he's done to me. He's going to do it to you.' "

Then the two women went to confront Bill together. According to Marci, when he swore his devotion to Marci, she did not believe him and left with Melanie.

"You know I'm going back with him," Marci says that Melanie told her.

"I told her, 'Good luck. This is what he's done to me,'" said Marci. "It probably wasn't the first time he was cheating on me."

Soon after the meeting, Marci filed for divorce. Years later she claimed Bill had thrown rocks through her window, prompting her to file a restraining order against him.

In early 1995, Sue Rice was working for a bank in Malden, South Carolina, when an irate customer with a thick Indian accent called about a bank error. He was very persistent, asking a stream of silly questions about his account.

Sue finally put him on hold, complaining to coworkers that he was a "real a–hole." When she got back on the line, he continued his barrage of stupid questions.

"I was getting ready to hang up," she remembered. "And suddenly he said, 'Hey, Sue—it's Bill McGuire.'"

Sue was stunned, having been completely taken in. It had been years since they had last spoken, so she was delighted he had tracked them down.

Then he told Sue he was divorcing Marci, and had met somebody.

"I was kind of surprised," she said. "But he said he loved [Marci] like a sister, but had never been in love with her."

Bill said he was living in an apartment in Edison with two roommates, and studying Pharmacy. Over the next few weeks they had several further conversations, but soon lost touch again when the Rices moved.

In 1995, soon after meeting Bill McGuire, Melanie Slate joined the Charles E. Gregory School of Nursing in Old Bridge, NJ, studying for her RN. She became friends with a tall, bearded young nursing student named James Finn.

"We sat next to each other in class," said Finn. "We eventually got to know each other very well."

Over the next few weeks, Finn fell "madly in love" with the beautiful student nurse with long cascading brown hair.

"I thought she was the best thing since sliced bread," Finn remembered.

Eventually, he asked Melanie out on a date and told her he loved her.

"I wanted to take our friendship to the next level," he said. "She always said, 'Let's stay friends.' And that's what we did. We were very close friends for a long time."

That Christmas, Melanie Slate gave James Finn a copy of the popular Stephen King novel *Dolores Claiborne*, about a woman who gets her abusive husband drunk and murders him.

And on an inside page she wrote the inscription:

Now here is a story of a woman with true strength and wisdom. You can learn a lot from her. I did.

Love,
Melanie

Melanie still lived at home with her mother and stepfather in Middletown, New Jersey. Although her relationship with Michael Cappararo had improved, he refused to allow her to move in with Bill McGuire, saying it went against his Catholic beliefs. So she frequently spent evenings at Bill's apartment, before going back to her parents'.

Most evenings Melanie worked as a waitress in a seafood restaurant in Edison, where she had become friends with the manager's girlfriend, Regina Knowles (not her real name), who often hung out at the bar after dinner.

"Everyone knew she was in nursing school," said Knowles, "so her ambitions were really clear-cut. She just always came across as a very genuine person."

Bill McGuire had previously worked at the same restaurant, before moving on to the Metuchen Inn.

"Bill had worked throughout the years in a number of fine dining establishments," said Regina, who knew him. "He was always trying to make the big bucks, so he worked at fine dining as opposed to the more casual, because the tips were better."

* * *

Through 1996, Melanie and Bill's relationship deepened, with an understanding that they would marry after they both graduated. Although they often argued, they seemed to be in love and devoted to each other.

"They had their issues," said Selene, who was now dating a successful builder in Brooklyn named Alex Trevizas. "Melanie was a very strong-headed person, but Bill pretty much overpowered her. And so they argued a lot about silly things, but that was just the nature of their relationship."

Melanie often discussed her tempestuous relationship with McGuire with James Finn.

"It was always a rocky relationship," Finn later remembered. "They've been fighting since day one, as she would always describe it. I was asking, 'Why are you staying with this guy if you fight all the time?' And she would always say, 'When it was great it was great, and when it's bad it's really bad.' That was their relationship in a nutshell."

But "Melanie eventually gave up on the arguments," said Selene. "She learned that she would never win, so there was no point." Over time, Melanie grew more passive-aggressive, finding it easier to hold her tongue.

On March 1, 1996, Bill McGuire was driving with a suspended license in Scotch Plains, New Jersey, when he was stopped by police for speeding. Aware he faced certain jail time, he pressured Melanie to tell police she had been driving his car, and later to lie under oath in court.

According to Union County court records, McGuire was subsequently arrested for "fabricating false testimony regarding circumstances surrounding a motor-vehicle stop . . . and discussing and/or preparing such testimony with witness identified as Melanie L. Slate." An attached probation report revealed that he had previously been arrested for "wrongful impersonation," relating to a disorderly persons offense.

He spent a day in jail, before being freed on $2,500 bail.

On November 12, 1997, he received three years' probation, and was fined $1,550 for the third-degree tampering with a witness. Melanie accepted Pre-Trial Intervention (PTI) in a plea agreement, where she testified in court, receiving a year's probation.

Under the New Jersey PTI program, first-time offenders are offered rehabilitation to solve any personal problems that may have led to the crime. When the defendant successfully completes the PTI program, the original charges are dismissed, leaving no record of the conviction.

"He had me perjure myself in open court . . . as a human shield," she would later explain, "to save his ass from a traffic ticket."

Regina Knowles believes that Melanie never forgave Bill for that.

"I think this was a turning point for them," she recounted. "That's where I think some of the abuse may have begun. Melanie's got a pretty heavy-duty level of integrity. She's not one to compromise."

In the summer of 1997, Melanie finally agreed to move in with Bill McGuire, once he found a new apartment. Now 33, McGuire had been living the bachelor life in a cramped apartment in Woodbridge, with two younger roommates who liked to party. He wanted a quieter environment to make a home with Melanie and pursue his studies.

Several years earlier, he had dropped out of his Pharmacy course at Rutgers. He was now working on a Bachelor's Degree in Management at the New Jersey Institute of Technology.

In August, he answered an advertisement for a room in a neighboring three-bedroom townhouse in the same Woodbridge complex that he had been living in. He was interviewed by the sub-lessee, Eric Soles, who had only moved in a couple of months earlier.

"I had to meet him before giving him the okay," remembered Soles, "and right off the bat, he seemed like a good guy."

McGuire told Soles he wanted to move his fiancée into the apartment, negotiating for the master bedroom so they would have more room.

That October, Melanie moved in with Bill, sharing a kitchen, living room and basement with Soles and another female room-mate, who was leaving.

"Bill and I hit it off because we're both wise-asses," said Soles. "We'd joke around with each other like that, and I can see how some people could think he was a little abrasive. But he really wasn't."

Soon after moving into the apartment, Melanie upset her new roommates by announcing that she wanted to redecorate and get new furniture.

"She was snobby," recalled Soles. "Bill seemed a lot more down to earth, but she was a lot more upper-crust, and put on airs. When she came in, she wanted to change everything. 'This is ugly! This needs fixing!' She wanted to put her stamp on the apartment, even though she was sharing it with other folks."

Bill and Melanie were rarely in the apartment, as both stud-ied hard, waiting tables evenings and weekends. McGuire was now working at the Paper Mill Playhouse for dinner theater, while Melanie was at the seafood restaurant.

The couple often double-dated with Selene and Alex Trevizas, going to movies and dining out in nice restaurants.

"They had a lot of fun," said Selene. "They were good to-gether."

They also cooked elaborate meals together, Bill being par-ticularly proud of his culinary prowess.

Although Soles got along better with McGuire, he eventu-ally became friendly with Melanie, as they both loved watch-ing *Ally McBeal* and *ER*.

But as Soles got to know them better, he realized there was often tension between Bill and Melanie. "I would never see them fighting," he said. "But you'd know they'd had an argu-ment and they weren't talking to each other. You didn't really hear anything, but you could see it on their faces."

EIGHT

Melanie Slate, RN

In the summer of 1997, Melanie Slate graduated second in her class, obtaining her nursing diploma from the Charles E. Gregory School of Nursing. Bill McGuire was there to see her receive her diploma.

"Melanie brought him along as a date that night," remembered James Finn. "It was the only time I ever met him."

In her last year at nursing school, Melanie had developed an interest in the OB/GYN fertility field.

When she became an RN, she applied for a position in the Infertility division of St. Barnabas Medical Center in Livingston, New Jersey, and was accepted.

"She was an egg donor first," remembered Lori Thomas, who started at St. Barnabas at the same time. "She worked in the egg donor division of Infertility, and I worked with straight In Vitro for fertilization patients. Our offices were next to each other."

The two young nurses became close over the next few months, traveling to infertility conferences all over the country. Melanie would often discuss Bill McGuire, saying they fought all the time.

"We were talking weddings," said Thomas. "But I remember her not talking good things about him."

From the beginning, Nurse Melanie Slate impressed her superiors with her natural intelligence and nursing ability. "She was a fantastic nurse," said Thomas. "I can't say anything bad about her as an RN." She had exceptional people skills and her often profane humor seemed to put patients at ease.

But Melanie could also use her razor-sharp wit as a vicious weapon, against anyone in the hospital who dared to cross her.

"I think Melanie had a little demon in her," said Lori Thomas. "She could be very mean and sarcastic about other nurses if she didn't like you. She'd humiliate people."

Soon after graduating nursing school, Melanie cooled off her relationship to her long-time admirer Jim Finn, who no longer had much to offer her.

"It just became an e-mail here, a phone call there," he remembered. "It really wasn't much at all."

It would be another eight years before she would need him again, and reconnect.

In late 1997, Bill McGuire got down on his knees and proposed to Melanie, and she accepted. He had already told roommate Eric Soles how he was now going to Atlantic City to try to win enough money for matching engagement rings.

Lori Thomas, who also got engaged around the same time, remembers Melanie coming into St. Barnabas, proudly announcing it to everyone.

"She showed off her diamond ring," said Thomas. "She was so happy."

But when she told her parents she was engaged, they were less than enthusiastic. Michael Cappararo did not consider Bill McGuire worthy of his stepdaughter. Bill, who had always longed for a strong father figure, embarked on a campaign to win Cappararo's approval.

"Michael didn't like Bill at all when they first met," said Jim Carmichael. "He was seeking Michael's approval. It wasn't until Bill made it clear that he was marrying her and they needed to get on board with each other, that things finally settled down."

The one thing the two men shared was a love of gambling in Atlantic City. And Michael started taking his future son-in-law to the casinos, providing a gambling master class and teaching him tricks to maximize casino comps.

McGuire told his sister Nancy Taylor how Cappararo had perfected a system of placing large sums of cash into the bank of one casino, while staying at another. He would later withdraw it, without using it to gamble, and under New Jersey state law a depositor must fill out a casino form, asking where he is staying.

"And you say, 'Well I'm staying at the Taj Mahal,'" said Nancy, "'but I like to gamble at the Grand.' They'll go, 'Well why don't you stay here? We'll give the penthouse here at the Grand, compliments of the house. Here's dinner, here's this, here's that.' That's how you get your comps, and not by what you win."

Eventually the Cappararos grudgingly accepted Bill McGuire, inviting him to their weekly family dinners.

"Melanie had a very tight relationship with her family," said Nancy, "and Bill became part of that. And growing up the way we did and not having a family, Bill liked that."

Around Christmas 1997, Sue Rice received another call at the bank, from a difficult customer with a thick Indian accent.

"I should have known," said Sue, who had moved back to Virginia Beach with Jon the previous year. "Bill had tracked us down again and in his Indian accent he said he was trying to use his ATM card."

When Sue politely asked his account number, the caller replied he did not have one.

"I'm like, 'I can't help you,'" she said. "I'm trying to just get him off the phone, and finally he goes, 'Hey, Sue, it's Bill McGuire.' I'm like, 'You jerk.'"

Sue then gave him the number of the restaurant Jon was working at, so Bill had a real Indian friend call and place a huge order for delivery.

"I knew Bill was behind it," remembered Jon. "I said, 'Okay, [we'll] send them right away.' So his friend handed the phone to Bill, who said, 'Do you know who this is?' I said, 'Yeah—it's Bill McGuire.'"

Bill then told his old friend he had gotten engaged, asking if he could bring Melanie down to Virginia Beach for a couple of days.

"That was when we reconnected," said Jon. "He would do the craziest things, but they were just so cool."

One Sunday afternoon in late January 1998, Bill and Melanie arrived at the Rices' Chesapeake home, bearing a bottle of Dom Pérignon champagne.

"When they walked through the door, Melanie was flustered," remembered Sue. "She had been driving and had gotten a speeding ticket in Delaware. She was so pretty, and looked like Julianna Margulies of *ER*. And I think, 'Bill's got something here.'"

At first Melanie seemed shy, hardly saying a word to anyone, as Bill began teasing her about her speeding ticket.

"But then she gave it right back to him," said Sue. "I'm like, 'Hey, I think I like this girl.' Here was his match. She was his mate. Yes."

Later over a delicious linguini shrimp dinner, prepared by Jon, Bill stood up, asking him to be his best man at the wedding.

"He got all teary-eyed," remembered Jon. "I had a bottle of very expensive wine we were holding back for a special occasion, and we toasted them with it."

Over the next several days Melanie relaxed, coming out of her shell and endearing herself to the Rices.

"We three had a relationship," said Sue. "And she was the new one. But she soon broke through that."

The next day, the Rices drove them to Colonial Williamsburg for a sightseeing tour. On the way back, a well-known Beatles song came on the radio, and Bill claimed to have no idea who it was.

"He could have been pulling the wool over our eyes," said Sue. "But Melanie, Jon and I were having so much fun teasing him. Melanie would say, 'Who is that, Bill?' And he would say he didn't remember, but it sounds familiar, and sing along with it."

Melanie would then tease him mercilessly, and their radio shtick became an ongoing joke between them.

Five months later, Melanie met Bill's sister Nancy Taylor.

"I liked her," remembered Nancy. "I thought she was lovely

back then. She struck me as smart and quiet. She was reserved and was not outgoing. She listened more than she talked, which is not a trait any of the McGuires have. But now that I look back, she was calculating."

During her two-night stay at their apartment, Nancy had a disagreement with her brother, and asked Melanie to reason with him.

"She wouldn't," said Nancy. "She was like, 'I have to stand by my husband.' They were just dating at the time, but it felt like they were married."

After discussions with Melanie's parents, the engaged couple decided on a strict Catholic wedding, enrolling for Pre-Cana classes at St. Joseph's Church, West Orange, where they would marry. It is common for Catholics to meet with a priest or deacon at least nine to twelve months before the wedding, for spiritual counseling. It is known as Pre-Cana, named after the town of Cana, where Jesus and his mother Mary attended a wedding feast and he changed the water into wine.

During their regular Sunday Pre-Cana meetings with the priest, the couple were instructed on the spiritual nature of a Catholic marriage. They were also told about natural family planning, as the Church strictly forbade any form of artificial contraception.

Soon after they started Pre-Cana, Melanie decided to have a baby. And without a word to Bill, she stopped using birth control, embarking on a course of fertility drugs that she obtained from the hospital. Later she confided her secret to Lisa Carmichael, who was now married to Bill's old Navy friend Jim.

"I know that she had decided to have a baby before she got married," said Lisa. "She decided she was ready to have a baby, so she started taking fertility drugs. She just couldn't wait until she was married like normal people do."

Regardless of her religious convictions, Melanie was having affairs with at least two married doctors at St. Barnabas. In October 1998, Lori Thomas accompanied Melanie and one of the doctors to a fertility conference in San Francisco.

"The two of them were together," said Thomas. "I saw them walking back to the hotel after an engagement one night. She was engaged and he was a married man, but he had a little extracurricular activity."

And according to Thomas, Melanie was also romantically involved with another St. Barnabas obstetrician.

"The doctors and the nurses all worked very closely together," explained Thomas. "People were jumping from bedroom to bedroom."

One night at dinner during the San Francisco conference, Nurse Melanie Slate was introduced to Dr. Bradley Miller, a renowned Washington, D.C.–based obstetrician. She made such a big impression on the tall, handsome—but married—fertility specialist, he would never forget that first fateful meeting.

By January 1999, everything was in place for Bill and Melanie's lavish June wedding. The 26-year-old future bride and her mother Linda had spent the last year making elaborate plans for the big day. They had booked the reception in the exclusive Highlawn Pavilion in West Orange with its dramatic sweeping views of the Manhattan skyline, picked out a wedding dress and sent out invitations to more than 100 guests.

Then one morning in early February, Cindy Ligosh got a frantic telephone call from her brother.

"Melanie had announced she was pregnant," remembered Cindy. "And my brother's flipping out. He's mad. The dress has been bought. The place has been booked—they were within four months of the wedding."

When Melanie had a miscarriage soon afterwards, Bill breathed a sigh of relief, telling her he did not want a child before they got married.

But Melanie ignored him and continued taking fertility drugs she obtained from work.

"Come April, I get another phone call from my brother," said Cindy. "She thinks she's pregnant again. And this time it turned out she was."

NINE

Reproductive Medicine Associates

In spring 1999, a group of ambitious St. Barnabas doctors broke away from the hospital, setting up a private infertility clinic in Morristown, New Jersey. They handpicked Melanie McGuire and eight other nurses to join them.

Reproductive Medicine Associates (RMA) was founded by St. Barnabas reproductive endocrinologist Dr. Richard Scott, with two other partners, Dr. Paul Bergh and Dr. Michael Drew.

And within a few years RMA would have satellite branches across America, establishing itself as one of the world's largest and most experienced infertility clinics, generating millions of dollars in revenue every year.

RMA offered patients a variety of cutting-edge methods to aid conception. It was a success from the very beginning, and Melanie Slate was considered one of its key team players.

"She was a great nurse," said Dr. Richard Scott. "Melanie had an extraordinary work ethic. She worked extremely hard."

Lori Thomas, who would join RMA a year later, said Melanie impressed everyone with her hard work and dedication.

"It was very different than working at St. Barnabas," she said. "It was a business."

Melanie shared an office with a Regent nurse named Joyce Maloney.

"We talked for hours about anything," remembered Maloney. "Family, friends, ongoing occurrences."

Soon after joining RMA, Melanie mailed out invitations to her upcoming wedding to almost every member of the staff, as well as many of her old St. Barnabas colleagues.

"We all got invitations," said Thomas. "However, there were rumors going about St. Barnabas that her marriage wouldn't last more than a year."

In May 1999, Bill and Melanie signed a lease on a new one-bedroom apartment in the Edison Woods apartment complex in New Jersey. And with Bill's encouragement, Eric Soles and his girlfriend moved into an apartment two floors below.

"It was right before they were getting married," remembered Soles. "Melanie seemed very happy. I don't know what his thoughts and dreams were about getting married, but it seemed like her fairy tale. She was more the driver of that wedding than Bill was."

As soon as they moved in, Melanie began shopping for expensive new furniture and wall hangings. According to Soles, Melanie would constantly buy new furniture, giving away the old stuff to friends.

At that time Melanie was the main breadwinner, earning far more than Bill, who was studying at New Jersey's Science & Technology University (NJIT) and working as a waiter at an expensive French restaurant. It was owned by a husband and wife team of restaurateurs and Bill was in charge of the front of the house.

"He was known as the 'rude waiter,'" remembered Sue Rice. "And people would come back and ask for him to serve them, so he could insult them."

Whenever he saw patrons sitting around at a table chatting after a meal, he would come over and berate them.

"Hey!" he would say. "Are you going to sit around here all night? I've got other people waiting! I've got to make money and we've got to turn this table." He developed a devoted set of customers who always requested the "rude waiter," tipping well for the pleasure of being insulted.

"It was entertaining," said Sue Rice. "He loved it and would say, 'They love it when I'm rude to them.'"

At that time Bill McGuire dreamed of opening his own restaurant, and he was always trying to get Regina Knowles and her husband Kevin to become his partners.

"There was always a scam," said Regina. " 'This restaurant's for sale' or 'That property's for sale'. It's like, 'Bill, we don't have the money.' But he'd say, 'Don't worry about it, I'll come up with the money part, you guys just run it.' "

Regina never trusted Bill, thinking he lived beyond his means and was not right for her friend.

"Something about Bill just always irked me," she explained. "I never really cared for him, and we got along for the sake of Melanie."

Regina never criticized Bill, as she did not want to risk losing Melanie's friendship.

"Quite frankly I never really understood their relationship, and we didn't feel he was right for her," she said. "But when someone who's close to you says they're in love and they make them happy, you keep your mouth shut."

Michael Cappararo also still had reservations about his prospective new son-in-law.

"He could be very likable," he later told ABC's *Primetime*. "And then on the other hand he could be very calculating. There was always something about a deal. There was always a deal."

Cappararo had grown up with his mother, two sisters and assorted cousins in the same building on Mulberry Street in Manhattan's Little Italy. His was a close-knit Italian family, and he often joked around about having ties to the Mafia.

When *The Sopranos* became a big hit for HBO, which was owned by Time Warner where he worked, Cappararo gave everyone *Sopranos* calendars and other memorabilia from the show.

Cindy Ligosh thinks her brother desperately wanted to impress Cappararo, to prove that he was good enough for his daughter.

"I don't know if it's a male thing or not," she said. "If you marry a girl whose father plays such a dominant part in her life, that you want to prove, 'Not only am I as good as you, I'm really one better.' I think Bill had that attitude. Michael had made it plain to him that he didn't think he was good enough for his daughter."

Melanie's best friend Selene said there was always tension between McGuire and his future father-in-law.

"They knocked heads a lot," she said. "That was the man his daughter had decided to marry . . . but he didn't think much of him at all."

In May 1999, RMA hired an accountant named Christine Richie (not her real name) to work as a financial coordinator, liaising between patients and insurance companies. For the next five years she would work closely with Nurse Slate, becoming close friends with her.

"She was just striking," remembered Richie. "She was thin and had very dark eyes, and really curly dark hair down to the middle of her back. And she was also very friendly."

Richie was immediately impressed by Melanie's sheer professional competence. "It was amazing," said Richie, "because she was one of the youngest nurses there, but she knew her business. She was meticulous and it was such a pleasure to work with her."

Where some of the other nurses had trouble navigating through essential financial documentation for insurance companies, Melanie was always on top of it.

"She knew what the answer was," said Richie, "what the situation was and what to do. There were sometimes problems with other nurses, but never with Melanie."

Richie thought so highly of her that when a friend had an infertility problem, Richie recommended Melanie.

"Melanie took care of her," she said. "And my girlfriend ended up having a beautiful baby girl from the IVF, and went back to have frozen eggs put in."

RMA was such a success, that over the next few years Dr. Richard Scott set up satellite offices in West Orange, Englewood and Somerset to serve the lucrative tristate market. Melanie Slate looked set for a long highly paid career.

"She made a home for herself at RMA," said Richie. "She was obviously adored by all the doctors, so she didn't have to worry about job security. And she continued to grow and excel."

In the weeks leading up to the wedding, Bill McGuire was in daily contact with his best man Jon Rice. The wedding was planned for Sunday, June 6, and Bill wanted the Rices to arrive in New Jersey on the Thursday before, so they could spend some quality time together.

The Rices, who were coming up from Virginia Beach, decided it would be the perfect opportunity for them to take a long anticipated trip to the Bahamas, where Jon's Aunt Peggy had a vacation home. So after getting his aunt's permission, Jon invited Bill and Melanie to spend their honeymoon with them on the Islands, and they immediately agreed.

"He hadn't planned anything," explained Jon. "I thought, 'The more the merrier.'"

Just before they got married, Melanie gave her future husband a smiling photo of herself, with the following inscription on the back.

> *Bill, as we prepare to start out our lives together, I just want you to know how much I love you and I couldn't have done it without you.*
>
> *Thank you for your undying love and support,*
>
> *Mel*

TEN

"From This Moment On"

On June 3, 1999—three days before they married—Bill McGuire declared bankruptcy, exploiting a loophole in the U.S. bankruptcy laws, which were about to change. A few months later Melanie also filed for bankruptcy.

"He was embarrassed," said Jon Rice. "He talked to me about it. He was always looking to either make money or get out of paying for something."

Bill also discussed it with his former roommate Eric Soles, describing it as a good financial move.

"I don't think it was really about money problems," said Soles. "It was just a way of consolidating some things. He knew he was getting married soon and it was almost a strategy."

He told his sister Cindy that being bankrupt would ensure a better interest rate in the future, when he and Melanie bought property.

"He didn't have money troubles," she said. "We used to do stocks when he was going to school and working as a waiter. The two of us would be on the phone, playing the stock market and trading online. Sometimes we'd lose and sometimes we'd win."

A few hours after filing bankruptcy papers, Bill and Melanie drove to the Newark airport to meet Jon and Sue Rice, who were arriving from Norfolk. Even before they left the terminal, Bill took his best man to one side to give him some important news.

"Well, she got pregnant," he announced. "She quit taking the pills without my knowledge and became pregnant."

The way Bill rationalized it to Jon, Melanie spent so much time with infertile women, she'd grown fearful of being able to have children herself.

Jon was shocked and upset, feeling this would ruin their upcoming trip to the Bahamas.

"It was going to be a party and a honeymoon," he explained. "The whole nine yards—drinking, eating a lot and snorkeling. And that's what we invited them to go down for."

That night Bill and Melanie took the Rices out for dinner, at the chic French restaurant where he worked. And during the meal, Sue—who did not know Melanie was pregnant—said they would soon be snorkeling in the Bahamas.

"Well, Melanie's not going to be able to," snapped Bill.

When Sue asked why, Bill said it was because she was pregnant.

"And," said Sue, "I just went, 'No way, Melanie! You couldn't wait?'"

That night, the Rices moved into the Woodbridge apartment, while Melanie stayed with her parents, where she would sleep until the wedding.

Friday was spent running last-minute errands for the wedding. Bill drove his best man into Manhattan to rent tuxedos, and Jon happened to ask if his mother Ruth was coming from Florida to see her only son get married. Bill said he had not invited his mother or sister Nancy, as he was not getting along with them at the moment. He then changed the subject.

"It wasn't something he really wanted to talk about at great length," remembered Rice. "And that's when I found out that he even had another sister named Nancy. You could tell there was a strain there. He didn't go into great detail, and I'm not going to press him either."

After the rehearsal dinner at Bill's restaurant, everyone went back to Bill's Woodbridge apartment, staying up late, drinking wine and reminiscing.

It was the first time Jim Carmichael had met Melanie, and they got on well.

"I thought she seemed very nice and sweet," he remembered. "But Melanie doesn't exude warmth. There's a coolness to her."

After a late start on Saturday, Bill took his friends to a Riverfest, before going to Michael and Linda Cappararo's home for a pre-wedding dinner. After the meal, Melanie and her 17-year-old half-brother Christopher retired into the living room to watch *Flintstones* cartoons, while everyone else sat around the kitchen table, chatting.

At one point, Cappararo gave his future son-in-law a fatherly lecture, joking that he'd better take care of his daughter or else. Then out of the blue, Bill shocked everyone, asking where Michael had been during Melanie's affair with her high school teacher.

"The conversation stopped short," remembered Sue Rice. "You could tell it was not something they wanted to [discuss]."

At 7:30 a.m. on her wedding day, Melanie drove to her gynecologist for a sonogram, which she would later proudly display at the reception.

"That was bizarre," remembered Cindy Ligosh. "And it bothered me. No bride has enough time on their wedding day to get ready, let alone get a sonogram. And then she brings it to the wedding to show people she was pregnant."

At precisely noon, Melanie entered St. Joseph's Catholic Church on the arm of her stepfather, Michael Cappararo. Every head turned as the beautiful bride, resplendent in a pure white lace wedding gown, complete with veil and a long train, slowly walked down the aisle, to the strains of "Here Comes the Bride." There was no hint whatsoever that the petite bride was two months pregnant.

With her long curly hair swept back under a pure white veil, Melanie was the spitting image of Snow White.

"She looked just like a princess," remembered Lisa Carmichael, who shot the wedding video. "Well, she was a size four, which is great for a wedding dress. She was so tiny."

Throughout the Mass and wedding vows, Melanie appeared

strangely emotionless, whereas the handsome tuxedoed groom was visibly moved by the occasion.

"Bill showed emotion," remembered Jim Carmichael, "which was new to me. He had tears in his eyes when she came down the aisle."

After exchanging vows and braided platinum wedding rings, Melanie suddenly appeared overcome by emotion, as she kissed her parents and grandmother Ann Moritz. Then the beaming groom went over to kiss them too. The maid of honor Selene Rodriguez rearranged Melanie's train, before the bride returned to the dais for the Reverend Kevin Schott to perform the Holy Mass.

"This celebration here has ended," declared the priest, finishing up the lengthy service. "Let us go forth today to rejoice in the marital love of Melanie and of Bill. Thanks be to God."

Outside St. Joseph's rectory the sun was shining down on a perfect June day. Bill and Melanie took their places on the receiving line, alongside her parents and grandmother, welcoming the guests as they filed out of the church. The smiling bride introduced her RMA colleagues to Bill, who politely shook their hands and thanked them for coming.

Outside the rectory, the newly married couple posed for photographs, and Bill clowned around for the camera. Then two stretch limousines arrived, and the bridal party got in, sipping champagne for the two-mile drive to the reception at the Highlawn Pavilion in West Orange.

On arrival, the bridal party went straight into the wine cellar for a special pre-reception party. By the time Bill and Melanie led them upstairs to the main reception, the rest of the 150 guests were eating hors d'oeuvres.

"It was a top-shelf open bar," remembered Sue Rice. "No expense was spared."

With sweeping views across the Hudson River to the Twin Towers and the dramatic Manhattan skyline, the wedding guests feasted on steak and lobster. The ecstatic bridegroom went from table to table, telling everyone it was the happiest day of his life.

After dinner the DJ cued up "From This Moment On," by Shania Twain, and to a round of applause, Bill and Melanie stepped out on the floor for their first dance as husband and wife, as night fell and the lights of Manhattan twinkled.

Then an emotional Michael Cappararo took the floor to slow dance to crooner Al Martino's "Daddy's Little Girl," with his stepdaughter.

For weeks, Jon Rice had been nervous about making his best man toast, even buying an instruction book to help him. After much thought and deliberation he had finally written one. But on entering the reception, Bill handed him a piece of paper with a toast written by his sister Cindy, telling him to read that.

"Cindy was really the mother hen," said Sue Rice. "She was playing the mother and that was her role."

After first thanking the bridesmaids, Jon asked the newly married couple to join hands.

"This is the last time Bill's going to have the upper hand," quipped Jon to much laughter. "Bill, you never forget what's worth remembering, and you never remember what's worth forgetting. And may the love you share forever remain as beautiful as Melanie looks today."

Then the pony-tailed MC took the music up a notch, playing the Four Seasons hit, "Oh, What a Night." And the newlyweds led a conga line around the hall to Ricky Martin's big hit "Livin' La Vida Loca."

Then to a round of applause, the bride and groom cut the three-tier wedding cake together and Melanie threw her bouquet, which was caught by Selene Rodriguez. Then, to the strains of "Mission Impossible," Bill gamely removed Melanie's garter from under her wedding dress, throwing it into the air to be caught by Selene's fiancé, Alex Trevizas.

"It was a fun reception," said Sue Rice. "Melanie and Bill were a beautiful couple, and I don't think they left each other's side the whole night."

Several weeks later, after seeing the wedding photographs, Bill called his sister Cindy in a terrible state, complaining that he couldn't find a single photograph of Melanie smiling for the thank you cards.

"Billy was very unhappy," she remembered. "And I wonder if her unsmiling face meant something."

At 6:30 the next morning, Bill and Melanie caught a flight from Newark to the Bahamas for their honeymoon. The newlyweds had spent their first married night together in their Woodbridge apartment, while the Rices moved into a hotel to give them privacy.

Melanie was exhausted, sleeping all the way to Fort Lauderdale. She later revived for the short flight to the Bahamas.

After they landed, they were met by Jon's Aunt Peggy, who drove them to her vacation home in her Jeep. But there was no air-conditioning in their room, and Bill was concerned about his pregnant new bride.

One day, Bill and Jon decided to go snorkeling off a reef, a half-mile off shore, where the marine life was supposed to be fantastic. The two men swam out as their wives stayed near the beach, paddling a kayak.

Then suddenly Bill started desperately waving his hands and yelling for help, screaming that Jon had gone under the water and not surfaced. Melanie then took control, ordering Sue to swim back to Aunt Peggy on the beach, saying she was going out to save him.

"She rowed out to Bill," remembered Sue. "And she's going against the waves."

Sue was amazed at Melanie's strength, rowing against the strong current, despite her small size and being pregnant. But when she reached the reef, Jon suddenly came up for air, totally oblivious to everyone's concern for him.

"They decided to leave the kayak there," said Sue. "So Melanie has to swim to the shore. And when she got there, Aunt Peggy was mad at Bill, for allowing her to go swimming while pregnant."

Most nights they would all go out to dinner with Aunt Peggy, drinking exotic cocktails. On one occasion, the middle-aged woman announced that she was unfit to drive her SUV. So Jon got into the driver's seat, although he had never driven on the left-hand side of the road before.

"Bill sobered up real quick," said Jon. "He was saying Melanie should drive, as she hadn't been drinking. But I said I hadn't driven yet."

When Jon insisted, turning on the ignition, Bill became furious, threatening to kill him if anything happened to his wife and unborn child.

"My family is in this car," declared Bill, close to tears. "My whole life is in this car."

The next day, after apologizing, Bill took everyone to the Atlantis resort and casino on Paradise Island in Nassau. As Jon and Sue didn't gamble, they went to see the aquarium, while Bill and Melanie hit the tables.

"Bill wanted to play blackjack," remembered Sue. "And he won a nice chunk of money and bought Melanie an emerald ring."

On Saturday night, Bill and Melanie went out for a romantic dinner at a Victorian-style restaurant, leaving the others at home, watching a movie. Then early the next morning they flew back to Newark, where they said their good-byes, before the Rices returned to Virginia.

It would be several years before Jon and Sue Rice saw their friends again, but by then everything would be different.

ELEVEN

Dr. Bradley Miller

On February 11, 2000, Melanie McGuire gave birth to a baby boy they named Jack, at Riverview Medical Center in Red Bank, New Jersey. Bill was delighted to have a son, immediately telephoning all his friends with the news.

"He wanted children," Melanie would later tell ABC *Primetime*. "He wanted to be a good father. The best times were after we got married and after our first son was born. The sun rose and set over that child."

Soon after Jack was born, Bill found a larger apartment at 1819 Forest Haven Boulevard in Edison. He was still working as a waiter, but was taking a business management course at NJIT in Newark. He seemed overjoyed to be a father and to finally have his own family.

"He loved being a father," remembered Jon Rice, who spoke to him regularly on the phone. "That was his crowning achievement."

After maternity leave, Melanie returned to RMA, immediately placing a photograph of Bill and her new baby on her desk. She had still not shed much of the weight she had put on during pregnancy, but it suited her, as she had been so thin before.

That July, Dr. Bradley Miller was recruited to RMA to head the new Gestational Carrier Program, where paid surrogates carry an infertile patient's egg to full-term delivery. Dr. Richard Scott had known Dr. Miller since the 1980s, when he'd trained the handsome young reproductive endocrinologist at the National Institute of Health's fellowship program.

"I recommended Dr. Miller," remembered Dr. Scott. "He was one of my fellows . . . an extraordinary physician."

After attending medical school in Detroit, Dr. Miller had served in the U.S. Navy, doing his entranceship in San Diego, where Bill McGuire had been stationed. He had then moved to the Bethesda Naval Hospital for his residency and fellowship, prior to joining RMA.

Dr. Scott placed great importance on the Gestational Carrier Program, immediately assigning his protégé Dr. Miller a handpicked team, including Melanie McGuire as his nurse and Christine Richie to handle insurance.

"That was a big deal financially," Richie explained. "It was *the* most expensive treatment."

New Jersey is one of the few states to allow surrogacy, in the wake of the landmark "Baby M" custody case. Baby M, whose real name is Melissa Stern, made headlines in 1986, after her surrogate mother Mary Beth Whitehead, refused to give her up after birth.

In 1987, a New Jersey court awarded custody of Baby M to William Stern and his wife Elizabeth, but the following year this was overturned by the State Supreme Court. The case was then remanded to Family Court, which awarded custody to William Stern and visitation rights to Whitehead.

In the aftermath of the infamous case, New Jersey passed a law permitting surrogacy agreements, and RMA was one of the few clinics to offer the treatment.

"It was a very complicated program," explained Richie. "It's very expensive and highly legal."

And the Gestational Carrier Program was big business, eventually making millionaires out of the three RMA partners and Dr. Miller, who would shortly be invited to become a partner.

Melanie soon struck up a rapport with the handsome distinguished-looking doctor, who remembered her from the 1998 San Francisco conference.

They worked well together. Dr. Miller enjoyed her irreverent, often X-rated, humor, which lightened the gravity of the complex medical procedures required.

Nurse McGuire's job was crucial to the success of the clinic's surrogate program, dealing with the third-party egg donors, the paid surrogates and the infertile clients. She had to keep track of every piece of the highly complex chain, putting her exceptional organizational skills to good use.

"She had massive responsibilities," said Richie. "It wasn't something that you would put in the hands of any nurse at that practice."

The Gestational Carrier Program drew many affluent clients from New York, where surrogacy laws were far stricter. The patients were often rich, as it cost more than $40,000, including surrogates' compensation and legal fees. And many patients were over 45 years old and could not use their own eggs, sending the costs even higher.

"So it was easy for a cycle of that magnitude to be sixty thousand dollars," said Richie, who handled all finances for Dr. Miller's team. "Remember, that's just one attempt, because there's no assurance of pregnancy. So an unlucky couple would have to start from the beginning again."

Nurse McGuire was well paid by RMA, earning more than her husband. She even received an extra $1,100 a week, just to carry a beeper and be on call on weekends.

As the program's nurse, she was privy to the most intimate details of her patients' lives. It was her job to help them vet prospective surrogates and then guide them through highly complicated medical procedures. Her down-to-earth humor and her gift for raising morale when patients were at their lowest ebb would endear her to all.

"She's an excellent nurse," Dr. Miller would later relate. "She took very good care of the patients and they all loved her. She was always somebody who just rose to the challenge and took on extra responsibility."

That July, Bill McGuire took Melanie and baby Jack to Orlando, Florida, to meet his mother Ruth. They visited Disney

World together, and Melanie appeared to get on well with her new mother-in-law.

Later, Bill would tell Jon Rice about the trip, saying they had dubbed his mother "the Lobster," as she ate little else except Dots candy.

After his marriage, Bill became close to Cindy, sometimes calling her ten times a day. She now acted as his confidante, and they would talk for hours at a time.

"He was a little chatterbox," she said. "Billy and I were just so much alike, and there's nothing better than having someone who thinks exactly like you do."

With his new maturity and sense of family responsibility, their old roles reversed.

"He was always there for you," she said. "Even though I was his older sister, it was like the strength of having an older brother. It was great."

At Christmas and Thanksgiving, Bill and Melanie would invite Cindy's family to the Cappararo home in Middletown for festivities.

"We used to go to her parents' house a lot," said Cindy. "I thought he was marrying into a very nice family. I loved her parents and her grandmother. They were very close, and Billy got along well with them."

Cindy especially liked Michael Cappararo, who she always made a point of sitting next to, as he was so entertaining.

But she found her new sister-in-law Melanie distant and aloof.

"We didn't have a close relationship," Cindy explained. "It wasn't a girl-friendly relationship where we'd gab on the phone. I usually spoke to my brother, or she'd get on the phone for a minute to talk about one little thing. And then she'd give the phone back to my brother."

When Cindy visited their apartment for dinner, Melanie usually remained in the background.

"We'd have dinner together and then she'd leave us alone," said Cindy. "She would busy herself with things, while Billy and I would hang out together."

Even though they were both working long hours with a young baby in day care, their Edison apartment, right off the busy Route 1, was always spotless.

"She's extremely organized," said Selene, who married Alex Trevizas soon after catching Melanie's wedding bouquet. "And that also had a lot to do with Bill, who was very, very neat. But he wanted Melanie to do the cleaning. He was a bit dominant, but Melanie allowed that."

After Jack was born, Bill McGuire felt it was time to quit the restaurant business for a more stable career. In late 2000, after graduating cum laude with a bachelor's degree in Management at NJIT, he accepted a $65,000-a-year job at the school, as an adjunct professor and programmer analyst.

"I hired him," said NJIT's associate vice president of information resource development, Tom Terry. "His position title was a 'programmer analyst,' but he actually worked as a troubleshooter for computers and PCs."

The institute had a lucrative contract with the New Jersey State Department of Health, purchasing and installing PCs at the twenty-five health departments dotted around the state. McGuire's job was to travel around the various departments, doing the installations and then troubleshooting any technical problems.

He single-handedly applied himself to his new job, as he had never done before.

"His job performance was excellent," said Terry. "He had a very good rapport with everyone."

Bill shared a cubicle with a senior program analyst named Jason Steinhauser, who was highly impressed with his computer expertise. For in addition to installing and maintaining client computers, Bill also ran the NJIT help desk and was in charge of its 1-800 number.

"People would call after hours and during weekends," said Steinhauser. "It's a twenty-four-seven e-mail system, and we didn't have a policy of 'Stop answering after five.'"

McGuire was given a Nextel Direct Connect phone and a

BlackBerry device, so he was in constant e-mail contact with the 120 users in his NJ LINCS health alert system.

"He was a power user," said Steinhauser. "And he was a social guy and had friends in the working community. I'm sure he was on some sort of joke list or forward list too."

TWELVE

A Double Life

In June 2001, Melanie became pregnant again, and Bill suspected that fertility drugs were responsible. This caused friction in the marriage, as Bill admonished her for not taking his wishes into consideration.

"He was not that thrilled that she got pregnant again," said Selene Trevizas. "I'd say everything seemed to be OK until her second child. I don't think it was the money, but he was fine with the child he had."

After Bill had resigned himself to becoming a father again, he began looking for ways to increase his income. The opportunity arose during a visit to a NJIT health clinic in Elizabeth, New Jersey, when he realized the need for a computer program that could cut out time-consuming paperwork.

When he returned to NJIT, he asked Jaychandra Tandava, a senior programmer in his office, to help him develop a software program for it.

"He said, 'Let's form a company and develop a program,'" said Tandava. "So that's where the idea of Jvista Software came into the picture."

In mid-2001, the two NJIT programmers founded the consulting company, with the full knowledge of their boss Tom Terry, who gave it his blessing. They set up a joint company bank account, with a float of $12,000 to $14,000.

A few months later, McGuire took a second job, working nights as a senior programmer for the Essex County Health

Department, earning almost as much as he did at NJIT. After signing off at NJIT at 4:00 p.m., he would moonlight in South Orange until 11:00 p.m. Then he'd go home to Melanie for a few hours' sleep before rising early, so he could start work again at 7:30 a.m.

Working such long hours, Bill and Melanie seldom saw each other during the week, and began to drift apart. Baby Jack now spent most of his time in day care, or being taken care of by his grandparents.

"She was pregnant," remembered Lori Thomas, who now shared an office with Melanie, "but I don't know if she was that happy. She never really talked about Bill."

But Melanie often criticized her husband to Christine Richie.

"I never met Billy," she said, "but he was always portrayed as a bit of a jerk."

Since starting the Gestational Carrier Program together, Melanie worked very closely with Dr. Brad Miller. They spent most of their working day together, soon discovering a strong mutual attraction.

"We were always flirtatious," admitted Dr. Miller, who had a young son the same age as Jack. "She had gotten me a birthday cake, and bought me a small gift for Christmas."

The chivalrous reproductive endocrinologist started acting more like a suitor and less like a boss.

"He was so kind and just very sweet," remembered Melanie. "I'd come back to my desk after a long meeting with a patient, and there'd be lunch sitting on my desk waiting for me. He was just very, very tender."

Melanie and Bill had now begun bickering again, each accusing the other of not pulling their weight in the marriage.

"I know that they argued," said Dr. Miller. "I heard her yelling on the phone."

One main concern was Jack, who at 18 months had still not started speaking. After a doctor tested his hearing and found it normal, Bill worried that the boy was spending too much time in day care.

About this time, Bill's sister Nancy Taylor was contemplating a move back to New Jersey with her two children. So she called him to see if he knew of any job opportunities.

"All he could think about was day care," she said. "Because they were paying an arm and a leg for [it]."

But his elder sister Cindy had a friend who was a nurse and mother of three young children, and in a similar position. She had solved it, working a 3:00-to-11:00 p.m. shift four days a week, making the same money, but enjoying far more quality time with her children.

But when Cindy suggested it to her sister-in-law as a possible solution, she was shocked by Melanie's reaction.

"What kind of life would that be for me?" Melanie snapped, walking out of the room without another word, and leaving Cindy dumbfounded.

"There's no response to that," said Cindy. "That someone would even think that and then verbalize it . . . But Melanie doesn't really engage in argument. That was the only time I said anything at all."

Bill also had a plan, inviting Selene and Alex Trevizas, who owned a thriving Brooklyn construction business, to become his partners in a day care center. They wrote a business plan and found a location, and then Bill called Nancy in Florida, inviting her to work in his new enterprise.

"He wanted Melanie too, so she could be with her baby," remembered Taylor, "but she did not want to give up her nursing job."

But when it came time for Bill to put up his share of the stake money, he suddenly pulled out.

"They had a certain amount of money and we had a certain amount of money," explained Selene. "And then all of a sudden their money was gone. He said they put it in one stock, and it went down and they lost everything. I thought that was weird."

In late 2001, RMA opened the first of three satellite offices in West Orange. And over the next two years the successful fertility clinic would expand to Somerset and Englewood.

Dr. Brad Miller's Gestational Carrier Program was such a success, he was invited to become a partner.

"That's how good he was," explained Christine Richie. "Forget millionaire—multimillionaire."

Dr. Miller and his wife Charla now lived the high life, with a luxury house in the exclusive town of Bridgewater, New Jersey, and his own private plane. And the sky seemed the limit for the dashing doctor from humble Maryland origins.

On February 3, 2002, Dr. Miller held a lavish Super Bowl party at his million-dollar house, throwing his doors open to all RMA employees and their spouses.

Melanie brought Bill along, introducing him to her new boss for the first time. Later he would tell his sister Cindy how much he had enjoyed himself at the party.

"He loved the doctor's house," said Cindy Ligosh, "and liked him and his wife. They had a son who was the same age as Jack, and he spoke to me about the similarities, and their strengths and weaknesses."

Melanie was also impressed with the Millers' lavish lifestyle, which seemed light years away from her nondescript Edison apartment.

Bill McGuire's horrendous driving record finally caught up with him that year, when he was suspended from driving in New Jersey for racking up 37 points. But after surrendering his license to the State of New Jersey Motor Vehicle Commission, he and Melanie drove to Pennsylvania, and, using her Aunt Barbara's East Stroudsburg address as proof of residence, illegally obtained Pennsylvania licenses and plates.

In early 2002, Michael Cappararo, approaching 60, retired from Time Warner. He and Linda sold their house in Middletown, moving to a gated retirement community in the scenic beach resort of Barnegat in south Jersey. Then, to the surprise of many, he got a job behind the counter of the local post office.

Bill was shocked, unable to comprehend why his father-in-law would be doing this. But it turned out the savvy Cappararo was teaching himself the package shipping business, eventually opening an E-Z Store with two partners in a Barnegat mall.

One of Bill's main gripes to Melanie was always having to visit her parents, instead of the other way around. "Billy used to complain that Michael and Linda never came to their home," said Cindy. "They would always go down there."

And now that the trip to Barnegat took far longer, this caused even more tension between them.

By mid-March, Melanie McGuire was thirty-eight weeks pregnant, and preparing to go on maternity leave. One day she was in Dr. Miller's office, when she mentioned she had a pinched nerve in her neck.

Without a word the handsome doctor stood up and came around behind her, to give her a back massage. And within seconds they lost control.

"We had oral sex in the office," Dr. Miller later admitted, "before she went on maternity leave."

On March 21, Melanie gave birth again at Riverview Medical Center to another baby boy, who they named Jason. Soon after the birth, they moved into a spacious three-story townhouse at 2902 Plaza Drive, Woodbridge.

"They were in one bedroom when they went to have their second child," said Bill's former roommate Eric Soles, who remained in close touch. "I know they were cramped for space."

Soon after Jason, or JT, as Melanie would always call him, was born, an excited Bill called Soles for a heart-to-heart conversation.

"He was home alone with the boys," remembered Soles, who could hear the baby crying in the background. "And we were talking about having kids and how it changes your life. He was just really into the kids. He loved being a father, and whenever he and I had conversations afterwards, the kids were always in the background."

When Melanie returned from maternity leave, she and Dr. Miller embarked on a wild passionate affair. But they had to keep it secret at RMA, as having an adulterous affair with his nurse violated his partnership agreement.

"It was difficult," explained the doctor. "We did have a lot of problems. We sometimes would see each other in the office. We would sometimes go out for lunch. Sometimes leave work a little early, or on a day off we'd spend half a day together."

Most evenings Dr. Miller would return home to his wife Charla, helping out with his young son. But whenever he and Melanie attended an RMA function, they would stop off at the Loop Inn on the U.S. 1 & 9 in Avenel, New Jersey, for sex.

Using the non-de-plume "Brian Mills," the doctor would check them into the sleazy motel, boasting adult theme rooms and champagne bedrooms. He always paid in cash to avoid any paper trail.

He also purchased, in cash, two separate cell phones with prepaid minutes on a family plan, so they could have their own private conversations. As their love affair progressed, they would call each other incessantly, spending hours on the phone every day.

But all this excitement and living dangerously was apparently affecting Melanie McGuire, who lost a shocking amount of weight after Jason was born.

"She was skin and bones," remembered Christine Richie. "We all went to a karaoke bar and I told her, 'Holy cow, you got so thin.' She had just come back from maternity leave, and I didn't know any of that was going on at all."

Although it had begun as pure lust, Melanie and Dr. Miller soon fell deeply in love with each other. Over the next three years, they lived a double life, becoming practiced at the art of deception.

THIRTEEN

The Mother Whisperer

Soon after Jason was born, Bill McGuire flew to Virginia for a long weekend, wanting to check out a classic red Mustang he'd found for sale on the Internet. It was the first time he had seen Jon Rice since the Bahamas honeymoon, two years earlier. After meeting him at the airport, Rice drove him to the house in Chesapeake, where Bill would be staying.

That night Jon and Sue took their best friend to a comedy club, where they sat at a table right by the stage.

"The whole time the comedian was picking on me," remembered Jon Rice. "Bill was rolling around and thought it was the funniest thing. It was just a fun time for the three of us."

Later that night, over a glass of Silver Oak red wine at their home, the Rices asked Bill to become godfather to their new-born son Austin.

"He was crying," remembered Jon. "We were all crying."

Then as they celebrated, Bill became very emotional and unusually serious. He began talking about domestic violence.

"We were just having a real heart-to-heart," remembered Sue. "And he talked about never hitting a woman, because he thought that was the lowest you could get."

Then Bill said that if Jon ever hit her, she should tell him immediately.

"I said Jon would never do that to me," Sue said. "And he said the worst thing you could do is hit a woman."

The next day when Bill McGuire took the Mustang for a test drive, it broke down. The embarrassed owner then had it repaired, but the same thing happened when Bill took it out again. He gave up on the idea of buying it.

Throughout the weekend, Bill telephoned Melanie incessantly, asking about his two sons. His old friends were delighted to see him so happy, and devoted to his wife and children.

"You would have thought Melanie was here," said Sue, "as much as he was talking to her on the phone."

Now settled in their new Woodbridge townhouse, Melanie had been busy buying furniture and furnishings for the spacious three-floor apartment. There was an expensive couch with matching armchairs for the living room, and a Thomasville bedroom set for the master bedroom.

With Bill working such long hours at his two jobs and new consultancy business, Melanie had little trouble concealing her affair. She and Dr. Miller were now spending as much time as possible at the Loop Inn, with Melanie then coming home, acting the part of good wife and mother.

And before long the lovers were planning a future together one day.

"I was deeply in love with him," Melanie would later tell ABC *Primetime*. "The understanding between us had always been that the children came first."

Soon after the affair began, Dr. Miller's wife Charla became pregnant with twin girls. After an amniocentesis, a problem was found, and one of the twins was later born with Down syndrome. Throughout his ordeal, Melanie was always there with a reassuring word of comfort.

"There was a lot of stress in the marriage," said Christine Richie. "But after the baby was born with Down syndrome, he did share it with everybody. It was very stressful. I never knew him to take a minute off of work, and he was taking care of it like any father would."

Melanie and her boss now spent so much time together that many at RMA were becoming suspicious.

"There were always rumors about them having an affair,"

said Richie, who worked closely with them both. "And people talked behind their backs, as they were spending a lot of time together. But she certainly never shared that with me."

Nurse Lori Thomas said their affair was an open secret at the clinic.

"Everybody knew," she said. "Were they indiscreet? Yes they were, and there were rumors around the office. She was always on the phone with him, and always in his office when he was in Morristown."

That summer, on Melanie's advice, Selene Trevizas became an RMA patient, doing in vitro with Dr. Miller.

"He was my doctor," said Selene, "and Melanie was my nurse."

Selene was immediately charmed by the handsome specialist, teasing her best friend that they would make the perfect couple, if they were not both already married.

"I told her that," said Selene, "and she used to tell me in her sarcastic way, 'Well, you know, maybe we are or maybe we will be.' But I always thought she was joking."

That Halloween, Angela Shiska flew into New Jersey with her husband Brad, to be screened as a possible paid surrogate for RMA's Gestational Carrier Program. After arriving at the Morristown clinic, they were interviewed by Nurse Melanie McGuire, to see if Angela was suitable.

"She came and greeted us in the waiting room," remembered Angela. "Then we sat down with her for the interview. I thought she was wonderful, because she approved me right away."

After passing the first hurdle, Melanie called in Dr. Miller and the intended parents from New York for the next stage of the process. From the way Dr. Miller interacted with his nurse, Angela wondered if there was something more than just a professional connection between them.

"I just had a feeling," she remembered. "From that first meeting I kind of suspected the relationship, but of course I would never vocalize it. When Melanie went to make the appointment for Dr. Miller, she almost told him what to do. 'OK, we're going to do this and we're going to do that.' It was kind of like a spouse would."

After being approved as a surrogate, Melanie was assigned as the Shiskas' coordinator, beginning an ongoing relationship between her and the couple.

"She was so excited about the possibility of us going through this joint venture of creating the baby," said Angela. "She reassured us that if we had any questions, or if we were scared, we should call her immediately. I just thought she was wonderful."

In her first attempt át in vitro, Angela became pregnant, but miscarried after six weeks, requiring a D&C procedure. But her second attempt was a success, and under Melanie's close supervision, she gave birth to a healthy baby for the New York couple.

"I call her 'the Mother Whisperer,'" said Angie. "She was extremely supportive."

That October, Sharon Elizabeth LaBlue, a systems engineer for a Nashville-based computer company, flew into Newark for a two-day business meeting at NJIT. In the wake of 9/11, Bill McGuire's NJ LINCS Health Alert Network was now part of the newly created Homeland Security, to keep vital communications going between local health departments in the event of a biological terrorist attack.

The attractive slim redhead's main point of contact at NJIT was Bill McGuire, who seemed especially charming during her presentation on her company's emergency notification technology system.

The two got along very well, and after finishing early on the second day of the meeting, McGuire invited her to lunch and then took her sightseeing.

At a jewelry store, McGuire showed her a ring with a large purple stone, saying he planned to buy it for his wife Melanie. He then invited Sharon to dinner, and she willingly accepted.

"We did have drinks," she said. "Margaritas."

After dinner, they went back to LaBlue's hotel room and had sex, and the next day she flew back to Nashville.

Over the next few weeks, Bill McGuire called her several times, suggesting another meeting.

"I asked him not to contact me anymore," she would later testify. "And I recommended that he and his wife seek marriage counseling."

That Christmas, Melanie McGuire and Dr. Brad Miller brought their respective spouses and children to Radio City Music Hall in New York City, for the holiday show.

"We went together as a family," Dr. Miller remembered. "[Melanie's] entire family had been over to my house for cookouts."

And soon afterwards, an unsuspecting Bill McGuire attended a low-stakes poker party at the Miller house, playing for quarters and dollars.

"They went over to the Millers' house a number of times," said Cindy Ligosh, "and they also came to [Bill's] house. You have to be so cool to do that."

But whenever Dr. Miller saw Bill with Melanie, he became uncomfortable.

"He acted affectionate [towards Melanie]," said Dr. Miller. "He would have his arm around her or hold her hand."

Melanie would also discuss her and Bill's sex life, describing to Dr. Miller what they did in bed.

"There were three occasions," related Dr. Miller, "that she told me, after their second child was born, that they had sex together."

Although the lovers still enjoyed regular trysts at the Loop Inn, they now started meeting each other in a family context with their children.

"I'd take the kids grocery shopping on the weekend," Melanie said. "He would try and meet me there. He went pumpkin-picking with us. He was every bit the family man, but somebody else's family."

And although Bill McGuire had no inkling of the affair, Dr. Miller's wife Charla suspected something was going on with his nurse.

"She had questions or suspicions," said Dr. Miller, "but I always reassured her that nothing was going on."

FOURTEEN

A Dream House

In March 2003, Bill McGuire drove Melanie and Jack to Virginia Beach for his godson Austin Rice's baptism, while baby Jason remained in New Jersey with his grandparents. They arrived late on a Friday afternoon, after Bill missed the turn-off, adding hours to the journey.

"Bill kept calling," remembered Sue Rice. " 'Sue, I'm going to take a shortcut,' but anyhow, he took the long way around."

After the birth of his second son, Bill had set himself a goal to be achieved within eighteen months' time.

"Bill badly wanted to put his wife and kids into a home before he turned forty," said Jim Carmichael. "Not something he rented, but something he owned. That was very important to him."

And he wanted to move to Virginia Beach, where property was far cheaper than New Jersey, and the dollar stretched further. Since his visit the year before, he had started saving for a down payment, and the Rices were sending him photographs of prospective houses on the market.

"He really wanted to move into the neighborhood," said Sue. "Owning a house was something he always wanted."

As soon as they arrived, an excited Sue started showing Melanie the *Virginian-Pilot* property pages.

"Melanie was the one that we would have to convince," said Sue. "Then Bill would have been here in a flash. But she just kind of blew it off: 'That's not going to happen.' "

The weekend trip was a disaster—just before leaving for the baptism, Melanie discovered that Jack had scalp ringworm.

"They were going nuts," remembered Jon. "They thought they were putting us in harm's way, and felt terrible."

After the baptism, Bill called his pharmacist brother-in-law Bill Ligosh for advice. Ligosh suggested using some ointment that Sue already had.

"But that wasn't good enough for Bill McGuire," said Sue. "They were just really freaking out, and they had to take him to a doc-in-a-box walk-in place for treatment."

Back in New Jersey, Bill McGuire tried to persuade Melanie to move to Virginia. He argued it would allow them to spend more time with the children, and raise their standard of living.

But Melanie, now in the midst of an intense love affair with Dr. Brad Miller, had no intention of leaving New Jersey.

"He really strongly wanted to move to Virginia," said his sister Cindy. "But she wouldn't hear of it. And they did get into arguments over that."

Whenever he raised the subject, Melanie adamantly refused to consider it, saying it would be too far away from her parents and friends.

"He was mad," said Cindy. "But he had no idea why she so adamantly didn't want to move down there."

Finally they compromised, agreeing to start looking for a house in New Jersey, so Melanie could stay at RMA and be near her parents and friends.

"She was like, 'OK, then we'll get the house,'" said Selene Trevizas. "But she wasn't involved in the house. He made it very clear that he'd take care of the house and she'd take care of the kids."

That June, Bill McGuire learned his mother was dying of diabetes and heart problems, and requested compassionate leave to visit her in Florida. But as he was working on an important project on a tight deadline, NJIT refused to let him visit her, and she died soon afterwards. This led to heated arguments in the office, and lasting tensions between McGuire and one of his superiors, whom he blamed.

Bill went to the funeral that July, in New Port Ritchey, Florida, where he was reunited with his sister Nancy Taylor. But Melanie had refused to go, or allow him to bring Jack.

"He was very upset," said Nancy. "Melanie was totally against it, and made up all these excuses. I know he felt bad," said Nancy.

It was a highly emotional occasion for the two siblings, made more so by a plan Bill had come up with.

"Nancy had always wanted my father to admit that he had molested her," said her sister Cindy, "but he never would. So after my mother passed away, my brother went to [her] house and told Nancy that he had found a letter that my father had dictated to a nurse on his deathbed, confessing. But there was never any letter."

Though Nancy believed the letter to be genuine, Bill had written the imaginary admission himself.

That would be the last time she would ever see her brother alive.

By this time, Melanie McGuire and Brad Miller had decided that they eventually wanted to divorce their partners, and have children together. Dr. Miller was now based in a new satellite RMA office in Somerset, New Jersey, giving him and Melanie more time together.

"We were hoping to be together in the future," Dr. Miller would later admit. "She was going to divorce Bill and then a while later I was going to divorce Charla. And the two of us would marry, buy a house together and ultimately have children."

They were now in constant contact, from 5:00 a.m., when Dr. Miller went to the gym, until they went to bed at night. They would call each other on their secret cell phones as many as eighteen times a day, as well as exchanging up to fifty e-mails.

Their affair was virtually an open secret at RMA. "I think a number of us were concerned," Dr. Richard Scott said, "that he might be having an affair with Melanie McGuire." One day Dr. Scott called Dr. Miller into his office to confront him about it.

Miller vehemently denied having an affair, saying he would never engage in such unprofessional conduct.

"I accepted it at that time at face value," said Dr. Scott.

A few weeks later, Dr. Scott became even more concerned about a possible affair, challenging Dr. Miller once again.

"Dr. Scott had suspicions," admitted Dr. Miller. "But any time he asked me about it, I denied it. One of us would be losing our job if we had admitted to an affair."

Perhaps *the* only person who did not suspect a thing was Bill McGuire.

"He had no clue," said his sister Cindy. "He was definitely no rube. And the thing that shocked me so much about it was that she was able to have an affair over a period of several years without him knowing."

That summer, Jim and Lisa Carmichael were attending a conference in Philadelphia with their daughter Chelsea, when they stayed at the McGuires' townhouse on the way home. During their weekend stay, they observed how devoted Bill was to Melanie.

"It wasn't idyllic . . . they clearly had problems," said Jim Carmichael. "But I think Bill was completely in love with her."

In hindsight, Carmichael believes that his savvy friend simply had no idea that Melanie was cheating.

"Bill was very street-wise, very smart," said Carmichael, now a prosecutor in Georgia. "Bill had [no] idea that Melanie was ever screwing around. And he's the kind of guy that would never have missed it."

During their stay, Melanie took Chelsea—then aged 12—and her oldest son Jack into Manhattan to visit the science museum. Chelsea immediately noticed how Melanie had two cell phones, making frequent calls with one of them.

After going to the museum, Melanie took the children to Krystal restaurant for a meal.

"She was nice enough," remembered Chelsea. "But I'm used to being around Mom, who's kind of a warm person."

When Melanie got the food, Chelsea pointed out it was far too hot for little Jack to eat, suggesting they let it cool down first.

"And she's like, 'Oh, exactly,'" remembered Chelsea. "And we cut it into little pieces. She seemed like she was trying really hard to make it look like she was the perfect mother. Everything had to be just right."

Bill McGuire was now spending more and more time in Atlantic City gambling, and he was on a winning streak. A rated player at the Trump Taj Mahal since 1994, during twelve visits he made in 2003 he won a total of $30,775, earmarked to go towards the new house when he found it.

His NJIT work involved him traveling between the various health departments, and whenever he was in south Jersey he'd stop off at Atlantic City and play the tables.

"He had this twenty-minute rule," said Cindy Ligosh. "And he would tell the valet, 'Don't bury my car.' He'd tip him ahead of time and say, 'I'm going to be out in twenty minutes.' And he figured, 'How much money can I win or lose in twenty minutes?'"

On Thursday, October 16, Jon and Susan Rice arrived in Atlantic City for a long weekend with Bill and Melanie McGuire. Bill had invited them to stay at the Taj Mahal as his personal guests, after they expressed interest in visiting it.

"I'm taking care of everything," he'd promised. "The hotel, the meals—everything's included. Just come on up."

It was the first time the Rices had seen Bill and Melanie in six months, and they appeared happy.

"We never saw them not having that ideal marriage," said Jon Rice. "They're still arm-in-arm. Bill would say something to Melanie, [who] would have a quick retort. It was fun to be around that couple."

On Thursday night, Bill took them for a champagne dinner at an Italian restaurant, where they reminisced about their Navy days. Bill said he had just received an e-mail from Marci, who had tracked him down through Classmates.com.

"He says, 'I heard from Marci,'" said Sue Rice. "'She's up in New York working as a nurse, and married.' I said, 'Really, did you respond back?' And he goes, 'Yeah, I sent her a quick thing. I felt like I needed to apologize if I was mean to her.'"

After dinner, Bill hit the baccarat tables and started gambling. He had brought $10,000 with him as stake money, telling his friend that he had to show he was serious to get all the casino comps.

Then Bill started winning.

"He could do no wrong," remembered Jon. "He won and then he left, saying he just made a bunch of people mad."

They then moved on to roulette, and Jon watched in admiration as Bill's winning streak continued. Then he started teaching Jon the game, telling him where to place his bet.

"We placed the bet and then the guy rolls the dice," said Jon. "OK, we just won two hundred dollars."

Then Bill took him to the craps table, telling him to sit down, and where to place his bet.

"And OK, we've just won another fifty dollars," said Jon. "That first night he won a bunch of money, just not even trying. And every time I would place a bet, I'd lose it, hands-down."

The next morning, after breakfast, Bill gave Jon a blackjack lesson, while Melanie and Sue went for a walk on the Boardwalk.

"We walked the entire thing until we got to a seedy part," remembered Sue. "And we went into various shops, getting the kids souvenirs and salt water taffy."

But almost the entire time Melanie was on her cell phone.

"Melanie would just go off by herself and talk," Sue said. "Or the phone would ring. I could tell it was a private conversation, as she would go to the other side of the shop."

On Friday night, Bill had arranged for the best seats in the house for a Matchbox Twenty concert. But after two songs, he and Jon went back to the tables, leaving their wives to watch the show alone.

On Saturday morning, Melanie suddenly announced that she was returning to Woodbridge, saying she wanted to pick up her boys from her parents' and clean the apartment. By now Bill was up $30,000, and she wanted to take it back with her, so he couldn't lose it.

When Bill refused, saying it would be dangerous to travel with so much cash, Melanie threw a tantrum.

"They had an argument about the money," said Jon, "because Melanie wanted to take it and put it in the bank. She left in a huff."

On Sunday, after Bill competed in a blackjack tournament, they drove back to Woodbridge. During the journey, Sue Rice sat in the back, next to one of Bill McGuire's three new matching dark green Kenneth Cole designer suitcases.

At one point, Melanie called, complaining that the furnace had gone out and there was no heat in the apartment. When they arrived back at Plaza Drive, Jon went down into the basement to look at the furnace, admiring a new Weider weight set Bill had recently bought.

"He had furniture, clothes and I saw some weights in a storage room," said Jon. "I remember thinking, 'Only Bill would have designer weights.'"

FIFTEEN

"You Think You Have Problems?"

All through the summer Bill McGuire searched for his dream house. He was helped by his sister Cindy, who was now working as a realtor in northern New Jersey, with inside access to the local property market.

"So I would meet him," she said, "and we'd go around to see the properties that he wanted to see."

Eventually, Bill put down an offer on a large house in Warren County, asking his boss Tom Terry for mortgage advice.

"Bill was very excited," said Terry. "And as I had purchased several houses, he came to me, asking for information about where he should be going for a loan. I was kind of a father figure since his father had passed away."

But during negotiations, Melanie started investigating her prospective new neighbors through tax records.

"All their neighbors were foreigners," said Cindy. "She made comments that the children won't have anyone to play with that spoke English. Billy loved the house, but they ended up getting into an argument and withdrew their offer."

Even though her husband was searching for an expensive house, Melanie was now contemplating divorce, informing Dr. Miller that she wanted to move into a new apartment with Jack and Jason. But she admitted being scared of Bill's reaction when he found out.

"Bill had told her if she ever got a divorce," said Dr. Miller, "that he would take the kids and disappear, and she would never see her children again."

She now publicly referred to Bill as "the Jerk," discussing her deteriorating marriage with several colleagues at RMA.

"I once talked to her about relationship problems I was having," said Lori Thomas. "And I remember her specifically saying, 'You think you have problems? Pull up a chair if you have a few hours.' I was like, 'Wow.' "

That Thanksgiving, Bill, Melanie and her stepfather Michael Cappararo attended an open house, for a half-million-dollar property in the select Asbury section of Franklin Township in Warren County. While Melanie and Cappararo remained downstairs, owner Peter Burnejko gave Bill a guided tour of the four-bedroom colonial house with vaulted ceilings, set in two acres.

"We made basic small talk," remembered Burnejko. "How big the house was, nice size rooms, stairs."

But Burnejko noticed Melanie's lack of interest during the twenty minutes they were there.

"She didn't ask any questions," he said. "Mr. McGuire asked the questions."

At that time the house at 29 Halls Mill Road was listed to a realtor, but when the contract ran out the second week of January 2004, Burnejko decided to sell it privately, and began advertising. He then received a call from Bill McGuire, saying he wanted to negotiate a price.

Three days later Bill arrived at the house alone, ready to make a deal.

"We had a contract form that I had purchased," said Burnejko. "And we discussed the price being $515,000 at the time."

Bill agreed to the price and signed the contract, leaving a $1,000 deposit. Over the next few weeks, he devoted himself to getting a mortgage and having the house appraised.

When Melanie told her friend Regina Knowles that they were buying a half-million-dollar house, she was flabbergasted.

"I said, 'What are you doing?' " said Knowles. " 'This mortgage is going to take up all of your money, how are you doing this?' And she said, 'Bill's taking care of everything.' "

Melanie was now actively exploring divorce, asking her nursing colleague Joyce Maloney—a recent divorcée—for advice.

"Melanie was really stressed out," she remembered. "We discussed her children, day-care issues and things like that."

But when Maloney said that her divorce had cost more than $100,000, Melanie looked shocked.

"She had a lot of concerns about the financial end," said Maloney.

To make things worse, Dr. Brad Miller was now having reservations about leaving his children, telling Melanie he wanted to wait between six months to a year after she left Bill before making his own move.

"I was internally conflicted," he explained. "As the kids were getting older . . . it would be harder and harder for me to consider divorcing my wife and leaving the children."

In January 2004, Melanie McGuire enrolled Jack—one month shy of his 4th birthday—at Kinder Kastle day care in Metuchen.

"I first met Melanie when she came to tour Kinder Kastle," said the director, Donna Todd. "Afterwards she sent her husband Bill for a short tour [and] I showed him the classroom."

Initially, Jack was placed with children of his own age, but there were problems.

"Jack had some difficulty in the classroom," said Todd. "He was a little frustrated. At that point I talked to him and moved him back to a younger age group."

At the same time, Melanie also found a speech therapist for Jack, who was still not talking properly. She was now convinced Jack was autistic.

"Bill would not acknowledge that," said Selene Trevizas, "and would not allow the boys to get tested. The school that Jack went to was concerned, and they asked Melanie . . . to get her son tested. But Bill refused. He said there's absolutely nothing wrong with his son."

Bill believed Jack merely lacked maternal attention.

In February, Bill McGuire telephoned the CTX Mortgage Company, asking for pre-approval on a $463,500 mortgage. He spoke to loan officer Eric Levy, who took his Social Security number and ran a credit check. Levy then mailed out a forty-page residential loan application, asking for personal financial information from Bill and Melanie, along with Bill's business card, but never heard another word.

As Bill McGuire grew more and more excited at the prospect of his new dream house, Melanie felt increasingly trapped. Although she was searching online for apartments, Dr. Miller refused, for the moment, to commit himself to leaving his wife and children.

But at RMA Melanie never let her guard down, working as hard as ever and being the consummate professional.

In February, a surrogate named Melissa Coulter and her husband Dean, flew in from Illinois for a screening meeting with Dr. Miller, Nurse McGuire and the intended parents. They first spent an hour with Melanie, as she explained the process, showing them the long needles used for intramuscular injections in the hip.

"She was very funny and patient," remembered Coulter. "She really engaged my husband Dean, who was terrified when he saw the points of the needles he would have to put into me. And she tried to joke to alleviate his fears, saying, 'Most husbands would love to get to jab their wives in the ass.'"

A few days later, Melanie called Jim Carmichael's wife Lisa in Georgia. The Carmichaels were desperately trying to have their fourth child and the fertility nurse had some suggestions.

"She was trying to give us pointers," remembered Lisa, "and had offered to send fertility drugs down to us. I was uncomfortable with that, because, at least in Georgia, that's illegal."

Melanie said it was "no big deal," as these were leftover drugs at RMA, offering to drop them in the mail. But Lisa declined, saying she did not want to break the law.

As a trusted nurse, Melanie had access to Dr. Miller's prescription pads, since part of her job was calling in medications to pharmacies. With his full permission, she would routinely copy his signature on prescriptions for drugs.

But she now started writing herself prescriptions for Xanax and other tranquilizers, which she was becoming increasingly dependent on.

Things were moving fast, as Bill secured a first mortgage on the Asbury house, and began looking for a second to complete the purchase. He had already gotten estimates from a moving company, and been granted a two-week vacation for the move at the end of April.

"It was like a dream house for him," said his colleague and business partner Jay Tandava. "He used to talk about this house to everybody in the office, even on the client side."

But as the new house became a reality, Melanie became more and more stressed out, viewing Bill McGuire as an obstacle to her happiness. She began planning an exit strategy from the marriage, so she could start a new life with Dr. Brad Miller.

On Sunday, March 28, 2004, Cindy Ligosh visited Melanie and Bill's Woodbridge townhouse for dinner. Later, as they sat in the living room talking and watching TV, Bill opened a bottle of red wine, and Melanie went off by herself.

At one point the subject of their late mother's estate came up. It had been agreed that the $100,000 estate would be divided, with Bill getting $30,000, and the rest being shared between Cindy and Nancy's children.

But Nancy was being a fly in the ointment, coming up with a succession of impractical schemes, which was slowing down the whole process.

"She was frustrating us a lot," explained Cindy. "And it was taking a very long time to settle the estate. It was no argument over money. It was just Nancy and her crazy ideas."

Then, as the wine flowed, they mischievously decided to

write their sister an imaginary letter from a prison psycho, as she was presently looking for romance in Internet chatrooms.

"It was brother-and-sister immature stuff," said Cindy. "An example of our dark humor."

So Cindy started playfully doodling on a little notepad, next to the telephone.

1 — letters from psycho in prison
2 — burnt ashes of letter from nurse
3 — taunt her w/she's lying

"It was just fantasy," said Cindy. "A letter from a psycho— 'Oh, she can have play pals from prison.' 'And let's burn that note.' But it was just fooling around in frustration."

Later that night, Bill fell asleep on the couch and Cindy left, writing a good-bye note below the "prison psycho" doodlings:

Went home to sleep. Talk to you tomorrow! Kiss the kids and special hug to Jack.

After Cindy left, Melanie came into the front room and saw the note, picking it up and reading it. She then brought it upstairs and hid it in a safe place, thinking it might be something she could put to good use later.

SIXTEEN

"How to Commit Murder"

Ten days later, Ruth McGuire's estate was settled, with her son receiving a $30,000 share. That week Melanie McGuire searched the Internet on her home computer for the sleep sedative Dalmane. She then filled out an RMA prescription for the powerful hypnotic in her late mother-in-law's name, giving her old Forest Haven Boulevard, Edison, address. She forged Dr. Miller's name to it, before dropping it off at a Walgreens at 1197 Amboy Avenue, Edison, collecting it twenty-five minutes later.

She had also reconnected with her old nursing school admirer James Finn, who still carried a torch for her. In the eight years since her graduation, Melanie had rarely been in touch, but suddenly in February 2004, she began sending him flirtatious e-mails.

"They really picked up a lot around April," remembered Finn, "and the tone changed. Things were not so good at home and her husband was acting strangely."

They eventually started talking on the phone, with Melanie complaining about Bill's heavy drinking and hallucinations. She told Finn—who she knew to be a keen firearms enthusiast—that she was afraid.

She also told him she was so stressed out, she was taking the anti-anxiety drugs Xanax and Ativan.

"She was very worried about buying that house," said Finn. "She thought it was going to overextend them financially. She knew they could make the payments, but she didn't think they were going to have much left over after that."

Two weeks before closing, the deal almost fell apart, after the house was appraised for only $500,000—$15,000 short of the agreed price. Cindy Ligosh, an experienced realtor, told her brother he was under no obligation to pay more than the appraisal price, but Bill disagreed, saying that he felt morally bound to pay the full amount.

"And I had a big argument with him," she remembered. "I said, 'It's only worth that, and you're not screwing him.' But Billy is the type that, if he makes the deal, he makes the deal. And if he gets screwed—too bad, he made the deal."

Finally he and Peter Burnejko compromised at $507,500, but the mortgage company refused to lower the price, leaving Bill to come up with the extra cash.

"He called me about two weeks before the closing," said Burnejko, "and said he could not afford to pay $515,000. My lawyer suggested a promissory note for $7,500. I said that would be fine."

Scrambling to meet the agreed down payment, Bill asked his colleague and Jvista partner Jay Tandava if he could borrow $10,000 from their joint company account.

"He said he was expecting money from his mother's will," said Tandava. "Then he said, 'Do you mind me taking out ten thousand dollars from the company's account?' I said no problem."

According to Cindy, the Capparoros had initially agreed to pay the closing costs as a housewarming gift, but then reneged. So Bill needed the extra $2,500 to cover that.

On Easter Sunday, April 11, Bill, Melanie and their two boys attended a barbecue at Selene and Alex Trevizas' house in Brooklyn.

As usual, Bill was upbeat and chatty, walking around with a beer in his hand, telling everyone about his new house.

"They seemed fine," Selene said. "He was really excited about the house.

"He was very mellow at that brunch," she added. "They had a couple of things that week, and then they were moving."

Back in Woodbridge later that night, prosecutors believe, Melanie McGuire went on the home computer and Googled "undetectable poisons." Then a few minutes later she ran a further search for "tomax/suicide."

Now that Melanie and Bill appeared to be going ahead to buy the new house, Dr. Bradley Miller was very upset. He just could not see the logic, as she was actively searching for an apartment on the Internet for her and the children to move into, But when he challenged her, she assured him her husband would never get the necessary financing for such an expensive house.

By now their affair was in overdrive.

"We would probably call each other ten to twenty times a day," said Dr. Miller. "If we were both in the office, we could have spoken many more times than that."

They also communicated through their RMA work phones, as well as a special T1 line between the Morristown and Somerset offices.

By mid-April, Melanie was complaining to her lover about Bill's unusual behavior.

"She said that he had been behaving more and more erratically," Dr. Miller would later testify. "He had some hallucinations. Bipolar behavior where he would be working through the night on the computer and then sleep long periods of time."

In mid-April, Melanie telephoned Jim Finn, asking how to buy guns.

"I'm a gun owner," he explained. "So it was a logical question to ask me."

The burly bearded registered nurse, who was working for a blood bank, gave her information on obtaining a gun permit in New Jersey. But he mentioned that it was far quicker and easier to get one in Pennsylvania, as all one needed was proof of residence.

Melanie, already in possession of a Pennsylvania driver's license bearing her Aunt Barbara's East Stroudsburg address, carefully noted everything he said, before changing the subject.

On Friday, April 16, she went on her home computer to investigate further. At 7:35 p.m., while Bill was still at work, she typed in the words, "where to purchase guns without a permit," on the MSN search site. Four minutes later, she looked up two official National Rifle Association sites, giving information about various types of weapons and state gun laws.

At 7:45 she tried another MSN search for "instant poisons," and a few minutes later looked up "gun laws in PA."

On Saturday afternoon—ten days before they were due to close on the new house—an upbeat Bill McGuire phoned the Rices in Virginia.

"When are you going to come and help us move?" Bill quipped when Sue answered the phone. And for the next one-and-a-half-hours, he chatted non-stop, as he packed up his entire kitchen.

"He was taking down the glasses," remembered Sue. "And you could just hear them while he's talking."

Melanie was at work, and Jack and Jason were playing in the background, and Sue had never heard her friend sound so happy.

During the conversation, they made plans to visit Bill and Melanie in their new house on Memorial Day weekend. Sue offered to help unpack, joking that Melanie was "so organized," they would probably be unpacked and settled in by then.

Then Jon got on the phone and spoke to his best friend for ten minutes.

"He said, 'You guys are not going to have to stay in a hotel,'" said Jon. " 'You're going to stay at the new house.' "

After putting down the phone with the Rices, Bill McGuire telephoned his sister Nancy in Florida. It would be the last time they ever spoke.

"He called me out of the blue," said Nancy. "And for some reason, he asked me what I really thought of him. And we had a personal conversation."

Bill and Nancy had always had a difficult relationship, with many of their recent phone calls ending with one hanging up on the other. But with their mother's estate settled, Bill seemed calmer and bursting with optimism.

"He was getting his life in order," remembered Nancy. "We didn't argue."

For the first time in many years they discussed their feelings, with Bill asking his sister her opinions on various things.

"And at the time, it touched me, and I didn't understand why. You know, it's just like some people know that they're going to die, and certain things just fall into place."

At 5:03 Sunday afternoon, Melanie McGuire went on her home computer. For the next two hours she conducted eighteen searches, gathering information. She first Googled how to purchase guns in New Jersey and Pennsylvania, before searching for "instant poisons," "toxic insulin levels," "fatal insulin doses," "fatal digoxin doses" and "instant undetectable poisons."

Then at 5:41 she typed in the words "how to commit suicide," followed four minutes later by "how to commit murder."

The next morning at 7:38, Jim Finn sent Melanie McGuire a humorous e-mail titled, "do you think she's angry?" together with a picture of U.S. Secretary of State Condoleezza Rice. Three hours later, Melanie cryptically replied:

ok, i need to know if you have a firearm in the house. condi and i are coming over.

That night, at 9:26, Jim Finn replied with a flirtatious e-mail, subject: You and Condi, humorously referring to firearms on his property:

Hmmm, maybe I should tread lightly here. Ok, yes there is a firearm in the house (and it's a really good one) and more ammo than I can comfortably mention. But . . . maybe this isn't the time for war. Maybe . . . maybe we can all . . . discuss this.

He then suggested Melanie come over with Condoleezza Rice, bringing ingredients to mix Malibu Bay Breezes. He promised to cook "you two hounds from hell" some of his "famous" pasta.

We'll eat, get drunk, and have a slugfest to settle this damn thing. And after that one or both of you might get lucky.;-)

At 9:48 the next morning, Melanie e-mailed, asking,

you around today?

And straight after receiving it, Finn called Melanie's cell phone.

"She described her husband starting to act strangely," Finn would later testify. "Drinking more, having drug use, and she's starting to get worried about her safety for herself and her children."

That night he followed up the phone call with an e-mail entitled "BTW" (By The Way):

After our talk, it occurred to me that we haven't seen each other in something like six years! I think it was 1998. It's time we got together. C'mon you're fun and I miss you. Now I know I've already made my yearly request to see you back in February and you turned me down as usual, but I'm not taking no for an answer on this one.

The next morning, at 9:49, Melanie sent him an e-mail from her RMA desktop computer:

actually, i was thinking about our conversation too and it has been too long. I definitely want to get together at some point soon, but there is lots going on right now that I need to tell you about. and I was thinking about taking you up on something we were joking about yesterday (if you were serious, that is—you might remember the conversation). if you're not comfortable doing it, I understand completely. i'll explain more when you're around and can talk. don't want to do too much on email. there is a lot going on right now at home, and we're set to settle on a house in the next week, i am seriously contemplating making heavy changes b/c there is a lot of weird stuff going on with him. i'm around at the office today, but i don't know what time you're working. tonight i have to give a lecture in ct, so I'll be pretty inaccessible. let me know when you're around and have some time.

Thirty-four minutes later she sent him a postscript:

i maybe in your area friday or saturday night to give an injection. i wouldn't be able to stay long, but if i'm heading down that way i could always pop in and say hey.

Twenty minutes later, Finn replied, expressing concern for Melanie after her last message:

So that's why my antenna went up yesterday. I know what you're talking about and if that's the subject then it's pretty serious. I'll definitely help, you got it. E-mail is definitely not secure so I understand that you want to go in depth (jeez, I feel like I'm in a Robert Ludlum espionage thriller!).:)

I will be home Friday afternoon/night and all of Saturday. I'd love to see you Mel even if it's only for five minutes, though I hope you have more time then that. Now for the obvious and most important . . . are you safe???????

Five minutes later Melanie replied, saying she would telephone him as soon as she could find a free office. And then, in an emotional phone conversation, she told him things were getting worse at home and she now wanted a divorce.

"She and her husband are fighting even more," said Finn. "They're about to close on a house. And she's talking about his crazy behavior, and I'm worrying about her safety. I'm telling her, 'Look, if you're afraid of this man, grab the kids and go to your mother's. Get the hell out of there. What are you waiting for?'"

He then advised her to buy a gun for protection against Bill, recommending a 40-caliber 9 mm semiautomatic, as she was so petite.

That night, at 9:56, Jim Finn followed up their telephone conversation with an e-mail, offering more help on buying firearms:

> I was thinking about things a lot today. Some of which I'd like to revise though the general theme is the same . . . just more urgent. I have some permit info you need and some ball park prices.
>
> The more I think about your situation the more I worry about you. So much so that I want to talk to you again. I'm at work all day Thursday. Should be home by 6pm or a little after. Call me. Ok.

On Saturday, April 24, Melanie McGuire started contacting gun stores in Pennsylvania. She first telephoned Jones Gun Shop in Allentown at 11:28 a.m. and then called C&D Guns in Bethlehem.

Later that morning, Melanie telephoned her RMA surrogate Melissa Coulter with the sad news that the transfer to the intended mother had not worked.

"She was very sweet and very calm," remembered Coulter. "She said, 'Mel, I'm sorry.'"

Melanie then offered to inform the intended mother, but Coulter said she wanted to do it.

"She said, 'OK, I'm going to give you five minutes and then I'm going to call you back to make sure you're OK.'"

Melissa Coulter says she was always struck by Melanie's empathy and how kind and comforting she always was.

"I asked her if there was anything I could do to make it work for sure," remembered the surrogate. "Melanie said, 'You know, science can only take us so far, and then we have to leave it to a higher power.'"

SEVENTEEN

The Gun

At 7:28 a.m. on Monday April 26—two days before the scheduled closing—Melanie McGuire telephoned John's Gun &
Tackle Room in Easton, Pennsylvania. Located just 60 miles
from Woodbridge, near the Pennsylvania border with New
Jersey, she could be there and back within a couple of hours.

Three hours later, after receiving a humorous picture e-mail
from Jim Finn entitled "Happy Monday," she replied, never
mentioning she was taking his advice and buying a weapon:

You're insane. But it made me laugh.

A minute later he responded, writing:

GOOD! You need to laugh.:)

Melanie immediately sent back a cryptic reply:

*last night he got up in the middle of the night saying he
heard a noise in the attic (no one is supposed to use the
attic, but all units have access). he told me he saw a
light there. where? there. babe, that's where the wall
meets the ceiling. it's sheetrock. if someone had a spot-
light behind it that was shining like the sun, you wouldn't
see it. i know, i guess i'm just paranoid. just?*

Finn replied:

> *Dude, he's losing it. I wouldn't leave my two kids alone*
> *with him. Sh*t, I wouldn't leave my cats either.*

A few minutes later, Melanie sent Finn another e-mail titled "yikes!":

> *he was talking about the move, and he said, just think,*
> *this will be the last one prior to the divorce.*

And when Finn e-mailed back, asking what she had said to Bill, Melanie wrote,

> *my parents walked up to us just then. that stopped the*
> *conversation.*

At 1:30 p.m., after picking up a new prescription for Xanax at Walgreens, Melanie McGuire got into her Nissan Pathfinder SUV and headed west on I-287 to Palmer Township, Pennsylvania. An hour later she pulled up outside John's Gun & Tackle Room on Freemansburg Avenue, just outside Easton.

She walked into the tiny store and was served by its elderly owner John Coscia, who would remember her.

"Not many women come into the shop to purchase a handgun," he explained. "She was well-dressed, and in all the years I worked here, she was the first registered nurse to buy a handgun."

Taking Jim Finn's advice, she selected a Taurus 85 smallframe revolver, costing $270, including tax. Weighing just 13.5 ounces, the five-round .38 Special is ultra-light, easily stored in a pocketbook. She also purchased a box of Ultramax wadcutter bullets, mainly used for target shooting, costing $9.95.

Before he could sell her the handgun, Coscia had her fill out a yellow federal form, as well as a Pennsylvania State one for handguns. To establish residency, Melanie used her driver's license, with her Aunt Barbara Martinez's Pine Creek Estates,

East Stroudsburg, address on it. She gave her occupation as "registered nurse," listing the fictitious 15 Kathleen Drive as her work address.

Then Coscia ran an instant NICS check to the state police computer by phone, giving Melanie's driver's license number. She was immediately approved.

At 3:10 p.m., after paying in cash, Melanie walked out of the store with the powerful .38 Special, and more than enough ammunition for what she had in mind.

That day she made eighteen telephone calls to Dr. Miller, spending a hundred minutes on the phone. But she never once mentioned buying a gun in Pennsylvania. She also talked to Jim Finn several more times, also without mentioning it.

That night, Melanie was back on her home computer, Googling information for various drugs. At 7:43 p.m. she made three searches for "insulin shock," followed by ones for sedatives, tranquilizers, barbiturates and Nembutal. Then at 8:30 she began investigating the powerful hypnotic sedative chloral hydrate.

Discovered in 1832, chloral hydrate is easily soluble in alcohol. Better known as a "Mickey Finn," the "date rape drug" also played a part in the deaths of Marilyn Monroe and Anna Nicole Smith.

At 8:42 Melanie Googled the effects of chloral hydrate, learning that when combined with alcohol, it will cause significant drowsiness.

Straight after reading this, Melanie got on the Walgreens official website, searching the store locator and looking up opening hours.

Then, investigators believe, Melanie McGuire forged an RMA prescription pad for 500 MG/5 ML of chloral hydrate syrup, more than five times the recommended adult dosage.

She made it out in the name of Tiffany Bain, a one-time RMA patient, whose information was readily available to her on the patient database.

She filled in Bain's correct birth date and home address,

but deliberately changed one digit on her phone number, in case the pharmacist ran a check. Then she signed Dr. Miller's name to it.

At 8:32 Tuesday morning, Jim Finn sent Melanie an e-mail, sarcastically asking if the attic light was out last night.

Two-and-a-half-hours later, she replied:

please, yes. now his paranoia is centering around his job.

At around noon, Melanie arrived at RMA's Morristown office, for lunch with Dr. Brad Miller. She told him the house closing would probably not go through tomorrow, as Bill was having problems with financing.

"Her impression was that the closing was not going to occur," Dr. Miller would later testify. "She had been looking for apartments online and she had several different possibilities."

Melanie said she had to be out of the Woodbridge apartment by the end of May. She would then tell Bill that she wanted a divorce, and move into a new apartment with Jack and Jason.

"I felt good," remembered Dr. Miller. "I thought that was the direction that we wanted to move in for the relationship."

EIGHTEEN

The Closing

At 8.20 on the Wednesday morning of the closing, Melanie McGuire dropped off her two boys at the Kinder Kastle school on Middlesex Avenue in Metuchen. She then drove 1.4 miles to Walgreens pharmacy at 905 New Durham Road, Edison, dropping off the chloral hydrate prescription at 8:32, and collecting it eighteen minutes later, after paying $9.99 in cash.

That morning, Bill McGuire was a bundle of nerves before leaving with Melanie for the 2:00 p.m. appointment for the closing. To occupy himself, he went for a haircut.

While he was out, Melanie telephoned Dr. Miller on their secret cell phones, one of many calls they would have that day.

"She said that they were going to go to the lawyer's office," said Dr. Miller, "and find out what the status of the closing was going to be. Again, she didn't feel like the closing was going to occur."

Melanie then told him not to worry, promising to call him later that day.

At about 2:00 p.m., Bill and Melanie drove to attorney Laurence R. Sheller's office in Princeton, New Jersey, to sign the closing papers. Despite a last-minute problem, everything was resolved. By 3:00 p.m. Bill and Melanie McGuire were the new owners of 29 Halls Mill Road in Asbury.

Later Sheller would describe the couple as being "upbeat" at the closing.

A few minutes after the closing, Melanie called Dr. Miller in a panic.

"She informed me that they had closed on the house," he would later testify. "She sounded upset. She told me that she didn't know she was going into the closing."

Melanie explained that she'd thought they were just going to discuss the house with their lawyer, but when they walked in, she was surprised that the seller's attorney was present. Then she'd started signing the papers with Bill, and it was too late.

"I became upset and started yelling at her," said Dr. Miller. "I said, 'You should go back in there and rip up the papers. Why do you want to buy a half-a-million-dollar house, if you ultimately want to get divorced from Bill? It just doesn't make any sense.'"

A few minutes later, at about 3:30, Melanie called her sister-in-law Cindy Ligosh in a totally different frame of mind. She announced that they had closed on the new house, giving Cindy a humorous account of what had taken place.

"I thought it was strange," remembered Cindy. "It was odd for her to initiate a phone call, and she recounted some funny story about the closing."

Later that afternoon, Melanie called Dr. Miller again. He was in a meeting when his cell phone rang, but he went into another room to take her call.

"She was on the way home from the closing," he remembered. "I could hear Bill in the car. He was on his cell phone. And she just said, 'Don't worry—everything's going to be fine.'"

After the closing, Melanie drove to Kinder Kastle to pick up Jack and Jason, while Bill returned to 2902 Plaza Drive, to make final arrangements for the Saturday move into the new house.

At 5:44 p.m., Bill made a fourteen-minute call to an old friend named Hayes Penn, who lived in Reading, Pennsylvania.

"He was very happy," Penn remembered. "He had just closed on his new house. We were just talking about how his new home would be closer to where my family lives. They would only be an hour. And also how good it was to be reacquainted."

At 5:59 p.m. Bill called Jon Rice with the good news. Sue was away on a business trip in Charlotte, Virginia, and Jon had just walked in from work when the phone rang.

"He was really excited and really jovial," remembered Jon. "It was awesome. He was so happy that he had achieved the dream that he's had for so many years to buy a house."

But after they'd been talking for ten minutes, Reagen, Jon's pet husky/German shepherd ran out the front door, making him cut the call short.

"I had to chase after her," said Jon. "I said, 'Bill, forgive me, I've got to go.'"

Then after congratulating Bill once again on the house, Jon put down the phone.

And he would be the last person, with the exception of Bill McGuire's murderer, to ever talk to him again.

NINETEEN

A Celebratory Toast

After Bill put down the phone with Jon Rice, prosecutors believe that Melanie McGuire started executing the meticulously planned murder of her husband. At about 6:00 p.m., with the children upstairs playing, they believe, Bill opened a bottle of red wine to celebrate the new house. Then somehow, when his back was turned, Melanie surreptitiously slipped enough of the red-colored liquid chloral hydrate into his glass to knock him out.

When Bill McGuire triumphantly raised his glass with Melanie to toast their family future, it was *the* happiest day of his life. He had achieved his goal of owning his own home before turning 40. It truly was a moment to savor.

Then Melanie sat on the couch with him, waiting for the powerful drug to take effect.

At 7:09 p.m., Bill McGuire's BlackBerry rang, but no one answered. It was a call from Peter Burnejko, to congratulate Bill on the deal going through, and to thank him. But when he called the McGuire home phone a minute later, Melanie answered.

"I [said], 'Congratulations, I hope you'll be happy in your new house,'" Burnejko later testified. "I didn't hear anything. There was silence on the other end."

Finally, he told her he'd catch up with Bill later, as they still had unfinished business on the house, which he would vacate that weekend.

An hour later, Melanie called Dr. Brad Miller on their private T-Mobile cell phones, for a fifteen-minute conversation.

"She said Bill had some wine," Dr. Miller recalled. "He was sleeping on the couch and when he woke up, they were going to have a discussion about the house."

And Melanie promised she would finally bring up the question of divorce, saying she would call him in the morning to tell him Bill's reaction.

At 4:59 the next morning, Dr. Brad Miller telephoned Melanie's private cell phone, on his way for a spin workout at the YMCA. When she didn't answer, he left a message, saying he loved her and to call him as soon as she could.

Desperate to hear what had happened when she'd asked Bill for a divorce, he left her two more messages in the next two-and-a-half hours.

At 6:17 a.m., prosecutors believe, Melanie began creating an elaborate alibi. She first went on Bill's BlackBerry and sent an e-mail to Bill's boss Ross Ninja, copying his immediate superior Tom Terry. The subject was: "Thursday, April 29: I will be out sick today."

But she had Tom Terry's e-mail address wrong, and there was an immediate message from the system administrator, saying it was undeliverable.

Then as her husband lay unconscious on the living room couch, Melanie prepared her two little boys for school. As they walked past him on the way out to the front door, Melanie told them to hush, as he was sleeping.

She then drove Jack and Jason to the Kinder Kastle in Metuchen, dropping them off at precisely 8:30 a.m. She told the day-care center's director Donna Todd that she was applying for a temporary restraining order against Bill, as he had been violent towards her the previous night.

Just before 9:00 a.m., Melanie called RMA attorney Melissa Brisman, saying she would not be into work that day. She then called Dr. Brad Miller.

"She sounded upset," said Dr. Miller. "She told me that Bill had left [and] went into more detail."

According to Melanie, Bill had woken up at about 4:00 a.m. and they had gotten into a "fight" over the house. At one point he'd told her that if she wasn't happy with him or the house, he was going to leave, and she could keep it.

"The dispute became physical," Dr. Miller continued. "He pushed her up against the wall. He put a dryer sheet in her mouth, and I believe she said he was even choking her."

Then her youngest son Jason had woken up crying. So she'd taken him into the bathroom and locked the door. For the next half an hour, they'd remained there, listening to "activity throughout the apartment," before hearing the front door slam shut. Only then had she come out.

Melanie then asked Dr. Miller to prescribe her some Xanax, to calm her down.

"As soon as I hung up the phone," said Dr. Miller, "I called in a prescription to a pharmacy near her for some Xanax."

On the handwritten prescription, Dr. Miller included his diagnosis, saying that 32-year-old Melanie McGuire

complains of extreme anxiety, palpitations, nausea and difficulty concentrating. She reports that the couple closed on a new house yesterday and later that night the couple got into an argument which became physical. She states that she was pushed against a wall and then slapped across the face. She denies having any injuries or pain at this time.

Dr. Miller then prescribed 0.25 mg of Xanax for "situational anxiety related to domestic violence," saying he had instructed Melanie to notify the appropriate authorities, and encouraged her to "seek counseling and/or psych care, as soon as possible."

After putting down the phone with Dr. Miller, Melanie called her son Jack's speech therapist Joanne Cascia's office, leaving a message to cancel that evening's scheduled 5:00 appointment and asking her to call back.

"I did call her back," Cascia would later testify. "She told me that the reason she was canceling was because she and her husband had had a fight the night before. He had walked out on her and she had not yet heard from him."

Then Melanie telephoned her friend Selene Trevizas, announcing that Bill had walked out and she was getting a divorce lawyer.

Later she called Regina Knowles with the news.

"Quite frankly," said Knowles, "when I heard that Bill was gone, I breathed a sigh of relief."

Exactly what happened next when Melanie McGuire arrived home after leaving the boys at day care, no one except Melanie McGuire will ever know. Investigators have reconstructed what they believe took place, using the evidence and scientific expert analysis.

They believe that Melanie had a so-far unidentified accomplice to help her create a false trail of clues and dispose of her husband's body.

While Bill McGuire lay unconscious on the living room couch, Melanie loaded the Taurus handgun that she had bought two days earlier, with wadcutter bullets. Then she aimed the powerful .38 Special at her husband's forehead, placed a green throw pillow over the barrel to dampen the noise, and pulled the trigger. The flat-top cylindered bullet—usually used for target practice—punched a perfect round hole through Bill McGuire's frontal bone, tearing through his brain, before exiting out the back of his head.

She then pointed the gun at his lower chest, firing into his abdomen just below his rib cage. The second bullet ripped through his lung before exiting out his back. Then she fired two more bullets into his chest at point blank range.

When the trained nurse was satisfied that her husband was dead, she began the grisly task of disposing of his remains. And with the children in day care, she and her alleged accomplice would have had hours to dismember the body at their leisure, leaving absolutely no traces of what she had done.

First she prepared the shower stall in the larger of the two bathrooms on the second floor, hanging old paint-stained dropcloths around it, to catch the blood. Then she blocked up the drain, to stop any incriminating biological matter from getting trapped there.

The shower stall would have provided the perfect environment for her gruesome work, as it meant the cutting could be done near ground level, with three walls and a shower door to contain blood spatter. Melanie utilized her medical training to create a "controlled environment," like a hospital mortuary, before making the first cut, so it would not end up looking like something out of a horror movie.

When she was ready, they undressed Bill, who weighed nearly 200 pounds. They left him only in his underpants, which were heavily soiled, as he'd been unconscious for hours.

Then they dragged him into the shower stall, but he was too big to fit lying down, so they placed him in a sitting position, with his knees bent, so the shower door would close.

Melanie then produced a short-bladed reciprocating power saw, plugging it into a power socket in the bathroom. After placing a hospital blanket over it to dampen the sound, she turned it on.

She first began cutting straight down through his lower left knee, front to back. But although the fine-toothed saw easily cut through the femur bone, it slid off the bloody flesh without cutting it. So she then cut through his flesh with a sharp bevel-edged knife. Bill's severed left leg was then bled out, before they cut off the right one below the knee in the same gruesome manner.

With the lower limbs severed, there was more room in the shower stall to operate. Now, deduce prosecutors, Melanie or her alleged accomplice pushed Bill's head down to the floor, and started sawing through his mid-backbone, before hacking through his organs and flesh with the knife. The thighs and lower body were positioned in such a way as to protect the shower fixture from being scratched by the saw.

After bleeding out the rest of the body, they began parceling up Bill McGuire's body parts in plastic trash bags. First *they wrapped a blue HCSC medical blanket over his face, before placing a kitchen garbage bag with yellow drawstrings over his head, and pulling it down over his shoulders and upper torso. Then they fitted a second one around the severed bottom part above his navel, pulling it up until the bags met, and tightening the drawstrings.*

Then they wrapped the head and upper torso in three larger industrial-sized heavy-duty trash bags, from a supply the McGuires had used for moving, before taping them shut with blue painter's tape.

They then packaged up the legs in more black trash bags, before parceling the middle torso—severed at both ends—and taping it shut.

"She was meticulous," New Jersey's Assistant Attorney General Patti Prezioso would later relate. "Once the body was cut and bled out and bagged, she could have simply surrounded [the pieces] with bags of ice."

Melanie then began to clean the bathroom, so no evidence of Bill's dismemberment would be found. She scrubbed and scrubbed the shower area and bathroom walls, until there was no trace of any blood or biological matter.

But she forgot to wipe the soles of her shoes. And later, when she placed Bill's BlackBerry and NJIT personal computer in the trunk of his Nissan Maxima, she inadvertently transferred small pieces of his flesh—"human sawdust," torn from his body by the saw—from the treads of her shoes onto the car rug.

After completing the acts prosecutors believe took place in her apartment, Melanie McGuire drove to Middlesex County Family Court, to obtain a temporary restraining order against her husband. But the line was too long, and she left, spending the rest of the afternoon calling divorce attorneys to represent her.

Melanie called Dr. Miller several times on their private cell phones that day, although they did not see each other. She told him that she wanted to go back to the townhouse and put away some things she needed, and look for an apartment.

"She wanted to get to the court to file a restraining order against him," remembered Dr. Miller. "She wanted to get to day care to make sure that Bill didn't have access to the kids."

At 5:30 p.m. Melanie picked up her two boys from day care, driving them to her parents' house in Barnegat, where they would spend the next few days.

TWENTY

The Perfect Murder

At 9:08 Thursday night, Melanie McGuire checked into the Red Roof Inn at 860 New Durham Road, Edison, with just an overnight bag. Not even one block away from the Walgreens where she had obtained the chloral hydrate the day before, it was a motel she knew well, as she had once stayed there with Dr. Miller.

Earlier, she had called her lover, saying she wanted to spend a couple of nights at the hotel, as she didn't want to stay at 2902 Plaza Drive, or go all the way to her parents' in Barnegat.

Melanie, who did not have a reservation, walked in and registered at the check-in for two nights, paying $136.78 in cash. She then walked through the parking lot to her room, calling her parents' home on her cell phone, and talking for nine minutes.

Then she lay down on the bed to take a nap, as she was exhausted.

Investigators believe that Melanie now staged the crucial next step in her perfect murder, with the help of her accomplice. She first removed the E-ZPass transponders from the windshield of both Bill's Nissan Maxima and her Pathfinder, carefully hiding them so they wouldn't register any hits that night that would track her movements.

Then, at about 11:00 p.m., she drove Bill's car 105 miles south to Atlantic City, followed by her accomplice in her SUV.

The plan was to abandon Bill's Maxima in the Flamingo Motel parking lot, so it would appear as if he had gone gambling in Atlantic City after the argument, before mysteriously disappearing.

At 12:41 on Friday morning, a time-lapse surveillance camera mounted above the car park photographed Bill McGuire's Nissan Maxima in the parking lot. Several minutes later, Melanie's black Pathfinder is seen pulling up alongside, stopping just long enough for her to get in, before heading back north.

When Melanie arrived back at the Red Roof Inn in the middle of the night, she parked outside her room, going in without anyone seeing her. Then she went to sleep for a few hours.

The next morning, she wrote a note to Bill's friend and business partner Jay Tandava, later pinning it on the door of his apartment at the other end of the Plaza Drive complex in Woodbridge, where he would find it when he came home from work.

Dear Jay:
I don't know if Bill has stopped by or called you, but a lot has happened. I know you are Bill's friend and I don't want to pull you into the middle of things. Bill has been behaving very erratically and strangely lately, at least with me. We had a terrible fight yesterday morning, and he left. I know he's taken off work for the next couple of weeks, which was supposed to be for the move, and I haven't heard from him.

I need your help in calling your friend and canceling the move tomorrow. Bill is welcome to reschedule when he comes back and gets his affairs in order, but I am not moving into this house or anywhere else right now.

Again, I apologize for putting you in this position. But I don't know your friend's name who was supposed to help us, and I don't want him wasting his time tomorrow coming to our place for nothing.

Thanks for helping. I am filing for divorce, but you've

always been a real friend to Bill, and our whole family.
And I thank you for that.

Melanie

p.s. If he does contact you, please tell him to let some-
one know where he is. He is going to be served with
some court documents, and I prefer to save him the em-
barrassment of having it done at work. Thanks, and
again, sorry to put you in the middle.

Later that morning, Melanie left another message on Jack's
speech therapist's office phone, asking her to call. When
Joanne Cascia returned the call soon afterwards, she asked if
Bill had come to the office, looking for her or the kids. Joanne
said he had not and promised to call if he did.

It was a beautiful sunny afternoon when Melanie McGuire arrived at Middlesex County Family Court in New Brunswick,
to take out a temporary restraining order (TRO) against her
husband. She first filled out a confidential victim's information
form, seeking a restraining order within a day, setting out the
circumstances.

She wrote that Bill had put her up against a wall, slapped
her in the face and then walked out. Then, in a separate question about any prior incidents of domestic violence, she wrote
that her husband had stuffed a dryer sheet into her mouth a few
months earlier.

The official form also asked if she or the defendant Bill
McGuire had access to a gun of any type, and she wrote "no."

But by the time she appeared before Judge Jessica R. Mayer
for the Family Court hearing a few minutes later, her story had
already changed.

After swearing on the Bible to tell the truth, Melanie began
by stating that she was in the process of retaining a divorce
attorney. Then, asked what had brought her to Family Court to
apply for a temporary restraining order, Melanie gave her version of what had happened after the closing.

Melanie, who was audiotaped, explained that, although they "argue pretty frequently," she would have expected Bill to lighten up after the closing, but he did not. She said they'd come home after the closing and "dozed off" on the couch, waking up early the next morning. When she was asked which morning, Melanie began to stumble on her words.

"Miss McGuire, you're safe here," said the judge to comfort her. "Don't worry, OK? I know it's emotional. You're going to get a temporary restraining order based on what I'm seeing so far, but I just need to develop the record."

"We were arguing about the house," Melanie continued, composing herself. "He said he had settled on this house so I could be near my family, and he hated my family, and that's an ongoing bone of contention with us."

She said earlier she had been folding laundry and a dryer sheet had gotten stuck in one of her baby's outfits, which was one of Bill's pet peeves.

"This is going to sound silly," she said. "He always comments on that. [That] I always forget to take the dryer sheet out, and how stupid I am, and what an awful mother."

Then, after saying he couldn't talk to her anymore, and couldn't rely on her for anything, she'd begun "yelling back," and an argument ensued.

"He grabbed me by the shoulders," she said, "and put me against the wall and [was] very menacing."

Then Judge Mayer asked if he had hit her.

"Not until—" she continued, gaining momentum, "well, I don't mean to sound like I had absolutely no part in this. I said some not nice things and at that point, yeah, he slapped me."

"Well, I've heard it all," said the judge, sympathetically. "What did you say to him?"

"I told him to go fuck himself," replied Melanie. "He told me I was a stupid cunt and slapped me in the face. Open hand."

She was screaming at Bill and he was walking away, when their 2-year-old son Jason came over.

"I just grabbed him," she said, "went into the kids' bathroom, locked the door. I heard him milling around. He took a shower, got his stuff. I mean, he wasn't in any rush. He didn't bolt out the door or anything. And I just stayed in there and stayed away from him until he left."

She said there had been no word from Bill since then, and her stepfather, Michael Cappararo, was presently changing the locks of their apartment, which they had to leave today.

Judge Mayer then asked if her husband had ever been physically abusive before. Melanie said it was the first time, although he had threatened to "smash my face in" several times recently.

Asked if there were any weapons, Melanie replied that there were none to her knowledge.

Although she had not heard Bill's side of things, Judge Mayer said Melanie had made out a prima facie case for assault and "terroristic" threats, and issued a temporary restraining order.

She then ordered Melanie to return to Family Court at 8:30 a.m. on May 11, with witnesses and the necessary documentation to apply for child and maintenance support. And she banned Bill McGuire from having any contact with her or his children.

But she did not order a search for any weapons, as Melanie had indicated that there were none.

Then, after awarding her temporary custody of the children, the judge asked for an address where the TRO could be officially served. Melanie said Bill might possibly go to their new house in Asbury, but was not sure.

"If you do get an address for him, Ms. McGuire," said Mayer, "call the police. Don't take matters into your own hands."

After leaving the Family Court, Melanie called Dr. Miller, who had house guests visiting from Hawaii and could not see her that day.

"She said she wanted to go back to the apartment and retrieve stuff," the doctor said. "I just told her I didn't want her to do it alone. I asked her to have Selene waiting for her outside while she went in, just in case Bill came back."

By Friday afternoon, Cindy Ligosh began to wonder why she hadn't heard from her brother since the Wednesday closing, leaving a message on his phone.

"I was thinking, 'It's really weird I haven't spoken to Bill,' " she remembered. "I started frantically calling his numbers. 'Why aren't I hearing from him?' "

That day Melanie telephoned Jim Finn, saying that Bill had walked out after slapping her and stuffing a dryer cloth in her mouth.

"She mentioned she had gotten a restraining order," he would later testify. "Again I recommended [purchasing] a handgun . . . to protect herself. And she would always say, 'I'm not ready to do that right now.' "

Then at 5:41 p.m. someone placed a phone call from Bill McGuire's Nextel cell phone to Jon Rice's house in Virginia. No one picked up and it was logged by the phone company as a one-minute call.

Later, back at the Red Roof Inn, Melanie called reception, saying she needed to keep her room an extra night until Sunday morning.

At 5:00 a.m. Saturday, May 1, Dr. Brad Miller got up at his usual time, telephoning Melanie McGuire on her cell phone. He had not seen her since Wednesday's closing, and wanted to meet her at the Red Roof Inn on his way to work.

"I wanted to find out which room she was staying in," said Dr. Miller. "She told me. I went there, parked the car and knocked on the door."

Melanie came to the door wearing flannel pajamas, and appeared heavily sedated. The television was on.

"I gave her a big hug," remembered the doctor, "and asked her if she was OK. She seemed very tired. Sort of out of it. She went back into the bed and I lay down next to her."

She went straight back to sleep and, after using the bathroom, Dr. Miller left to start his shift at RMA. That weekend he was on third call, and in charge of the clinic.

At 11:00 a.m., Melanie walked up to the reception desk, paying $68.39 in cash to cover that night's stay. Three hours later she met Dr. Miller for lunch at a nearby mall.

Melanie suggested they meet at the Menlo Park Mall in

Edison, as she had to open a new bank account. The doctor arrived there first, buying sandwiches in a deli, before sitting outside in the park to wait for her.

"I waited probably twenty to thirty minutes for her to show up," he recalled. "It was taking longer than expected to get her bank account opened."

She finally arrived at about 3:30 p.m. and stayed a few minutes, before saying she had to leave. Then after kissing her good-bye, Dr. Miller drove back to his house to entertain his guests before they flew back to Hawaii the next morning.

By Saturday afternoon, Cindy Ligosh was really getting worried about her brother, after not receiving any answer to her messages.

"I was going crazy," she said. "I spoke to him almost every day, and here he had closed on a new home, and I heard nothing. So I called Melanie's parents' house and left a message."

Just after midnight, Melanie McGuire and her stepfather, Michael Cappararo, set off for Atlantic City in her Nissan Pathfinder. At 12:54 on Sunday morning, her E-ZPass transponder registered a hit at a tollbooth on the Atlantic City Expressway. Sixteen minutes later the McGuires' home phone at the Plaza Drive apartment received a one-minute unanswered call from Bill's personal cell phone. Later, Melanie would claim to have tried to take a photograph of the caller ID, but it had failed to come out.

Exactly what they were doing in Atlantic City that night remains a mystery. But prosecutors believe they'd driven to the Flamingo Motel and Bill McGuire's Nissan Maxima. Then Melanie planted glossy travel pamphlets about hotels in Atlantic City and Virginia in the front seat, making it appear that he had left home to go to one of those destinations.

She also placed a vial of chloral hydrate and a syringe in the glove compartment, so he would look like a drug abuser. And she put Bill's BlackBerry and NJIT computer in the trunk.

After planting the red herrings in her dead husband's car, Melanie returned to the Red Roof Inn for a few hours' sleep.

At about 10:00 a.m., Sunday, May 2, Melanie McGuire checked out of the Red Roof Inn. After picking up a prescription for 0.25 mg. tablets of Xanax from Walgreens in Edison, investigators believe she returned to the Woodbridge apartment, to begin the gruesome task of disposing of Bill McGuire's body. For the next seven-and-a-half hours, her movements remain unaccounted for.

Melanie, who was well acquainted with the Chesapeake Bay Bridge-Tunnel from her trips to Virginia Beach with Bill, had decided it would be the perfect place to dump her husband's body parts. She also relished the be-careful-what-you-wish-for irony that his final resting place would be Virginia.

First she brought their matching set of Kenneth Cole Reaction suitcases up from the basement—the same luggage they had used a few months earlier, during their Atlantic City weekend with the Rices.

Working in the bathroom where the three trash bag–wrapped body parts were still preserved in ice buckets, she first placed his heavy head and upper torso in the largest of the green cases. To help weigh it down in the deep Chesapeake waters, she placed one of Bill's 5.5-pound Weider weights in the outside top pocket. Then she packed the two lower legs in the smallest case, before placing the mid-torso in the middle-sized bag.

For the rest of the day she re-cleaned the bathroom, scrubbing the shower stand and the tiles to get rid of all evidence. But the strong smell of bleach would linger for several weeks.

Soon after 5:00 p.m., investigators believe, Melanie left the Woodbridge apartment, heading south to her parents' house in Barnegat, where her two boys were still staying. Her E-ZPass transponder registered hits on the Raritan South Toll Plaza at 5:33 p.m., the Asbury Park Toll Plaza at 5:51 p.m., and the Barnegat Toll Plaza at 6:23 p.m.

At 9:00 p.m., Melanie called Cindy Ligosh, returning the

anxious message she'd left on the Cappararos' phone a day earlier.

"And she said, 'I thought you knew,'" said Cindy. "I said, 'Know what?' And she said, 'Your brother's left.' Then she told me this bizarre story."

In this version, Melanie said they had fallen asleep on the couch after the closing, waking up at about 1:00 a.m. They were walking upstairs, when she told him he must be very happy he'd accomplished his goal of buying a house. Bill then told her that it was not the house he'd wanted, and they got into an argument.

Then, in the upstairs hall, he had seen a pile of clean laundry outside one of the bedrooms, and a dryer sheet sticking out of a sleeve. He'd then started berating her as a bad mother, slapped her and shoved the dryer sheet in her mouth.

"And I'm thinking, 'I haven't heard from him in all these days,'" said Cindy. "Part of me knows that he would never strike a woman. He would never do that."

Cindy was also certain her brother would never walk out on Melanie without taking his kids.

"That just didn't fly with me," said Cindy. "I only had her word. They had just closed on a new house, I had no idea there was anything wrong. And I'm thinking, 'Did he? Did he hit her and was so embarrassed that he's not calling me?'"

Then she asked for the license plate number of Bill's Nissan Maxima, so she could look for him, but Melanie said she could not remember them.

"Melanie has a memory like a steel trap," said Cindy. "She has a degree in statistics and such a good head for numbers, she used to memorize the VIN numbers off of cars. 'I can't remember.' How convenient."

She also said she could not remember the name of Bill's car insurance company or Jon Rice's phone number, in case he'd gone to Virginia.

But during the conversation, Melanie mentioned being at the Woodbridge apartment early that morning, when the telephone had rung and Bill's cell number came up on caller ID.

"It showed that he had called the apartment and there was no message," said Cindy. "She said that her attorney told her to take a picture of it, but the picture didn't turn out."

When Cindy put down the phone she was convinced that something was wrong, although she had no reason to doubt Melanie's word. So for the next few days she kept on calling Bill's phone, leaving message after message, until his message box was full.

"I called, I called, I called," she remembered. "One day I left a message, saying, 'I wish you were dead!' And then I called right back and said I didn't mean it. But I was so angry and frustrated. All the worry he was putting everyone through . . ."

TWENTY-ONE

The Chesapeake Bay Bridge-Tunnel

On Monday, May 3, at 8:34 a.m. Melanie McGuire's Nissan Pathfinder passed through the Barnegat Toll Plaza, heading north on the Garden State Parkway. Strapped safely in the back seat were Jack and Jason. An hour and ten minutes later she dropped them off at Kinder Kastle in Metuchen.

Then, investigators believe, she spent the day—the first day of Bill McGuire's two-week vacation—at the Woodbridge apartment, cleaning up and making final arrangements to dispose of his body. She also spent a total of two hours and fourteen minutes on the telephone.

Late in the afternoon, Melanie arrived back at Kinder Kastle to pick up Jack and Jason. At 5:18 p.m. she passed through the Raritan tollbooth on the Garden State Parkway, driving south about ten miles to the Cheesequake Rest Area, for a pre-arranged meeting with her parents. There she handed over the boys, who would spend the night in Barnegat.

Then, investigators believe, Melanie returned to 2902 Plaza Drive, loading the three suitcases with her husband's remains in the trunk.

At about 8:00 p.m., she headed south for the 330-mile drive to the Chesapeake Bay. It was soon dark, as she glided the Pathfinder down the New Jersey Turnpike into Delaware, before joining the blandly interminable U.S. 13, which plows through Maryland and into Virginia, winding up at the Chesapeake Bay Bridge-Tunnel.

Around midnight Melanie paid the toll and drove onto the bridge. There would have been little traffic around when she pulled into the first lay-by and stopped. It was dimly lit, with just one overhead street lamp shining on the EMERGENCY STOPPING ONLY sign.

From her vantage point she could see traffic coming up behind her, although she could not be seen by oncoming traffic from the other bridge, running parallel.

She then got out of her Pathfinder, going around to the back, and opened the trunk. Then with adrenaline coursing through her body, she pulled out the largest suitcase, letting it drop on the floor. She could hear the swirling waters below, as she hauled the case over the low barrier, letting it drop into the Chesapeake Bay seventy-five feet below. Then she dropped the other two suitcases over the side of the bridge, before getting back into her SUV and driving on.

Melanie had to travel almost the entire length of the Bridge-Tunnel before reaching the Sea Gull Pier Restaurant and gift shop. It was three-and-a-half miles short of Virginia Beach, and the only place on the bridge to make a U-turn.

Finally, investigators believe that after stopping to freshen up, Melanie turned around for the six-hour journey back to New Jersey.

At midday on Tuesday, May 4, a weary Melanie McGuire drove through the Lincoln Tunnel into Manhattan, meeting Selene Trevizas for lunch at the Red Lobster in Times Square.

"She seemed OK," remembered Selene. "She told me what happened and said she needed to get a lawyer to file for divorce."

Melanie told her best friend she didn't know what she was going to do with the new house, but would stay with her parents until she could find a place of her own. She said she had to get her life in order, and she was still a little afraid of seeing Bill.

"She's like 'He left,'" said Selene, " 'and I assume he's gone for good, but with Bill I don't know.' "

TWENTY-TWO

"It Smelled Like a Morgue"

On Wednesday, May 5—the day the first suitcase was discovered floating in the Chesapeake Bay—Cindy Ligosh went to RMA's office in Morristown to meet Melanie McGuire, who gave her the keys to the new Asbury house.

"I wanted to go up and see if he was there," Ligosh explained.

And during their meeting, Melanie—who had earlier forged a prescription for 0.5 mg. of Xanax, double what Dr. Miller had prescribed—appeared totally unconcerned that her husband had been missing almost a week.

"She was done with him," said Cindy. "Her attitude at that point was, 'He hit me, it's over.' But she was just very calm, cool, collected and cold."

Then Melanie suggested that Bill may have had a girlfriend, saying he had had his teeth whitened just before he'd left. And she informed Cindy she had discovered a $5,000 check, showing that he had been gambling in Atlantic City, with money from the Jvista business account.

"So she's pointing me in all these different directions," said Cindy, "but she's not giving me any information."

That night Cindy and her husband Bill drove to 29 Halls Mill Road, Asbury.

"We just looked through it," remembered Cindy. "To see if there was any evidence at all, in case he was camping out there—a sleeping bag, food or something. But there was nothing."

And former owner Peter Burnejko was also concerned that he hadn't heard anything after leaving numerous messages for Bill.

"He never returned the calls," he would later testify. "He always made it a point to call back within an hour or two."

Two days later, Jay Tandava arrived home from work to find another note from Melanie McGuire taped to his front door, with her and Cindy Ligosh's home phone numbers on it.

Dear Jay,
We're wondering if you have heard from Bill at all. He hasn't called me (which doesn't surprise me), but he hasn't made contact w/ his sister, either, and they're very close. She is understandably worried. Can you let us know if you've heard anything from him? I know he's not due back at work for another week or so, but she just wants to know if he's ok. Both our numbers are below.

Also I need to ask you a personal question. Bill had told me he took 1/2 of the $ from the Jvista account. I am wondering if that is correct. I'm trying to figure things out financially, and I just want to know if that's right.

If you do speak to him, please tell him at least to call his sister. Thanks, and I'm sorry to keep bothering you.

Melanie

With each passing day, Cindy Ligosh became more and more concerned about her brother. And she was finding Melanie McGuire less than forthright, and uncharacteristically forgetful.

"She didn't do one thing to find him," remembered Cindy. "Nothing. She had no interest and never called the police, even if only for her children's sake."

Finally, after tracking down his car license information, she got on her computer and started accessing information on casinos in Atlantic City, just in case he had gone there. But she was overwhelmed, discovering that there were more than a dozen casinos, as well as a large parking lot at the airport.

Finally, in desperation, she called Melanie, saying she needed some help, as she just did not know where to begin.

"I went there once with my brother," she said. "I'm not familiar with Atlantic City at all. But Melanie offered no help."

Once again Cindy asked for Jon Rice's number, but Melanie was evasive, saying she believed he lived somewhere in Virginia that began with a "C."

On the Saturday afternoon of May 8—three days after the first suitcase surfaced—Cindy went online and found Jon Rice's phone number in Chesapeake. She called him, asking if he knew where her brother was.

"Jon said, 'He's not here,'" remembered Sue Rice. "'He should be in his new home, right?'"

Then Cindy told them Melanie's story of an argument with Bill, and how he had slapped her in the face before walking out.

"I was surprised," said Sue Rice, "that it was Cindy, who we hardly knew, calling us and not Melanie. If they had an argument, like Melanie is saying, and Bill walked out, why didn't she call his best friend?"

Then Sue asked Cindy for any phone numbers she had that might help, writing them down on a paper towel.

"Immediately after we hang up, we try to get Bill on his cell phone," said Jon Rice. "We're like, 'Bill, it doesn't matter what you did. It doesn't matter what's going on. Please just contact us.'"

That evening, at 8:14, Bill McGuire's blue Nissan Maxima was towed from the Flamingo Motel parking lot on Pacific Avenue, by Fourteen Towing Services at the request of management. The car, with Pennsylvania plates, had two child safety seats in the rear and was in good condition. After first checking with the Atlantic City Police Department to see if it was stolen, Fourteen Towing Services employee Anthony Miranda attached dollies to the car, towing it to a holding area about three miles away.

Sunday, May 9, was Mother's Day and the Rices had just gotten home from church when Melanie called.

"Well, she told me her story," remembered Jon, "that Bill had gotten physical."

Concerned for Melanie, Jon good-naturedly asked if there was anything they could do for her.

"Don't worry about me," she snapped. "You need to worry about Bill, because I'm not going to."

When Jon asked exactly what she meant, Melanie said she was not taking him back, as he'd crossed the line and hit her.

By the end of the forty-minute conversation, Jon and Sue were both stunned about Melanie's accusations, as Bill had always abhorred any violence towards women.

"We just saw them five months earlier," said Jon, "and they were arm-in-arm and just having a great time. And now she's telling me that Bill was this monster that we never knew. It just didn't ring true."

On Monday, May 17, Bill McGuire was due back at work at NJIT. At 10:00 a.m. Melanie telephoned his boss Tom Terry.

"And her question to me was, have I seen Bill," Terry would later testify, "and did he show up for work? I said no."

The next day, Melanie McGuire made another late-night trip to Atlantic City, this time with Selene Trevizas.

"Yeah, I went with her," said Selene. "When she went the first time, she told me. I asked her, 'Why would you do that?' And she said, 'I just want to know where he was.'"

Later that week, Melanie met Cindy Ligosh again at RMA, bringing Bill's mail in case there were any leads to his whereabouts. She brought it in a plastic bag, upending it on a table, as if it were contaminated.

"There was a bill from a credit card company and a piece of junk mail," recalled Cindy. "There was also a Federal Express letter from his boss, saying if he didn't show up for work by such-and-such a date he was fired."

Cindy was surprised at how little mail there had been since Bill's disappearance, as she wanted to trace any credit card receipts, and she asked why.

"Melanie said they didn't really use credit cards," said Cindy. "And she was keeping an eye on the checkbook, which he hadn't used."

The two women now spoke daily, often for more than an hour. But it was always Melanie initiating the calls.

"I would talk about my job," said Cindy. "She would talk about the kids, but the minute I turned the conversation to Billy, all of a sudden she would have to get off the phone. 'Oh, someone's calling me,' or 'One of the kids is up, I'll be right there.'"

At that point, Cindy never thought her brother was in real danger, speculating that he was either in Atlantic City or on an island just to get away.

"I had nothing to go on," said Cindy, "other than what she said. And I had no reason to believe she was lying. Although everything she said was *so* bizarre."

Every day she called his cell phone, praying he'd answer, but there was always a message announcing that there was no more space to leave messages.

Cindy was too scared to call the police to report her brother missing, as both he and Melanie were driving on illegal Pennsylvania licenses and insurance.

"I figured if I called, he'll get summoned," she said. "And that's not going to be good, so I didn't."

A few days later, Melanie McGuire reserved a U-Haul truck for the Saturday of Memorial Day weekend, when she had to vacate the Woodbridge townhouse. Dr. Brad Miller had kindly agreed to help move all her and Bill's possessions into storage. Melanie was busy getting the townhouse packed up, cleaning and preparing for her upcoming move.

"Dr. Miller and myself packed the house," recalled Selene Trevizas. "We did everything. I packed all of Bill's clothes. I packed his closet. The apartment was a disaster when I got there—boxes and stuff everywhere, because they were in the middle of packing."

Selene said she and Melanie first cleaned the apartment, before the Cappararos arrived to paint certain areas.

"I cleaned and packed both bathrooms," she said. "As neat as Melanie was, that bathroom wasn't in prime shape. I was the one that cleaned it."

Melanie was also selling off all her possessions, so there would be nothing left to remind her of Bill McGuire.

"We were in the office," remembered Nurse Lori Thomas, "and she said, 'I'm selling my furniture. I'm going to buy all new stuff.' That he'd probably left with another woman and she wanted to sell everything."

Thomas, who had just moved in with her boyfriend, was interested in a three-piece marble-topped Thomasville living room set, and arranged to view it.

The following Sunday afternoon, with temperatures in the 80s, Lori Thomas and her boyfriend arrived at Melanie's townhouse with the U-Haul truck, to collect the furniture. The front door was open, so they walked in to find Melanie and Selene busy cleaning the house in tank tops, cut-off jeans and yellow surgical gloves.

They went into the kitchen, where Melanie offered them bottled water to cool off with.

"She said, 'Go into the fridge and help yourself,'" remembered Thomas. "On the kitchen table there were black garbage bags in a box."

Then Thomas asked if they could look around the three-level townhouse. Melanie appeared reluctant at first, but finally led them upstairs, where Selene was cleaning.

"She showed us each bedroom," said Lori. "The boys' bedroom still had their toys packed up. And then I went into a second bedroom and there were Bill's clothes, in black garbage bags right by the closet."

Then Lori peeked in the walk-in closet, where there were still a couple of his dress shirts hanging up.

"And Melanie said, 'Do you want some men's clothing?'" said Thomas. "And I said, 'No.'"

Melanie then took the couple into the master bedroom, asking if Lori wanted to buy her Thomasville bedroom set. But she declined, as they had just bought one.

Then Thomas and her boyfriend walked into the master bathroom.

"It smelled like a morgue," said the nurse. "There was just this horrible strong smell of bleach. It was just horrible."

Lori's eyes started to sting and she had to get out of the bathroom, as the heat made the smell even more intense. When they came downstairs, Lori asked if they could look at the basement, but Melanie refused, saying it was too disorganized.

They then went to the living room, to negotiate a price for the furniture.

"She wanted a thousand dollars," remembered Lori, "but [I got] it for nine hundred dollars because there were little nicks here and there."

As they left, Melanie gave them several HCSC hospital blankets from RMA, to wrap up the marble tabletops to protect them on the drive home.

That same day, the Virginia Beach Homicide Unit was investigating Bill McGuire, after Jon and Sue Rice had identified him as the possible suitcase victim the night before. While they were awaiting the results of the fingerprint comparisons, Detective Ray Pickell asked Detective Sergeant Joseph Joraskie of the Woodbridge Police Department to make discreet inquiries.

After discovering that Melanie McGuire had taken out a restraining order against her husband three weeks earlier, Joraskie drove to 2902 Plaza Drive, leaving his business card in the front door, as there was no one there.

The next morning, he arrived at the Woodbridge police station to find a message on his answering machine from Melanie McGuire, giving a call-back number. But when he dialed it, it wasn't working.

So he tracked her down from Michael and Linda Cappararo's Barnegat address, which she had given on her temporary restraining order, leaving another message at their number.

"I received a call from Melanie McGuire," Detective Sergeant Joraskie recalled. "She assumed I had reached out to her in reference to the temporary restraining order that she had obtained against her husband. She said, 'I can't think of any other reason that you would be calling me.'"

The detective said the restraining order was now three weeks old, and the police did not like for them to go that long without being served. Then he asked if she had any idea where he might be.

"She told me she didn't know where he was," said Joraskie. "But suggested I look in either Atlantic City or Virginia Beach. I inquired as to why she suggested those two locations, and she said because he loved to gamble and he always wanted to live in Virginia."

She then asked him to let her know if police managed to find her husband, as she had hired a divorce attorney and wanted to serve papers.

After putting down the phone, Joraskie immediately called Detective Pickell in Virginia Beach, telling him about the conversation, and that Melanie McGuire had taken out a restraining order against her husband on April 30.

"That was suspicious," said Detective Pickell, "in the fact that she had filed a restraining order against him, and now we've got his body. I mean, that's something you can't overlook by any means."

On Monday, May 24, Tom Terry e-mailed Melanie, saying she could collect her husband's personal possessions at her convenience. He also regretted that he would have to postpone her luncheon invitation:

Maybe some other time for lunch. I will probably be in Morristown next week. Also we have collected all of his personal [belongings], consisting of 8 to 10 books, some Double A batteries, a pocket flashlight, a USB hub, wireless mouse, keyboard, eye drops and Sudafed. I'll keep them in a box until the end of June or deliver them to you if you desire.

Thirty-seven minutes after receiving the e-mail, Melanie forwarded it to Dr. Miller with a note:

Bill's boss offered to take me to lunch. Sweet old guy. This e-mail upset me a lot. I don't know why exactly.

The next day, Melanie McGuire's newly hired attorney, Risa A. Kleiner, filed divorce papers in the Superior Court of New Jersey. They accused Bill McGuire of being an inveterate gambler and chronic alcoholic, with a long-term pattern of violent behavior. Melanie requested sole custody of their children, and half of everything he owned.

The eleven-page divorce action stated:

The defendant has been guilty of extreme cruelty toward the plaintiff.

She alleged that in 2000, just as they were becoming solvent again after declaring bankruptcy, Bill started to gamble heavily:

Defendant's irresponsible gambling was extremely distressful to plaintiff, and caused her to constantly worry about their financial future.

She accused Bill of repeated "argumentative behavior" throughout the marriage, leading to the "alienation" of their friends and family, and of being a heavy drinker.

It continued:

One night in or about the Spring of 2002, defendant was returning home from a night job at a restaurant when the police pulled him over for speeding. He knew the points, when added to his existing points, would cause his driver's license to be suspended.

Melanie claimed Bill had called her around midnight, screaming that the ticket was her fault, as she had not wanted to move to Virginia. Then as the argument escalated, she hung up on him.

> *Undaunted, defendant called back and screamed multiple obscenities into the answering machine, threatening to kill [her] when he got home. Plaintiff was terrified and took the children from their beds in the middle of the night. She proceeded to drive around while trying to decide what to do.*

When Bill had come home and found her gone, he called her parents, who then urged her to go back. But

> *Defendant's volatile behavior caused plaintiff to fear for her life.*

Bill's behavior became even more erratic in the early spring of 2003, when he became "obsessed" with buying a house. As the action described it:

> *He would sit for hours at the laptop looking for real estate listings. He would go for periods of not sleeping for up to 48 hours.*

She claimed her husband's "extreme, self-absorbed behavior" meant she had to do everything around the house, as well as caring for the children.

In Melanie's version of events, things had become even worse in 2004, when they decided to buy 29 Halls Mill Road. She said she'd expressed concern at whether they could afford it, but Bill insisted they could.

> *Defendant insisted on handling the negotiation. And whenever plaintiff disagreed with his strategy, defendant became so enraged and irrational that he flew into a rage, jumping up and down and screaming like a child.*

By the spring, according to Melanie, Bill began exhibiting "extremely bizarre" behavior, making Melanie feel "tense and on edge."

Bill was also verbally abusive, it read, accusing her of being "stupid," and saying he was tired of being a parent to her. He said that even his first wife Marci was not as stupid as Melanie was.

She also accused Bill of intimidating their older son Jack because he stuttered, telling him, "Talk like a big boy, not a baby."

Finally she reiterated her version of events following the closing of the new house, but this time with dramatic new embellishments.

In the three weeks since the "domestic violence incident," she claimed, there had only been one call from Bill's cell phone to the Woodbridge apartment.

And even though Melanie had never officially reported Bill missing, she said the police had been unable to locate him to serve the restraining order.

Plaintiff has reason to believe that defendant may have no intention of returning, as he has not provided any financial support for her or the children or [made] any arrangements to contribute toward the family's expenses since his abrupt departure.

The above acts of extreme cruelty make it improper and unreasonable to expect the plaintiff to continue to cohabit with the defendant.

TWENTY-THREE

Moving Day

By Wednesday, May 26, as Virginia Beach Detective Ray Pickell prepared to go to New Jersey, Woodbridge police insisted on making the official death notification to Melanie McGuire. That morning Barnegat police patrolman Richard Nowak went to Melanie's parents' home at 22 Aqua View Lane, Barnegat, and rang the front doorbell.

"Her father answered the door and advised me she wasn't home," remembered Nowak. "I said I had some important information for her."

A few hours later, after learning that Barnegat police wanted to see her, she telephoned Dr. Brad Miller.

"She was going to meet with them," he said, "and then call me back."

That evening, Melanie arrived at Barnegat police headquarters with her stepfather Michael Cappararo. Patrolman Nowak took her into an office and informed her that her husband Bill was dead, without saying exactly how he had been found.

"She was crying," he would later testify. "Her father was consoling her. She didn't faint, knees didn't buckle or anything like that."

And as she was helped out of the police station by her stepfather, Nowak told them to contact Detective Sergeant Joseph Joraskie of Woodbridge police as soon as possible.

Back at her parents', a tearful Melanie McGuire called her lover with the news of Bill's death.

"She told me that the police had informed her that Bill was dead," he said. "That he was found in the water."

Later that night, Michael Cappararo telephoned Jon Rice in Virginia Beach, fishing for information about how he had identified Bill from the Virginia Beach police sketch. Rice was stunned. For Detective Pickell had still not confirmed that the man found in the three suitcases was indeed his best friend.

"They had to tell the family first," said Jon. "But Michael says, 'I understand you ID'd Bill's body.'"

Rice said that was wrong, and he had merely been shown some pictures. Then Cappararo said detectives had told him that Jon had been 95 percent certain the sketch was Bill and had identified him.

"That didn't happen like that at all," Jon told him, "so I don't know where you're getting your information, but you're not right."

After learning of Bill McGuire's death, Jon and Susan Rice were devastated. They immediately called Detective. Pickell in Virginia Beach, who offered his condolences.

"I started drinking real heavy that night," remembered Jon. "We didn't go to bed until about two or three o'clock in the morning."

At 6:30 a.m., after a sleepless night, Jon Rice called Cindy Ligosh on her cell phone, giving her the tragic news of her brother's death. He carefully spared her the details of how the body had been found.

"He said they'd found Billy in the water," recalled Cindy. "And I thought he had committed suicide. He'd drowned himself."

Her initial reaction was that Melanie's story of him attacking her was true, and he had killed himself out of guilt.

"And then I'm thinking, 'Oh my God. I wasn't there for him. And I'm leaving him all my "Hope you're dead" messages.'"

And for the next two days, Cindy Ligosh thought her brother had taken his own life.

On Thursday, Melanie McGuire went on compassionate leave from RMA, as the Human Resources department sent out an e-mail informing all employees of Bill's passing.

That day, Melanie began calling friends to tell them that her husband was dead. But she never called his sister Cindy.

"I was shocked," Selene Trevizas remembered. "My first instinct was that he got himself in trouble gambling. That's the only thing that I could have thought of what happened to him."

After getting the call, Selene drove straight to the Cappararos' house in Barnegat, to be with her friend.

"She was a mess," recalled Selene. "She was like almost in shock, I think."

But other friends would question just how genuine her grief really was. James Finn received a call from Melanie, coldly stating, "He's dead."

"My first gut-level impression of that statement was that it was phony," he would testify later. "I felt like I was the director saying, 'Action.' And she went, 'He's dead!' It sounded so phony to me."

When Dr. Brad Miller told his wife Charla that he would be helping Melanie McGuire move her things into storage the Saturday of Memorial Day weekend, she was not happy.

"I had several discussions with Charla," explained the doctor. "And she didn't want me to go."

Charla had always been suspicious of her husband's relationship with Melanie, and now with her husband dead, she was even more worried. But the doctor insisted, saying that he had given his word and he had to help her in her time of need.

Later Melanie would inform him how her stepfather had wept with emotion after hearing he would be helping her move.

On Friday night, after finishing work at RMA, Dr. Miller collected the rental truck from U-Haul, putting it on his credit card. Then he drove it back to his house, parking it in his driveway.

Early the next morning, Dr. Miller—who had taken the weekend off—drove it to 2902 Plaza Drive. There waiting for him were Michael and Linda Cappararo, and Selene's husband Alex Trevizas, along with several of his construction employees, who would be doing the heavy lifting. They had brought along two large pick-up trucks in addition to the smaller U-Haul.

Melanie did not come, saying she had to babysit Jack and Jason, although Dr. Miller did see her later that day, giving her a silver and opal ring that he had bought as a love token.

Selene Trevizas' cousin Justin Marrero also helped with the move, driving one of the trucks as a favor. He helped carry out furniture, china and Bill's large Weider weight set, which Dr. Miller had disassembled in the basement earlier.

"The entire apartment was moved," Dr. Miller said. "There were six or seven people through that apartment that day."

While Justin Marrero was carrying out the half-a-dozen large heavy-duty black trash bags packed with Bill's clothes, he was offered them, as otherwise they would be thrown away. Marrero accepted, later bringing them back to his Brooklyn apartment.

The move took most of the day. While her stuff was being taken to the storage center, Melanie went shopping at a Toys "R" Us with her two boys, where she called the Rices. The previous night she had left an emotional message on their phone, but they had been told by detectives not to be in contact with her, as it was a murder investigation.

But when Melanie's name came up on their caller ID, Sue answered, deciding she had to be supportive.

"Melanie said the Virginia Beach police were going to come the following Tuesday and interview her," remembered Sue. "But she didn't say anything at all about how the body was found. I thought that was just horrifying."

Then Melanie said she had to go, as she had to take baby Jason back to her parents'.

After putting down the phone, Sue was livid, believing that

Melanie still had no idea of exactly how Bill's body had been found. They decided to warn Melanie's parents to have a doctor or a priest with her when the Virginia Beach police arrived. But when Sue telephoned the Cappararos, Michael answered, angry that the Rices had broken the news to Cindy two days earlier.

"He was yelling at me," said Sue. "He said Jon had no right to call Cindy to [tell] her it's her brother. And I'm like, 'Hold up there a second. This is his best friend. Jon drank half of the Texas fifth and he got sick that morning. Of course he's going to call Cindy, the next closest person to Bill outside of Melanie.'"

When Cappararo finally calmed down, Sue expressed her concern about Melanie hearing the "really awful news."

When Sue speculated that Bill might have been the target of a Mafia hit, Cappararo replied that he did not think so, as he was just a small-time gambler.

Cindy Ligosh soon discovered the horrific truth of how her brother's body had washed up in the Chesapeake in three suitcases. Her husband Bill's sister had done some research on the computer, reading the Virginia Beach newspaper stories. When Bill and her son Max walked in from work at 5:00 p.m. with ashen faces, Cindy immediately knew something was wrong.

"Then they told me how this happened," she said. "That he had been found in pieces."

And the split second she heard how Bill had died, Cindy knew exactly who was responsible.

"It was Melanie," said Cindy. "It then started clicking, clicking, clicking in my head. All of these things that were very suspicious in the weeks he was missing. It just started to make sense why she was saying things that I did not think were true, and why she was behaving the way she was.

"And then I started calling Virginia Beach [police], because she was moving out of the townhouse, and evidence could be destroyed. I was calling like crazy. 'She's moving! She's moving! She's moving!' But no one was picking up."

Over the next few days, Nurse Melanie McGuire's devoted network of surrogates became alarmed when she stopped responding to e-mails. That was unusual, as Melanie always answered e-mails almost immediately, day or night.

One by one they called each other, discovering that Nurse McGuire had not returned anyone's messages.

"I called and left an e-mail," remembered Melissa Coulter, "and another and another. Finally my intended mom called the clinic, and they explained that she had a family emergency. That her husband had passed unexpectedly."

So another nurse was assigned to temporarily take over Melanie's duties, until she could return to work.

"That was horrible," said Coulter. "The woman was awful. Terrible. And I guess it just made us appreciate how very good Melanie was at her job."

On Memorial Day, after handing over the keys to 2902 Plaza Drive, Melanie McGuire felt under pressure. Things were not going according to plan, and she cursed the fact that Bill's body had surfaced. It was as if he were coming after her one last time from the grave.

Apprehensive about her upcoming interview with Virginia Beach police, she contacted her divorce attorney Risa Kleiner for advice. She also forged one more prescription for double-strength Xanax on an RMA pad, as well as one for a supply of the once-a-week contraceptive Ortho Evra® Patch, having them filled at Rite-Aid pharmacy on West Bay Avenue, in Barnegat.

TWENTY-FOUR

Detective Pickell

At midday on Tuesday, June 1, 2004, Detective Ray Pickell set off in an unmarked Virginia Beach police car for New Jersey, to investigate William McGuire's murder. He brought along Detective Tommy Shattuck, who was raised in Woodbridge and knew the area.

They arrived in the early evening, driving straight to the Woodbridge police station, meeting Detective Sergeant Joseph Joraskie, who would be representing the State of New Jersey in the investigation.

Detective Pickell had planned to set up a murder headquarters at Woodbridge police station, but was told there was no office or computer available. So Detective Shattuck's mother kindly agreed to let them use a room in her house as a base for the investigation, giving them use of her computer, scanner and fax machine.

That would be the beginning of an uneasy relationship between the Virginia Beach Homicide Bureau and the Woodbridge Police Department.

"Some police departments bend over backwards and provide you with whatever you need," explained Detective Pickell, "because they know you are out-of-town and don't have the resources. So we ended up having to basically work out of his mother's house. You adapt to your surroundings, I guess."

That night, the three detectives drove to Teaneck, New Jersey, to interview Cindy Ligosh in her husband's pharmacy store. Over the last few days, Cindy had spoken to Detective Pickell by phone on numerous occasions, telling him she was certain Melanie had committed the murder.

"We went through what we thought would have happened since my brother was missing," remembered Cindy. "I filled him in as much as possible, and gave him answers to any questions that he had."

Detective Pickell first asked if Melanie was having an affair. Cindy told him she was certain she wasn't, advising him not to waste any time on that.

"I was convinced she wasn't having an affair," said Cindy. "And it wasn't because I knew her so well, but my brother was too smart. Now we all laugh and look at his picture and we're like, 'Yeah . . . not so smart after all.' "

Cindy's main concern was jurisdiction. For although Bill's body had washed up in Virginia, she was certain Melanie had murdered him in New Jersey. But Detective Pickell assured her that Virginia Beach Homicide, with an annual average of a hundred murders, had far better resources to deal with a homicide investigation than Woodbridge, which had about one a year.

"I remember kissing [Detective Pickell] on the cheek and telling him he was our hero," said Cindy. " 'Now go get her!' "

One thing that stayed with Detective Pickell after the interview, was that Cindy told him he closely resembled Bill McGuire.

"I didn't like that," said Pickell. "That struck me with thinking, 'Well if she killed her husband, she doesn't want to look at me.' "

So he told his relatively inexperienced younger partner Detective Shattuck that he would mainly deal with Melanie McGuire.

After interviewing Cindy Ligosh, the detectives drove to 2902 Plaza Drive, on a late-night reconnaissance mission. They met with the complex superintendent, who informed them that Melanie had handed back the keys to the apartment a few days earlier and it was now empty.

Then the two Virginia Beach detectives drove back to

Tommy Shattuck's mother's house, for a well-earned night's sleep.

"It was a long day," said Detective Pickell.

The next morning, Detectives Pickell, Shattuck and Joraskie drove to NJIT on Summit Street in Newark, to meet with Bill McGuire's colleagues. They first interviewed Jaychandra Tandava, who told them he and Bill had been good friends and gave them the two notes Melanie had pinned to his front door after the disappearance.

Then they met Bill's boss and mentor Tom Terry in his office.

"They questioned me at length about Bill," he remembered. "They requested information about his cell phone usage in general, and I was able to show them the bills."

Terry also told them how Melanie had telephoned him soon after Bill's body was identified, asking how she could apply for his life insurance.

"And I told her to call Human Resources," said Terry. "That was not something I would handle."

On their way back to Woodbridge, Detective Pickell called Melanie McGuire's cell phone, to arrange an interview. He also wanted his number to show up later on her phone records, which he planned to get, so he could see all her recent ingoing and outgoing calls.

"She actually answered," said the detective. "I identified myself and asked if we could meet today, and what would be a good time. She said she would have to call me back."

Thirty minutes later, Detective Pickell received a call from Melanie's divorce attorney Risa Kleiner, scheduling an interview in her office at 5:00 p.m. that afternoon.

That brief call from her attorney made the detective even more suspicious.

"Now it's becoming obvious there's some reason why you don't want to talk to me by yourself," reasoned Detective Pickell. "Let's face it—if someone's loved one turned up dead, and you really had nothing to do with it, you would surely make whatever arrangements you needed to get with the investigator, wherever, whenever. Without an attorney, just to find out as much as you could, or provide information."

At exactly 5:00 p.m., the detectives drew up in front of the Wilentz, Goldman & Spitzer law offices at 90 Woodbridge Center Drive, right next door to the McGuires' recently vacated townhouse in Woodbridge. They went up to suite 900 and were placed in a waiting area by the receptionist.

A few minutes later, they were told that Melanie McGuire was having second thoughts about being interviewed.

"They wanted to cancel it," said Detective Pickell. "But I told them, 'Look, I've driven a long way, and this is a murder investigation of her husband.'"

Forty-five minutes after they arrived, the detectives were brought into a small conference room with a large table with several chairs around it. Detective Pickell positioned himself at the head of the table, with Shattuck and Joraskie at either side of him. He noted how the McGuire townhouse was visible from the window.

Then Melanie McGuire walked in with her divorce lawyer Risa Kleiner, and a criminal attorney named John Hogan.

"That was also suspicious," explained Pickell. "When we do finally sit down and talk to her, we're not only greeted by one attorney, but two, and one being criminal."

From the beginning, Melanie appeared "stand-offish" and "evasive."

After introducing themselves, Detective Pickell asked how long she had been married to Bill, and about their marriage.

"She said it wasn't a very happy marriage," said Pickell.

Then he asked about her husband's car. Melanie replied that he'd driven a blue 2002 Nissan Maxima with Pennsylvania tags. When asked why PA plates, she replied that he had been trying to avoid the higher New Jersey insurance premium.

At one point in the interview, Melanie asked if they had recovered her husband's vehicle. Detective Pickell told her that was why they needed to talk to her, as they didn't have a description of Bill's car.

"She said something to the effect that he gambled," said Pickell. "More than likely you're going to find the car in Atlantic City, because he had a heavy gambling problem and would often frequent the casinos there."

She was then asked about the last time she had seen Bill. And again she related her version of what had happened after the closing.

"Her arms were crossed and she was visibly shaking," recalled Detective Pickell, who observed her closely. "And at no point did she ever cry. She tried to, trust me. I watched her eyes and no tears came out. She tried to look consoling, but she just wasn't a very good actress."

Then Detective Sergeant Joraskie asked if she or Bill had any guns in their apartment.

"She said no," Joraskie would later testify. "I asked a second follow-up question [of whether] there were any hunting weapons, as opposed to small guns, and she said no to that as well."

Melanie was then asked if they had a matching set of three suitcases. She said no, they only had some mixed pieces of luggage.

Joraskie sensed Melanie's annoyance at being questioned.

"She seemed upset and angry," he recalled, "specifically when I would ask questions of her. She seemed upset, but not emotionally upset, more [that she] didn't want to be in this situation."

But when asked about her husband's character and personal habits, Melanie was more forthcoming.

"She stated he was able to piss people off easily [and] he was a jerk," said Joraskie. "At work he was unliked, and his boss was looking to fire him. And in general, that he wasn't a friendly person or a happy person."

At the end of the twenty-minute interview, Detective Pickell asked Melanie's permission to search her storage locker, and she consented.

When the three detectives left her attorney's office, they were all convinced she had been lying.

"It was a very short interview," said Detective Pickell. "Obviously much shorter than I suspected it was going to be. I found her to be evasive. You asked a question and it was a very short answer, instead of elaborating a little bit. That surprised me, because not even her attorneys were interrupting [to say,] 'You're asking something inappropriate here.'"

His young partner Detective Shattuck later described Melanie's performance as "a charade."

"She was trying to play the role of a grieved and shocked widow," he said. "But in my experience, when you cry, there's usually tears involved. And she was not crying. She was just kind of moaning."

From now on, Melanie McGuire would be their prime suspect in the murder of her husband.

An hour later, Melanie McGuire called her sister-in-law Cindy Ligosh, telling her about the interview. Cindy played dumb, not letting on that she had already met the detectives the day before.

"I was asking her questions," said Cindy. "'What's [Pickell] like?' 'Do you think he's really competent?'"

"Oh, I'm sure they are busy little bees," she replied condescendingly.

Melanie was angry, saying she'd felt like she was walking into an ambush, expecting them to slap the cuffs on her at any moment. Cindy played along, as she would for the next year, never letting on that she suspected Melanie had cold-bloodedly murdered and dismembered her brother.

It was already dark when the three detectives arrived at 2902 Plaza Drive with a three-man forensic team, to conduct a luminol search for any traces of blood in the three-level townhouse. They had not informed Melanie McGuire—her permission was not required, as she no longer lived there.

"It was immaculately cleaned," Detective Sergeant Joraskie would later testify. [The] hardwood floors on the main living area were extremely clean and shiny. The walls were all freshly painted white. It was very clean."

The detectives were particularly interested in the second-floor bathrooms, which were immaculately clean. There were a couple of false luminol positives, caused by the heavy bleaching that had been done.

While they were testing the entire apartment for blood, Detective Sergeant Joraskie, who did not have protective gear, began canvassing neighbors, asking if they had seen or heard any suspicious activity at the McGuires' apartment recently.

After several hours of testing, the forensic team found no traces of blood, and finished up the search. As it was well past midnight the two Virginia Beach detectives returned to Detective Shattuck's mother's house to check e-mails and get a few hours' sleep.

TWENTY-FIVE

Prime Suspect

The next morning, Thursday, June 3, the sensational story of Bill McGuire's murder broke in New Jersey.

"Suitcases Held Jersey Man's Body," trumpeted the Newark *Star-Ledger* on its front page. The *Home News Tribune* ran the headline, "Suitcase Corpse Traced: Woodbridge man's remains found in the Chesapeake Bay."

Woodbridge police appeared to distance themselves from the gory murder, claiming only to have learned that McGuire was missing the day before, when they'd been contacted by police from Virginia Beach.

Woodbridge Police Captain Charles Rowinski told *The Star-Ledger* that there was "no indication" of any crime having been committed in the township.

"We've got nothing on [Bill McGuire]," he told staff writer Tom Haydon.

Virginia Beach police spokesman Don Rimer refused to release any more details, saying the murder investigation was continuing.

"Our homicide squad," he said, "is working in cooperation with various New Jersey law enforcement agencies."

That morning, NJIT issued a statement on its adjunct professor's untimely death.

"The NJIT community is shocked by the loss of a life so full of promise," said spokesperson Jean M. Llewellyn, "and extends its deepest sympathies to his family, friends and co-workers."

At 9:00 a.m., Detectives Pickell and Shattuck arrived at Arthur's Self Storage on Highway 1 in Edison, New Jersey, where they were met by Melanie McGuire and criminal attorney John Hogan. Melanie unlocked her large storage unit, 3161, packed to the ceiling with furniture and belongings from the townhouse.

"Our main focus of the search was to look for her husband's property," said Detective Pickell. "And look for weapons, whether it be a handgun, a rifle [or] bullets."

Melanie pointed out a blue 3 foot–by–2 foot plastic Tupperware container, saying it contained all her husband's personal effects. Detective Shattuck had to crawl up over piles of furniture and other stuff to retrieve it.

"I was making small talk to Mr. Hogan and Ms. McGuire," remembered Detective Pickell, "but I was watching what was being taken out."

The container held all Bill McGuire's naval mementoes and photographs, including his discharge papers. There were also old photographs of him and Melanie as well as other personal effects.

After looking through the locker, Detective Pickell asked where Bill's clothes were.

"She said she had given away all his clothes," said Pickell. "The only property that was left was in the container."

Then suddenly, Melanie volunteered that she had been thinking about yesterday's interview, and remembered they did own a set of green matching suitcases. It was "name brand," she explained, as Bill only bought designer products.

Then Detective Pickell asked her to look at a photograph of one of the suitcases found in the Chesapeake, and after consulting with the attorney, she agreed to.

"I showed her a picture of the first suitcase," said Detective Pickell. "It was in good shape, so there was nothing vile about it. She said it looked like the luggage they owned, but she wasn't one-thousand-percent sure."

At one point during the search, Detective Pickell went to

the restroom, as a ruse to go and interview the storage facility manager. He discovered that Melanie also had a second, smaller storage locker that she had failed to mention.

On the way out after the search, Pickell casually asked if she had another unit, and she admitted that she did.

"She was surprised," Pickell remembered. "She looks at her attorney first, and then says, 'Oh, yeah, I do have a second one.' So that information wasn't offered to us."

And in that small storage unit, Detective Shattuck discovered Bill McGuire's dark leather tri-fold wallet, containing his Social Security card, medical card and photographs of Melanie and their children, as well as several business cards. But the young detective put it back in the storage locker, and it would be another year before other detectives would give it a closer look.

While his partner was searching the second unit, Detective Pickell asked about mattresses, as he had seen none in storage. Melanie said that her boss, Dr. Brad Miller, had disposed of them during the move. She then gave him Dr. Miller's phone number. Later that day Pickell called, having a brief conversation with the doctor.

"Call it detective's intuition," said Pickell, "but some people's information flows when you're telling the truth, and there's nothing to hold back information on. But it was really choppy when I spoke to Dr. Miller. And you just get one of those feelings like, 'I really need to talk to this guy in person.' But I never did."

That day things started to go wrong for Melanie McGuire. Her first interview with law enforcement had shaken her, although she was certain she could easily outsmart those "busy bees."

After returning from the search of her storage lockers, she received her monthly E-ZPass bill and was shocked to see it contained two 45-cent charges—for her trips to Atlantic City on May 2 and 18.

She panicked, calling the E-ZPass customer service department on her cell phone at 4:11 p.m. to contest them. She told the customer specialist that there had been a mistake, as she'd never traveled to Atlantic City on those dates, and demanding they be removed from her bill immediately. But she was told that the toll had registered her E-ZPass transponder number, and nothing could be done to remove it.

Later that evening, Detective Ray Pickell learned that Bill McGuire's Nissan Maxima had been towed on May 8 from the Flamingo Motel parking lot in Atlantic City. So the two Virginia Beach detectives immediately drove the 104 miles to the gambling resort, arriving just before midnight.

They went straight to the Flamingo Motel on Pacific Avenue, determining that there was a security camera covering the parking lot. Then Pickell spoke to two employees of the towing company, ascertaining that McGuire's blue Maxima had been parked at the last parking space at the south side of the building. Finally Detective Pickell contacted the hotel manager, arranging to view the surveillance tape the next morning.

It was 2:30 Friday morning by the time the two detectives checked into a hotel that had been arranged by the Atlantic City P.D., for a few hours' sleep.

Since arriving in New Jersey on Tuesday, Pickell and Shattuck had had little downtime, working long exhaustive hours on the investigation.

"There was so much traveling back and forth," explained Detective Pickell. "Normally you have time to grab a beer after work. But we didn't have time to do that. It was like, 'Let's grab some food at the drive-through and go.'"

The next morning, after breakfast, Pickell and Shattuck walked into the reception area at the Flamingo Motel, where the day shift manager Asmat Hussain was on duty. He showed them the hotel's ancient computer surveillance system, on which the videotapes had already been transferred. Pickell soon found footage of Bill McGuire's Nissan Maxima being parked at 12:41 a.m. on April 30, and then towed on May 8 at 7:05 p.m. But he ran into problems accessing the images off the computer hard drive, calling in a computer forensic expert from Newark.

Detective Pickell finally made do with just downloading the first few minutes, after Bill McGuire's car had been parked, onto VHS, as that was better than nothing.

After finishing up at the Flamingo, Detective Pickell wanted to forensically process Bill McGuire's car for any clues it might hold. Under Virginia law he could have gone ahead and done it, but New Jersey required he get written consent from Melanie McGuire, or a search warrant.

So not wanting to waste time preparing a search warrant and getting it signed by a judge, the detective decided to ask Melanie for permission.

Before committing herself, Melanie said she first had to make a phone call. A few minutes later she called back and agreed, arranging to meet the two detectives at an exit off the Garden State Parkway to sign the consent form.

During the short meeting at the exit several hours later, Detective Shattuck went into Melanie's car to help her with the paperwork. She immediately began flirting with the handsome young homicide detective.

"She was extremely nervous," remembered Detective Shattuck. "I was in the car with her by myself and just making small talk, when she goes, 'You know, you're kind of cute.' And right there, it struck me—she's trying to get me to believe her story by flirting with me.

"That's kind of an inappropriate comment to make, when you have a homicide investigator in your car on the Garden State Parkway. And at that point she knew we were investigating her. There was no confusion about what our motives were."

After leaving Melanie McGuire, the two detectives drove back to Atlantic City, going straight to the police forensics office, where Bill McGuire's car was waiting in a bay. Atlantic City police forensic technicians first photographed the Nissan Maxima inside and outside. Then they did the sweep— vacuuming the rugs and carpets for any trace evidence, before processing for fingerprints.

Then Detectives Pickell and Shattuck thoroughly searched the vehicle. In the glove box, hidden under some paperwork, they discovered a small glass vial with a black cap, containing some pinkish clear liquid. Next to it was a syringe.

On the front passenger seat were two brochures, one from

Atlantic City and the other from Virginia. In the center console was Bill McGuire's E-ZPass transponder. In the back were two baby seats. Inside the trunk they found Bill McGuire's BlackBerry and a computer bag with his PC inside.

Then they drove back to Woodbridge, spending the night at Detective Shattuck's mother's house.

On Saturday, June 5, the two Virginia Beach detectives drove to Brooklyn, to interview Selene and Alex Trevizas, who had been given Bill's Weider weight set by Melanie.

"So I looked at those weights," said Detective Pickell, "and they weren't the weights we were looking for."

But during the interview, Selene told Detective Pickell that her cousin Justin Marrero had also taken some of the weights when he had helped in the move.

"So from Selene's house we traveled further into Brooklyn to see Justin Marrero," said Detective Pickell. "We asked if we could see the weights, but those weren't the ones either."

But there, lined up against the wall, they saw about ten heavy-duty black trash bags, packed with Bill McGuire's clothing.

"It didn't click with me to take them," remembered Detective Pickell. "Maybe just being exhausted."

After leaving Marrero's house, they headed back to Virginia Beach. A few hours later, they were discussing the case as they crossed into Virginia, when the significance of the black trash bags full of the victim's clothes dawned on them.

"It just hit me all of a sudden," remembered Detective Pickell. "Oh God! Why didn't we grab those bags? I swear I just felt like slamming on the brakes and turning back around."

Ultimately, they were just too exhausted to drive back to Brooklyn. So they called Detective Sergeant Joe Joraskie, asking him to collect them, which he did later that day.

On Saturday morning, the *Home News Tribune* carried a front-page story with the headline, "Authorities Locate Dead Man's Car in A.C." When Melanie McGuire read the story by staff writer Ken Serrano, she was livid. For it revealed that police were now studying surveillance tapes of the Flamingo

Motel car lot, showing Bill McGuire's car being parked at 12:41 a.m. on Friday, April 30.

"Surveillance cameras scanned the busy motel parking lot," a Fourteen Towing Services employee was quoted as saying. "They could yield important clues for investigators."

Now fearing she had been captured on videotape leaving the car, Melanie began concocting an elaborate story to explain her being there so soon after Bill's disappearance.

Soon afterwards, Melanie telephoned Dr. Brad Miller, saying she had something important to tell him relating to Bill's murder.

"She said we needed to meet and have a discussion," Dr. Miller would later testify. "She just said she had to share something with me."

They agreed to meet that night in the parking lot of the McDonald's at Exit 13 on Interstate 287.

Melanie arrived first in her Nissan Pathfinder, and as soon as her lover drew into the lot, she got into his car. Then she began describing a trip to Atlantic City, the night after Bill had left.

"She had gone to Atlantic City," said Dr. Miller. "There was a particular area where they would park outside of a casino that they would frequent."

Melanie explained that her purpose in going was revenge. She'd planned to find his car and then move it, saying she was "angry and upset" that he had walked out on her and his kids. She had managed to find Bill's car, she told him, moving it to the Flamingo Motel parking lot. There had been two or three cell phones in the front seat, which she had thrown out.

But after moving the car, she forgot where she had left her Nissan Pathfinder, deciding to get a cab back to Woodbridge, 104 miles away.

"She told me that at that point it was late at night," said Dr. Miller. "She was tired. She went to a casino and hailed a cab, and asked [it] to take her back to Woodbridge."

According to Melanie, she had fallen asleep during the cab ride back. But when she got off at the Woodbridge train station, she felt refreshed and hailed an off-duty cab, taking it straight back to Atlantic City.

"She did find her car," said Dr. Miller, "and drove it back to the Red Roof Inn that night."

Then Melanie told him about her second trip to Atlantic City.

"She said she also went down there on Saturday at around midnight with her stepfather," said Dr. Miller. "And again they were going down to see if the car had been moved. If they could find out where Billy was. She said they saw the car there, but did not find Billy.

"The last thing she mentioned to me was that she went down to Atlantic City on [May] eighteenth, again just to see if the car had been moved."

Dr. Miller then asked why she had not told him earlier.

"She told me that she didn't want me to be upset," he would later testify. "That she didn't want me to think that she was going back to find Bill, bring him back and rekindle the relationship."

Dr. Miller thought her story implausible and told her so, saying he didn't think anybody was going to believe her. He suggested they look for the two cab drivers who'd driven her, as a precaution.

During the conversation, Melanie admitted reading the newspaper article about a man being seen on surveillance videotape, moving Bill's car.

"I just asked her how they could confuse her with a male," he said. "She said she didn't know, but for sure it was her that moved Bill's car."

Then, just before Dr. Miller returned to his car to drive home, Melanie became unusually enigmatic.

"She said there was one other thing she needed to share with me," he said. "But she wasn't going to do that until this was all over. And that it's something she wanted me to know, but couldn't tell me for my own protection."

For the next few weeks, whenever they saw each other, a curious Dr. Miller would pepper her with questions. But she would always refuse to tell him, saying it was just too dangerous.

TWENTY-SIX

A Jurisdictional Problem

On Thursday, June 10, *The New York Times* carried an explosive interview with Bill McGuire's first wife Marci, in a story headlined, "Light Is Shed On Victim, But No Clues In Murder." Now remarried to Darryl Paulk and living in Milford, New York, she painted a dark picture of her first husband, saying he'd probably gotten what he deserved.

"I was a wreck by the time I got out of that marriage," she told the reporter. "He emotionally and physically abused me."

The story focused on the parallels between Marci's and Melanie's alleged bitter marital experiences with Bill McGuire. The story contained damaging extracts from Melanie McGuire's divorce action, with accusations of Bill's alleged heavy drinking and gambling problems.

It was something of a public relations triumph for Melanie, who was portrayed throughout as the injured party:

While the police try to determine who killed the [NJIT] computer specialist whose body was found in three suitcases off the Virginia coast last month, his wife and former wife have painted a portrait of a man who grew increasingly erratic and aggressive during the past two decades.

The article noted that Marci Paulk had unsuccessfully filed a restraining order against Bill in 1995, after he'd thrown rocks through her window.

Two days earlier, Paulk had given another interview to *The Star-Ledger*, claiming that Bill had e-mailed her brother Leonard Polsky, apologizing for the way he had treated her during the marriage.

"It was very, very strange," Marci was quoted as saying. "He wanted to make amends for everything."

And she said neither she nor her brother had bothered to respond.

In the days after Detective Ray Pickell returned to Virginia Beach to work the murder investigation from there, Cindy Ligosh decided to trap Melanie into incriminating herself. She now spoke to her sister-in-law daily, always putting on an act and being nice.

"When the case was down in Virginia," said Ligosh, "I would call her up and say, 'You've got to call [Detective Pickell]. You're his wife. They're not listening to me, Melanie, you need to put the pressure on.' "

Then Melanie would always reply that the Virginia Beach detectives knew what they were doing, and she should let them do their job.

Cindy would ask her if she was afraid for herself and the boys, if the murderer was still out there.

"Of course I am," Melanie would reply, before changing the subject.

On one occasion, Cindy and a friend went to 29 Halls Mill Road, going inside to videotape, thinking Bill might have been butchered there.

"I was looking for blood," she remembered. "This was the new house. I'm thinking, 'Where else can you do something like this?' You need privacy."

Cindy called Detective Pickell in Virginia Beach at least twice a week for progress reports on his investigation. She even volunteered to go undercover. Pickell told her she was free to do so, but he must have no knowledge, or anything she discovered would be inadmissible in court.

One day she went to New York, buying a miniature microphone and tape recorder from a spy shop. Later she taped several telephone conversations with Melanie.

"Every time I brought up Billy, she would not discuss it at all in any way," remembered Cindy. "She would talk about nothing. She would shut me down. I never got anything on her."

From the outset, Cindy had decided never to directly confront her sister-in-law with her suspicions.

"I wanted to keep my enemies close," she explained.

So Cindy pursued an ongoing telephone relationship with Melanie, hoping that one day she might let down her guard and incriminate herself.

When Cindy first voiced her suspicions about Melanie to Jon and Sue Rice, they refused to believe it. They loved Melanie as Bill's wife, believing her incapable of such an inhuman act.

But the more conversations they had with Melanie, the more surprised they became by her total apathy.

"She never wanted to know who did this," remembered Jon. "If my wife turned up in that state, I would be concerned for my family. Wouldn't you want to know who did this, so you could protect yourself?"

Whenever Sue pleaded with her to come down to Virginia Beach and help the detectives, Melanie would cut her short, saying, "I just can't think of that right now, Sue. I'm a single mom."

Then Sue would call Cindy Ligosh, telling her about her conversations with Melanie. And Cindy would keep telling her Melanie was the murderer.

"So she's trying to bring me into the fold," said Sue. "I'm teetering, going back and forth. And Jon's like, 'No.' He's solid on Melanie."

But that would soon change.

In mid-June, Nurse Melanie McGuire returned to work at RMA, and her old colleagues were shocked at her appearance. She had lost even more weight, and was no longer the sharp-as-a-whip, wise-cracking Melanie everybody had known.

Christine Richie, who had left RMA during Melanie's leave of absence, was still in close touch with her old colleagues.

"People called me from RMA, saying, 'Oh my God! She looks like a skeleton,'" said Richie. "'We feel so bad for her.'"

Soon after she returned to work, surrogate Melissa Coulter gave her condolences to Melanie on the phone.

"I said, 'I don't mean to pry,'" said Coulter, "'but my intended mom found out about your husband and I'm so sorry.' She was very quiet and then said, 'I really appreciate that. It's been a hard time, but I'm back to work.'

"To me that seemed appropriate. She's been off for about a month and seemed a little less Melanie. She didn't seem quite as quick to joke as before."

But whatever pressures Melanie was under after the death of her husband, her exemplary work performance remained unchanged.

"That's one thing with Melanie," said Lori Thomas. "Nothing ever affected her job. It's like she came into work and turned the light switch on."

Without Bill McGuire around, it became far easier for Melanie to pursue her love affair with Dr. Brad Miller. And he was highly supportive, always there with advice and a considerate word.

But Melanie's cryptic statement about keeping a big secret from him for his own protection bothered him.

"The curiosity was eating away at me," he remembered. "At one point I confronted her. I said, 'I need to know. You need to tell me what this other item is.'"

Then Melanie told him she had bought a .38 handgun and ammunition around the time they were closing on the house. She said Bill had wanted a firearm to protect the family, as they were moving out to a rural area.

"I told her she'd never mentioned anything about this before," said Dr. Miller. "And she said it's a discussion that they had also had with Selene and Alex, [who] had guns in their household to protect their family."

By the beginning of July—nearly two months after the first suitcase had washed up in the Chesapeake Bay—the investigation looked in danger of stalling because of multi-jurisdictional problems. Although Virginia Beach homicide was still leading the investigation, as Bill McGuire's body had been found there, his wife Melanie was the last known person to have seen him alive—in Woodbridge, New Jersey. To complicate things even further, his car had been found one hundred miles away, in Atlantic City.

"You need a crime scene," Woodbridge Police Captain Rowinski told the Associated Press. "If we don't know where the killing took place, unless someone confesses, it would be very difficult to solve."

Early on in the investigation, the New Jersey State Police tracked the case, seeing if they wanted to get involved.

"They were going over the jurisdiction," said New Jersey State Police Detective Sergeant David Dalrymple. "I looked into it to see if we wanted to offer assistance."

But ultimately it was decided to take a wait-and-see approach, allowing Virginia Beach detectives time to investigate.

TWENTY-SEVEN

"I'm a Single Mother"

The first week of July, Virginia police finally released Bill McGuire's body back to his family. Melanie, who had complained about the high cost of bringing her husband's body home to New Jersey, announced that there would not be a funeral because of media coverage.

"And Cindy fought that," remembered Sue Rice. " 'You are absolutely going to have a service for my brother.' "

Eventually Melanie capitulated, quickly arranging to have her husband's remains cremated first, before a free burial at a veterans' cemetery in south Jersey. She even tried to discourage the Rices from attending, saying it was a long way for them to come.

"That was so strange," said Sue Rice. "She didn't want us to come up. She didn't want anybody there except her."

Melanie never contacted any of Bill's friends to tell them about his death, and it would be another year before Jim Carmichael learned of it.

As the deceased's widow, Melanie controlled the funeral arrangements, refusing to have any chapel visitation for the family to say their final good-byes to Bill.

"She did the planning," recalled Cindy Ligosh. "She complained about the price and told me her father was footing the bill."

Once the funeral date was set, Cindy called her sister Nancy in Florida, finally breaking the terrible news that their brother had been murdered.

When Nancy Taylor first heard what had happened to her younger brother, she just didn't believe it.

"I didn't even know he was missing," said Nancy. "I got off the phone and went and looked online."

In the days leading up to the funeral, the two estranged sisters bonded together, forging a far closer relationship than ever before. And they were both convinced Melanie was Bill's killer.

The Friday before the funeral, Melanie telephoned the Rices, asking for a photograph of Bill, saying she couldn't find one.

"I'm like, 'What are you talking about?' " said Sue. " '*You*, Miss Photograph? You've got to have a picture in every room of Bill and the children. *You* don't have a picture of Bill?' "

Then two hours later, Melanie called back in a conciliatory mood, inviting Jon Rice to deliver Bill's eulogy.

Melanie McGuire had selected the Brigadier General William C. Doyle Veterans Memorial Cemetery as her husband's final resting place. Located in Wrightstown, New Jersey, it was dedicated in May 1986 by then-Governor Thomas H. Kean, as "a lasting memorial to those men and women who put their lives on the line to defend our country's honor and freedom." It provided ex-servicemen in all branches of the U.S. armed forces with a simple slat bronze marker on a marble base, at no cost to the next of kin.

On Monday, July 12, Melanie drove there with her stepbrother Christopher and best friend Selene. Her mother and stepfather arrived separately from Barnegat. And right behind the grieving widow's SUV was a Woodbridge police car, with several detectives inside to observe.

It was raining heavily, as Cindy Ligosh, her husband Bill and children Max and Laura parked at the bottom of a hill, where the chapel stood. Ahead of them were several other funeral parties, waiting to be summoned up to the chapel.

"It was a busy day," remembered Cindy, "so you have to queue at the bottom, and then they tell you when to go up and park."

The service was scheduled for 2:00 p.m., but Bill's sister Nancy's flight from Florida had been delayed because of bad weather. When she couldn't reach Cindy, she called the cemetery office, pleading with them not to begin until she could get there.

"I was hysterical," said Nancy. "I'm on the phone, frantic, with the funeral director. 'Don't let them start without me!'"

As it was so wet, all the mourners remained in their vehicles until summoned. Then they slowly drove up the hill in a procession to the chapel parking lot.

"I hadn't seen Melanie," said Cindy, who was sitting in the driver's seat, waiting to be called to the chapel. "And suddenly I heard a knock at the window, and it's Melanie, her father and [step]brother. It was the first contact I had had with Melanie after I found out Bill had been murdered.

"We rolled down the window and her father said, 'We have to leave.' And my mouth dropped. It's about four o'clock. We haven't buried Bill yet and Michael's like, 'We have to go and pick up the kids at day care.'"

Cindy was "speechless" that Melanie would even contemplate leaving before the service had even begun. She reasoned with her sister-in-law, saying that the day care would understand if she was late because of her husband's funeral. She even offered to give them a thousand dollars to look after Jack and Jason for the extra hour or so.

"It's so hard," sighed Michael Cappararo, as Cindy pressed the button to close the window.

"He was just whining," she remembered. "And I just rolled up the window. I turned my back on them. And they proceeded down to speak to other people in cars."

Then Cindy got out of her car and walked over to Jon and Sue Rice, telling them about the conversation she had just had with Melanie and her parents.

"Cindy had suspicions all along," said Sue Rice. "So now I'm watching her."

* * *

About half an hour later, Nancy Taylor finally arrived, and Bill McGuire's funeral party took their seats in the tiny chapel. Melanie had not brought any flowers, so Cindy Ligosh had arranged to have one lavish arrangement of different colored roses from her, Nancy and Jack and Jason.

At the front of the chapel was a smiling photograph of Bill and Melanie in Atlantic City that Jon Rice had taken the previous year, during their trip there. Next to it was a small urn, containing Bill McGuire's ashes.

Few mourners attended the brief service, but his NJIT work colleagues Jaychandra Tandava and Tom Terry were there to pay their last respects.

"It was very small," Tandava remembered. "And it happened very fast."

Just before the service started, the grieving widow came over to embrace her sister-in-law Nancy, who recoiled in horror.

"At that point I had made up my mind she was the murderer," said Nancy. "I wasn't ready to deal with her."

Several days earlier, Melanie had assured Cindy that she would tell the military chaplain a little about Bill's life, so he could speak a few nice words about him at the service. But it soon became obvious the chaplain had no idea who had died, even having to ask Melanie her husband's name at one point.

Then, Jon Rice stood up to deliver his tearful eulogy to his best friend.

"Hi. My name is Jon Rice and I'm here today to celebrate Bill McGuire's life. Bill was a husband to a beautiful wife, Melanie. Bill was a father of two wonderful boys, Jack and JT. Talking with him, they were his crowning achievement.

"Bill was a brother to Cindy and to Nancy. His relationship with Cindy was one that I was jealous of, and I wish I had with my own sister. Bill was a proud uncle. He often spoke of his niece and nephew's accomplishments. Bill was a godfather to my youngest son Austin, and he was my best friend.

"Bill was proud of his position and the work he did at the university. I met Bill over twenty years ago. He was always the

center of attention because of his sense of humor. After two years of tech school in Vallejo, California, we both became Delta System technicians. We were transferred to the U.S.S. America where he spent over three years on the ship. We visited various ports in Spain, England, Italy and the French Riviera.

"In 1986 we were involved in the conflict with Muammar Quaddafi, and together we crossed the Line of Death. We both got out of the Navy and we went our separate ways. However, Bill had the uncanny way and the ability of always keeping up with Sue and I.

"I could tell you a hundred different stories about Bill. Bill and I shared a lot of great memories. Like me, Bill was not a perfect person, but he was a perfect friend."

After the moving eulogy, the mourners went outside to the grave, where a small urn containing Bill's ashes would be buried. As the chaplain presented Melanie with a folded American flag, she suddenly screamed.

"All of a sudden, she let out this bizarre yell," remembered Cindy. "And everyone just looked at her. 'Where did that come from?' Because she had not shed a tear. It was her only emotional moment. But it wasn't as if she burst into tears or anything. She just let out some kind of sound."

The whole service lasted just twenty minutes from start to end, and afterwards Melanie and her mother Linda approached Cindy outside the chapel.

"She came up to me and hugged me," said Cindy. "And I just whispered in her ear something to the effect, 'I can't do this . . . I'll break down.' It was really an excuse to break away from her. I wanted to strangle her. I wanted to strangle her."

Jon and Sue Rice were among the last mourners to leave, as they wanted to retrieve the photo of Bill they had brought. Then Melanie and her parents came over and hugged them, thanking Jon for his eulogy.

Finally Melanie got into her Pathfinder by herself and started driving away.

Five-year-old Bill McGuire was always getting into mischief.
Courtesy of Cindy Ligosh

Little Bill McGuire with his sisters Cindy (left) and Nancy (right).
Courtesy of Cindy Ligosh

On March 23, 1986, Petty Officer Bill McGuire crossed Libyan dictator General Qaddafi's infamous "Line of Death." *Courtesy of Cindy Ligosh*

Bill and Melanie were very much in love on their wedding day.
Courtesy of James and Lisa Carmichael

Michael and Linda Cappararo never approved of their daughter Melanie's marriage to Bill McGuire. *Courtesy of James and Lisa Carmichael*

Bill and Melanie's apartment at 2902 Plaza Drive, Woodbridge, where prosecutors believe she drugged and then shot her husband dead, before dismembering his body.
Courtesy of the New Jersey Attorney General's Office

The $500,000 house at 29 Halls Mill Road, in Warren County, NJ, that Bill McGuire completed hours before his murder.

Courtesy of the New Jersey Attorney General's Office

The signed receipt of the Taurus handgun Melanie McGuire bought in Pennsylvania on Monday, April 26, 2004—just three days before Bill's murder.

Courtesy of the New Jersey Attorney General's Office

The Chesapeake Bay Bridge Tunnel in Virginia Beach, where prosecutors believe Melanie threw Bill's body over the side in three matching suitcases.

Courtesy of John Glatt

The first suitcase was brought ashore at Vista Circle, Virginia Beach.

Courtesy of the New Jersey Attorney General's Office

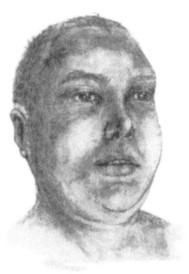

One of Bill McGuire's body parts wrapped up in a trash bag inside a suitcase.

Courtesy of the New Jersey Attorney General's Office

The artist impression of the suitcase victim was seen by Sue Rice, who instantly recognized it as Bill McGuire.

Courtesy of the New Jersey Attorney General's Office

Seven minute pieces of Bill McGuire's "human sawdust" that prosecutors contend Melanie trod into his car on the soles of her shoes.

Courtesy of the New Jersey Attorney General's Office

The Middlesex County Courthouse in New Brunswick, NJ, where Melanie went on trial for murder in March 2007.

Courtesy of John Glatt

Prosecutor Patti Prezioso, who left no stone unturned to get a murder conviction against Melanie McGuire.

Courtesy of the Court Video Pool

Celebrity lawyer Joe Tacopina gave his client Melanie McGuire the best defense money can buy.

Courtesy of the Court Video Pool

Melanie's first court appearance after her dramatic arrest.
Courtesy of the New Jersey Attorney General's Office

Dr. Brad Miller, who had a passionate extramarital love affair with Melanie McGuire.

Courtesy of the Court Video Pool

Bill McGuire's friends and family celebrate after the guilty verdict.

Courtesy of James and Lisa Carmichael

Jon and Sue Rice at their Chesapeake home hold up their favorite picture of Bill McGuire.

Courtesy of Gail Freund

Bill McGuire's old Navy buddy, James Carmichael, with Cindy Ligosh.

Courtesy of James and Lisa Carmichael

Melanie McGuire will be eligible for parole when she's 101 years old.

Courtesy of the New Jersey Attorney General's Office

Bill McGuire's friend gave him a final toast at his last resting place.

Courtesy of James and Lisa Carmichael

As she passed Jon and Sue Rice, she suddenly waved good-bye.

"She was grinning like a Cheshire cat," remembered Sue. "It was evil. It was *the* most eeriest smile."

Instinctively, Sue grabbed Laura Ligosh, who was standing next to her, telling her to look at Melanie.

"And I said, 'Laura, I have to have somebody witness that with me. Look at her drive off from here with this smile: "I've got[ten] away with it."' I'll never forget it. To me, that's what clinched it, that she had murdered Bill."

And following right behind Melanie's SUV was the Woodbridge police car.

After Melanie's strange outburst at the graveside, Cindy Ligosh told her husband Bill to somehow get the American flag away from Melanie. When he came home later, he was proudly holding the flag in his hand, which Cindy later gave Jack and Jason, as a treasured memento of their father.

The following night, after the Rices returned to Virginia Beach, they received a phone call from Melanie McGuire. She seemed upbeat, and after thanking Jon for his eulogy, asked what they had thought of the funeral. When Sue asked if she wanted her "honest opinion," Melanie said that she did.

"It was the most despicable thing I've ever seen," Sue told her. "Twenty minutes. Bill deserved so much more, as to how he was killed and how he was dismembered."

Sue said that if Melanie had needed money to give Bill a decent funeral, she'd only have had to ask Cindy, who would gladly have paid for it.

"And there was a little bit of sighing," she remembered. "And then Melanie says, 'Well, Sue, I just can't think of that now. I'm a single mother. I put my husband in the grave, and now I've got to get on with my life.'"

Sue was astonished by her reaction, saying that they had to find out who had murdered Bill.

"We need your help," said Sue. "Come down here [to Virginia Beach]."

Then Melanie repeated that she was too busy now. Saying that she had to go, she hung up the phone.

"That was the last time I ever spoke to her," said Sue. "And when I put down the phone, I looked at Jon and said, 'She did it. She's the one that did it.'"

TWENTY-EIGHT

Moving On

A week after Bill McGuire's funeral, Melanie put their new house at 29 Halls Mill Road on the market, without ever having set foot in it since her husband's death. She was looking to make a tidy profit, listing it with Coldwell Banker Realty at $525,000—$17,500 more than they had paid.

Since the funeral, Melanie told friends she was moving on with her life. And in late July, she and the boys moved out of her parents' house into a new apartment in Perth Amboy, until she could find somewhere more permanent.

Now, prosecutors believe, she became convinced she had been photographed on the Delaware Memorial Bridge, which links Delaware to New Jersey, or by one of the numerous speed-trap cameras on I-13, during her drive to Virginia Beach with Bill's body. So she concocted another story, accounting for her being in Delaware on the morning of May 4, the day before the first suitcase surfaced.

She suddenly told Dr. Brad Miller that a couple of days after Bill's disappearance, she had gone on a furniture-buying trip to Delaware, as there was no sales tax there.

"She wanted to replace the furniture that she and Bill had bought together," he said. "[That conversation] was probably two or three weeks after I knew about the gun."

On Tuesday August 31—four months after Bill McGuire's murder—Cindy Ligosh and her husband Bill went to Virginia

Beach, looking for answers. Cindy was becoming increasingly frustrated at the apparent lack of progress Virginia Beach police were making, so she had gone to the press.

"I wasn't getting the answers," she explained. "Things that I felt should have been done were not being done."

Cindy was also suspicious about whether Virginia Beach Homicide had bothered to view the Chesapeake Bay Bridge-Tunnel surveillance tape, which could have proved that Melanie's Nissan Pathfinder had been there in early May. So on the way over, she stopped at the bridge's small police station, to speak to an officer.

She was told that homicide investigators had only taken one day's worth of tape, but by now, all other video for that time period had been destroyed.

Cindy and Bill stayed at the Rices' house in Chesapeake. They were soon joined by Newark *Star-Ledger* staff reporter Suleman Din, who had traveled down from New Jersey, after being promised a major exclusive.

Over the next three years, the Canadian-born journalist in his late twenties would write many column inches on the story, becoming extremely close to the Ligosh family.

That afternoon, the Ligoshes and the Rices arrived at Virginia Beach police headquarters for a private meeting with Harvey Bryant, an attorney for the Commonwealth of Virginia, and several detectives.

It was a "cordial" meeting, but the authorities refused to divulge what, if any, progress was being made in the investigation.

Straight after the meeting, Cindy and Jon sat for an interview at a local TV station, before returning to Chesapeake. There at the Rice home, Suleman Din got his exclusive, learning how Jon and Sue had identified Bill McGuire.

The next morning, *The Star-Ledger* ran a front-page human interest story on Cindy Ligosh's mission to solve her brother's murder.

When Cindy returned to New Jersey, she fell into a deep depression. She stopped going to work and stayed at home all day, watching Court TV and true crime programs.

"All I did was watch crime shows," she remembered, "morning, noon and night. I couldn't tear myself away. I just sat there in the dark and watched the shows. And was afraid to go to sleep in case I missed something."

She still regularly called Detective Ray Pickell and Detective Sergeant Joe Joraskie of the Woodbridge Police Department for progress reports. Detective Pickell too was becoming frustrated, realizing that it should be New Jersey handling the investigation, not Virginia Beach.

"I spoke to Cindy by phone I don't know how many times," said Pickell. "I kept on saying, 'Cindy, it's New Jersey's case. You've got to get them on the ball there.'"

On September 24, a frustrated Cindy Ligosh made a second trip to Virginia Beach, meeting with Ray Pickell and his immediate bosses.

"I was so angry," remembered Cindy. "I went down because they were ready to get rid of it."

At the intense meeting, also attended by the Rices, Sue frequently had to rein in Cindy.

"Cindy's a Jersey girl, and very vocal," said Sue. "So I'm holding her back."

Detective Pickell's superiors told her that the investigation was on hold, and the only way it was going to continue would be if New Jersey took over.

"All of us agreed that we were strictly the dumping site," Detective Pickell would later explain. "We sat down at a meeting with Cindy and said, 'We're out. We can't investigate it from here.'"

After the meeting, Cindy was devastated, believing that Melanie McGuire now appeared to be getting away with Bill's murder.

A few days later, the Commonwealth of Virginia sent an official letter to Peter C. Harvey, the New Jersey attorney general. It notified him that, as there was a "high probability" that Bill McGuire had been murdered in New Jersey, Virginia Beach would no longer investigate.

Commonwealth attorney Harvey Bryant, wrote:

The Virginia beach Police Department and my office are in agreement that no further investigation of this case in Virginia Beach is warranted. We strongly suggest [New Jersey] take a look at what our investigation shows.

The letter was copied to Middlesex County Prosecutor Bruce Kaplan and Woodbridge Police Chief William Trenery, placing the investigative ball squarely in their court. But Woodbridge police, with little experience of homicide investigations, did not want to get involved.

"No evidence we have uncovered indicates that Mr. McGuire was murdered in the township," Woodbridge Deputy Police Chief Philip Dinicola told *The Sentinel* ten days later when the story broke. "Therefore we have no legal grounds to commence an investigation."

When reporters tried to contact the victim's widow for comment, Melanie McGuire was unavailable.

Furious that Virginia Beach had stopped the investigation, Cindy Ligosh and her sister Nancy Taylor now went to the FBI's Newark office, meeting special agents to try to persuade them to take over. They also met with New Jersey State Assemblyman Christopher Connors, who pledged his help. In addition, they consulted a psychic.

"There was no way in hell," said Ligosh, "I was going to let it be dropped."

Then on September 8, 2004, the New Jersey Office of the Attorney General announced that a yet-to-be-determined state law enforcement agency, would take over the investigation into the murder of William McGuire. John Hagerty, a spokesman for the attorney general's office, thanked Virginia Beach police for providing them with "very good information."

"It is safe to say that New Jersey law enforcement," he told *The Star-Ledger*, "will be carrying further the investigation, based upon what Virginia has provided."

Cindy Ligosh was delighted, saying that the investigation had always belonged to New Jersey.

"I think my complaining and going to the newspapers may have worked," she said. "I think [Virginia investigators] were eager to get rid of me, maybe. Really, it wasn't their case."

If Melanie McGuire had thought the investigation into her husband's murder would just go away, she was sadly mistaken. By now, she had hired a criminal attorney named Michael Pappa, as well as being in close touch with R. Armen McOmber, her old friend at Middletown High School South, now an attorney in Red Bank, New Jersey.

In late September, she met Jim Finn for lunch at the Middletown Diner. It was the first time she had been in touch since her telephone call, informing him that Bill was dead. They had not seen each other since nursing school.

"We gave each other a hug," he remembered. "'How are you doing?'"

Then they sat down, and after ordering lunch, discussed the murder case and investigation. During the conversation, a man entered the diner, sitting down at the next table, just a few feet away.

"[Melanie] started to get very tense and very nervous," remembered Finn. "Her voice got very low and she said she didn't know if that guy was a cop, and if he was listening to our conversation or not. She appeared to become paranoid."

Melanie was now taking more and more Xanax, relying on the powerful tranquilizer to get her through the day. Every day she dropped Jack and Jason off at Kinder Kastle, usually arriving late at RMA, between 9:30 and 10:00 a.m. Then she would leave at 5:30 p.m. to pick up the kids.

In mid-October, James Carmichael decided to call his old friend Bill McGuire. They had last spoken at the end of March, and since then, Carmichael and his wife Lisa had moved to a new house, and he'd been busy setting up a legal practice in Georgia. When he couldn't find Bill's phone number, he left a message on Jon Rice's answering machine.

After Bill's death, Jon had tried unsuccessfully to track down their old friend to tell him the terrible news. When he came home and heard Carmichael's message, he had a panic attack.

After composing himself, Jon picked up the telephone and made *the* most difficult call of his life.

At first Carmichael thought it was a practical joke, so a tearful Jon put Sue on the line to tell him it was true.

"I was just so stunned," remembered Carmichael. "Not emotional, but just so stunned not to have been there."

When he finally got off the phone, he went online at his computer.

"So I logged on and here are all these articles about this thing that had happened," he said. "Melanie had never contacted us. She told everyone she couldn't remember our names, and she didn't know how to contact us. She didn't know who we were."

PART THREE

The Investigation

TWENTY-NINE

"Who Killed the Man in the Suitcases?"

On Sunday, October 31, 2004, the six-month anniversary of Bill McGuire's disappearance, Suleman Din wrote a 2,500-word story for *The Star-Ledger*, asking, "Who Killed the Man in the Suitcases?"

> *Somebody is getting away with murder. Six months after the remains of William T. McGuire were found in the waters off Virginia Beach, police have not determined who shot and dismembered the 39-year-old Middlesex County man.*

The article made a strong point that with each passing day, the chances of finding Bill McGuire's killer grew more remote.

The same day the article appeared, the Trenton-based New Jersey Division of Criminal Justice said it would announce next week which law enforcement agency would be leading the investigation.

"Someone in New Jersey is going to investigate this," said a spokesman. "We just haven't decided who or how."

After the New Jersey Division of Criminal Justice agreed to take over the investigation, Attorney General Peter Harvey had to decide which county prosecutor to assign it to. This presented a real problem. So far the evidence in Bill McGuire's murder had involved three counties: Warren County, where he had just closed on a house; Atlantic County, where his car had been recovered; and Middlesex County, where he had lived and where his wife Melanie was the last person known to have seen him before the murder.

New Jersey is one of the few states where the Division of Criminal Justice, part of the attorney general's office, employs prosecutors who have statewide jurisdiction.

So Attorney General Harvey instructed then–Director of the Division of Criminal Justice Vaughn L. McKoy to assign it to one of his prosecutors. He immediately asked Patti Prezioso, one of his most experienced assistant attorney generals, to take over the investigation.

Born in 1963, Patricia Prezioso graduated from the State University of New York at Albany in 1985, with a minor in Chemistry. She then enrolled at Brooklyn Law School, where she received a Juris Doctorate three years later.

In 1988, at the age of 25, she was hired by Manhattan District Attorney Robert Morgenthau as an assistant district attorney, spending the next fourteen years specializing in homicide and sex crimes.

"That's always been my love," she would later explain. "Homicides and rapes, I think, are such devastating crimes. And a lot of times, people say, 'How can you do such grueling work?' But to be the person who can offer help— I don't think victims and survivors ever truly get closure, but they get some feeling of satisfaction, knowing that someone cares about them."

A driven workaholic with unbounded nervous energy, Prezioso made a name for herself in the New York County District Attorney's Office, serving as criminal court supervisor, as well as running all training programs for more than six hundred attorneys. It was there that she met her future husband and father of her two children, who was also an assistant district attorney.

In May 2002, she was recruited by New Jersey Attorney General Peter Harvey for a tough assignment, troubleshooting procedures for gathering evidence in homicide investigations in the busy Essex County Prosecutor's Office. A year later, she was placed in charge of the ambitious New Jersey DNA program, with a brief to collect DNA samples from 120,000 New Jersey prison inmates.

"So my plate was full," said Prezioso. "I was struggling at the time with making sure that I was doing my job. I had about 180 employees that reported to me."

When her boss Vaughn McKoy first approached her to organize a task squad to investigate the Bill McGuire murder, she was hesitant. At that time the Division of Criminal Justice had no homicide squad, and she was already busy setting up a New Jersey cold case unit.

But her superiors believed that the McGuire case would be the perfect vehicle, giving investigators experience of running a cold case.

A couple of days after McKoy had asked her to run the McGuire investigation, Prezioso was working late in her office when there was a knock on the door, and Attorney General Peter Harvey walked in.

"Patricia," he told her, "I need you to do this. The victim's family is feeling that no one's paying attention."

The attorney general told her that he believed she was the best person for the job, promising to provide her with all necessary resources.

Prezioso agreed to start setting up a homicide task force right away.

"He always called me 'Patricia,'" she would later remember. "And he says it in exactly the way my [late] mother always said it. So I will always have a very soft spot in my heart for Peter Harvey."

Assistant Attorney General Patti Prezioso soon got down to work. After first reading a "cursory overview" of the Virginia Beach investigation, she telephoned Detective Ray Pickell in Virginia Beach for a fuller briefing. Then she requested that the elite New Jersey State Police assist the Division of Criminal Justice in the investigation.

At the beginning of November, Prezioso called a special meeting in a conference room at the New Jersey Forensic Science Technology Center in Hamilton. That "infamous" first meeting was attended by New Jersey State Police Lieutenant Paul Morris and Detective Sergeant First Class David Dalrymple, head of the Major Crime Unit, who had initially tracked the case. Also present were: Thomas Lesniak of the forensic science department, an expert in toolmarks and trace evidence; Investigator Donald Macciocca of the Division of Criminal Justice; and Detective Sergeant Joseph Joraskie of the Woodbridge Police Department, who had accompanied Virginia Beach homicide detectives in June on their original investigation.

It was the first time Assistant Attorney General Prezioso and Detective Sergeant Dalrymple, who would jointly lead the homicide task force, had ever met. And they initially got off on the wrong foot.

"He called me 'Patsy,'" remembered Prezioso. "I'm not 'Patsy.'"

At that first meeting, the investigators examined all the investigative reports from Virginia Beach. Then they began to formulate a plan of action for what promised to be a highly complex and lengthy investigation.

They also looked at the 221 items of evidence that had come from Virginia Beach. These included the three matching Kenneth Cole suitcases, four large black plastic trash bags and four smaller ones, vacuumings and sweepings from Bill McGuire's Maxima, a pair of underpants and fragments of nail polish.

"We worked it as if it was a cold case," explained Detective Sergeant Dalrymple. "It was a severe disadvantage. Even though it was relatively fresh, it's six months old, and you're putting your set of eyes on it for the first time."

One of the main problems for the investigators was the heavy press coverage that the case had generated in New Jersey.

"At that point we hadn't seen the case yet," said Dalrymple. "It was explained to us. One of the things I'm experienced at is how best to exploit the potential of the evidence."

The New Jersey State Police forensic science laboratory is

state-of-the-art, and from the outset it was determined that no expense would be spared to bring Bill McGuire's killer or killers to justice.

"We specialize in managing large-scale complex investigations," said Dalrymple, "and I have contacts all over the country and internationally . . . we wanted to go to every step. If something's necessary, it's going to get done."

When Detective Sergeant Dalrymple started reading the full Virginia Beach case reports, no one immediately jumped out at him as a suspect.

But that would soon change.

A couple of weeks after the meeting, Investigator Don Macciocca went to Virginia Beach to start collecting the evidence. He met with Assistant Medical Examiner Dr. Wendy Gunther, who gave him two vials of blood and a vial of urine, taken from Bill McGuire's body during autopsy. The vials were then sealed in plastic containers, and placed in an icepack for the trip back, where they were later tested by Dr. George Jackson, director of the State Toxicology Lab.

A month later, Macciocca returned to Virginia Beach, collecting various tissue samples extracted during the autopsy. While there, he interviewed Jon and Sue Rice at their house, and informed Jon that telephone records showed he was the last person to talk to Bill McGuire, except for his murderer.

Back at the New Jersey State Police headquarters in West Trenton, Detective Sergeant Dave Dalrymple began checking to see if anyone mentioned in the Virginia Beach reports owned a firearm.

"One thing we knew from the Virginia Beach report is that two projectiles were found during the autopsy," he explained. "And those two were both .thirty-eight wadcutters. One of them was very well preserved, almost pristine, and the other one was also in very good shape."

From his twenty years' experience as a police officer, Detective Dalrymple was certain the shooter had little knowledge of firearms, as wadcutter bullets are only used for close-range low-velocity target shooting.

First Detective Dalrymple checked to see if any one of the dozen names in the Virginia Beach report had ever purchased a firearm in New Jersey. When he came up negative, the detective, aware of the laxer gun laws across the Pennsylvania border, where Bill and Melanie McGuire had drivers' licenses, asked the Pennsylvania State Police to run some names through its database.

"And we were lucky enough," said the detective, "to find Melanie McGuire had purchased a .thirty-eight-caliber hand-gun, two days prior [to the murder]."

Records revealed that Melanie had purchased a Taurus, one of the eight different manufacturers ballistic experts had determined manufactured the murder weapon.

"And that's when we started giving her a hard look," he said. "We started viewing her as a potential suspect."

On Thursday, December 2, the *Home News Tribune* ran a page-three story announcing that the New Jersey Division of Criminal Justice had assigned four investigators to look into Bill McGuire's untimely death.

"This is an extremely active investigation," said division spokesman John Hagerty, "and it's moving forward. We've had extensive meetings with Virginia officials and have gotten their input and insights."

Without naming any of the new task force members assigned to the case, Hagerty told reporter Ken Serrano that it included an assistant attorney general, a deputy attorney general and investigators from the New Jersey State Police, who would offer forensic analysis.

When Melanie McGuire read the story, she was horrified. For the next three months she sat tight and waited for homicide detectives to come calling.

THIRTY

A Covert Operation

At the beginning of 2005, with Melanie McGuire firmly in their sights, the task force embarked on an elaborate covert operation to trap her. Over the next few weeks, investigators would obtain a mountain of cell phone and E-ZPass records for Bill and Melanie McGuire, Linda and Michael Cappararo, and others close to them. Within a forty-day period, they would also record more than five hundred hours of Melanie's telephone conversations.

"We were also doing surveillance," Detective Sergeant Dalrymple said. "We were doing whatever we could to gather information, but without playing our hand or showing our involvement."

One problem was that the investigators had little idea of the relationships between Melanie and everyone connected to the case.

"We didn't know who was who," explained Dalrymple. "So to be covert, we were doing things designed not to arouse the suspicions of anybody listed in that report."

Detective Sergeant Dalrymple was especially careful, going to interview John Coscia, the owner of John's Gun & Tackle Room, where Melanie McGuire had bought the .38 Taurus.

"We didn't know if there was a relationship between Ms. McGuire and the gun shop owner," he said. "Like, why that gun shop?"

So initially investigators were very hesitant to interview Coscia, in case he told Melanie, setting back the investigation.

But eventually, in February, after reviewing all her phone records and seeing just one call to the gun shop, Detective Dalrymple went to Pennsylvania and John's Gun & Tackle Room.

"It's very mom-and-pop," remembered Dalrymple. "And a miracle to even find it."

The elderly Coscia easily picked Melanie McGuire's picture out of a photo lineup, telling the detectives he had never sold a gun to a well-dressed nurse before.

Then he gave the investigators the paperwork she had filled out for the handgun and ammunition. The detective noted that she had obtained her Pennsylvania driver's license illegally, using her aunt's address, where Melanie had never lived. She had also written down a false workplace.

"Why is she going to [Pennsylvania]," said Dalrymple, "instead of just purchasing it legally in New Jersey? So now it's very suspicious. Why is she doing this?"

Soon after the New Jersey Task Force was set up, Cindy Ligosh was summoned to the Division of Criminal Justice to meet Patti Prezioso, David Dalrymple and victims' advocate Gail Faille.

"I remember sitting down in Patti's office," said Cindy. "We were talking and I was really emotional."

But at that time, the investigators were careful what they told Cindy. It would be another six months before she learned that Melanie had bought a gun just a couple of days before Bill McGuire's murder.

During those crucial first few months of the investigation, Patti Prezioso and David Dalrymple met regularly. There was some friction between them, as they were both used to being in charge.

"There were a lot of very heated moments," remembered Prezioso. "He was reminding me all the time that I'm not a cop, and I'm reminding him he's not a lawyer."

But gradually they both learned to respect each other professionally, cementing a close working relationship that would be essential to the outcome of the case.

New Jersey State Police forensic scientist Thomas Lesniak was the task force's gatekeeper. He was in charge of receiving all evidence, evaluating it and then sending it out for specialized analysis. Under state police protocol he used the Laboratory Information Management System (LIMS), which assigns bar codes to all the evidence, allowing it to be tracked through the investigation.

Working from his laboratory in Trenton, the crime-scene analyst first established twelve sterilized set-up rooms, where he could examine each particular piece of evidence.

Each of the three suitcases had its own room. He began their examination by covering a long trestle table with brown wrapping paper, with large sheets of white paper over that.

"Then I placed the thirty-inch case on the table," he recounted, "and visually examined it. I found a ten-inch long brown hair and mounted it on a glass slide."

Lesniak then used sticky tape to collect any trace evidence, and a large stainless-steel spatula to scrape off debris.

"I would hit it very hard," he would later testify.

He also examined the blue painter's tape, found with one of the trash bags, under a trace microscope.

"I removed an animal hair," he said, "a purple fiber and a particle of red-colored nail polish."

He then opened the case, scraping the inside thoroughly, before inspecting the wheels for any trace evidence. He found another hair wrapped around one of them, which he sent off for further analysis. He carried out similar checks on the other two suitcases in separate rooms.

He then turned his attention to the large black plastic trash bags that Bill McGuire's body parts had been wrapped in. After photographing them on a large sheet of paper, he collected as much trace evidence as possible.

"I saw dry human remains," he remembered. "Hair, dried blood and sand. They had a foul odor."

The trash bags were then taken by hand by State Investigator Irving MacConnell to a laboratory in Toronto, Ontario, Canada, where they underwent vacuum metal deposition (VMD) also known as "gold dusting." This state-of-the-art process works at the atomic level, revealing latent prints that otherwise go unseen.

When the results came back in early January 2005, they revealed some palm prints, but none belonging to Melanie McGuire.

Soon after her husband's death, Melanie McGuire had started taking her little boys to various doctors, trying to get them diagnosed as autistic. She would provide false family histories, saying that their father had been bipolar and had committed suicide.

After selling 29 Halls Mill Road, Melanie McGuire began looking for a new home. Her friend Regina Knowles suggested she move to Brick, as it had a well-regarded school for autistic children.

But it was also an 80-mile commute to and from her job at RMA in Morristown, as well as an hour away from her parents' in Barnegat—and that meant that Jack and Jason would have to spend even more time in day care.

"I convinced her to move down there for the boys," said Knowles. "We had several lengthy conversations, and I said, 'Look, Brick has one of the best special needs education programs in the state—number one.'"

Knowles, who lived close by, also offered to look after the boys whenever needed.

In late January 2005, Melanie found a $300,000 house she liked on Constitution Drive in Brick. The seller was an old Middletown High School South friend named Stacey Schleicher. Melanie brought her stepfather Michael Cappararo along to meet Schleicher, explaining that she had sold their home after her husband had died. She was now living in an apartment in Perth Amboy, but wanted a nice area to raise her two boys in.

"When she said that, my eyes welled up," remembered Schleicher. "I thought she was so brave, being widowed and trying to raise two children on her own."

Then Melanie McGuire took her hand and calmly told her, "It's OK."

So much information was now coming into the investigation that there was a real danger it could get out of control.

"This case was a bear," remembered Detective Sergeant Dalrymple. "It was hard to handle. So much going on at once."

So Investigator Don Macciocca, the tall self-effacing Division of Criminal Justice investigator, was assigned to construct an Excel database, capable of holding every fact in the labyrinthine investigation.

"That seemed innocuous at the time," said Dalrymple. "It was more of a chore. But his database was pivotal to the prosecution, because there's no way one person can remember all this stuff. And the organization he did was crucial."

Over the course of the multi-faceted investigation, detectives could access Macciocca's database from anywhere, referencing and cross-referencing anything to do with it.

"You could search it soup to nuts," said Dalrymple. "It was exhaustive, and without it, I don't know what we would have done."

Once the investigation found its rhythm, detectives met once a month in Trenton, comparing notes and planning the next course of action. But whenever something important came up, a special meeting was called.

The task force members from the Division of Criminal Justice and the New Jersey State Police soon meshed into one tightly efficient unit, working together with no sense of competition.

"It was collaborative and cooperative," explained Dalrymple. "We're all strong-willed, and we all come up with different ideas, but I think that's why we're so successful."

In February, Detective John Pizzuro of the New Jersey State Police joined the task force, in charge of all wiretapping and surveillance on Melanie McGuire, who was already being followed, and those close to her.

"My role," explained Detective Pizzuro, "was to supervise the staff monitoring telephones, review all the conversations and make sure logs were generated."

It had been decided to initiate the wiretapping phase of the investigation on Tuesday, March 8. Leading up to that, detectives had set up all the equipment. Then, with a subject under surveillance, a detective would telephone, while another observed him—or *her*—answering the call. In that way there would be no doubt about whose voice would be on the wiretaps.

On March 8, when detectives had the wiretaps up and running, they provided "stimulation" to elicit conversations between Melanie McGuire and others.

"We did two things that day," explained case manager Dalrymple, "and both of them were innocuous."

The first one was to have Joe Joraskie telephone Selene Trevizas, requesting an interview. The second was for Dalrymple and a Pennsylvania state trooper to visit Melanie McGuire's Aunt Barbara Martinez's house in East Stroudsburg, Pennsylvania—the address on her driver's license.

Earlier, Detective Sergeant Dalrymple had discovered that John Coscia, who had sold Melanie the gun, had recently been robbed in his store. So the detective went to see Melanie's family on the pretext of investigating the robbery, knowing it would be easy for them to check up on it later on the Internet.

At precisely 4:00 p.m., Dalrymple and a Pennsylvania state trooper arrived at the house, and were let in by Melanie's Uncle Raphael Martinez, who brought them into the living room, where they saw Barbara Martinez and her son Jeff.

"I asked if Melanie McGuire resided there," said Dalrymple. "I said, 'We're checking on paperwork because this store was robbed.'"

After a short conversation with Melanie's aunt, Dalrymple left the house, immediately contacting his wiretap managers, to let them know the bait had been set. Then he sat back to wait for the reaction.

THIRTY-ONE

"Another Bill McGuire Special"

Straight after receiving Joe Joraskie's telephone call, an anxious Selene Trevizas called Melanie McGuire. In turn, McGuire telephoned her attorney Mike Pappa and old high school friend Armen McOmber, leaving urgent messages for them to call.

And at 4:23 p.m., the task force monitors were listening in when she telephoned her boss and boyfriend Dr. Brad Miller, on their private cell phone line.

"The cops called Selene," she told Dr. Miller, sounding panicked. "It's the detective from Woodbridge and some other guy. Of course, Selene can't remember anything."

"OK," said Dr. Miller coolly, "we were sort of expecting that."

Then after asking Melanie if she had called the two attorneys, he said he would prepare for his call by detectives.

"Um, maybe," replied Melanie. "Maybe not."

"Did you call your parents?" asked the doctor.

"Not yet," replied Melanie.

"Offhand," continued Doctor Miller, "I think [the police are] not gonna find anything new or discover anything new."

Then Melanie ended the call, saying McOmber was on the other line, and she'd call back later.

A few minutes later, Melanie again called Dr. Miller.

"So what did Armen think?" he asked.

"He thinks this is par for the course, that we should have

anticipated this. We sort of lulled ourselves into a false sense of [security] . . . thinking it would go away."

Melanie said she felt as though the police were targeting her through Selene, her closest friend.

"I'm sure they don't have many other people to target," replied Dr. Miller.

Selene had been contacted by Detective Joraskie, she said, adding that he had been really aggressive.

"That's the one that left the card at the door?" asked Dr. Miller. "That's when they knew."

Then Dr. Miller asked if she had called her parents yet, speculating that the police probably didn't have any new evidence.

"All right," said Melanie. "I'll call you back."

A few minutes later, she telephoned Selene, saying that although Mike Pappa was in Aruba, one of his colleagues had offered some guidance: Selene should return Joraskie's call, otherwise he'd just turn up on her doorstep.

"Everybody's feeling, by and large," said Melanie, "is that you should probably at least meet with a lawyer ahead of time, who might cut it off at the knees and say . . . 'You talked to her already.'"

"Doesn't that look suspicious?" asked Selene.

"It doesn't matter what it looks like," said Melanie sharply. "Because this guy Joraskie was the one who questioned me with Virginia [detectives]. He's really aggressive and he's a dick. He's a real dick."

Then Melanie told her not even to mention getting an attorney.

"Just say, 'Listen, this week is really bad, with therapy and the kids' and whatever. 'Can we set it up for Tuesday next week?' Armen's point was, they waited nine months, they can wait a week."

Selene agreed to stall for time, saying she would tell Detective Joraskie that it would have to be next weekend if he wanted to speak to her husband Alex, too.

A few minutes later, Melanie telephoned her stepfather Michael Cappararo, at work.

"E-Z Store, Michael," said Cappararo.

"It's your daughter, not your wife," said Melanie. "The cops called Selene."

Melanie explained that Detective Joraskie wanted to go to Brooklyn to interview Selene and Alex, saying McOmber had advised her to stall until attorney Pappa returned from his Aruba vacation.

"You know, the feeling is," said Melanie, "if she gets counsel out there in Brooklyn, the meeting will never take place."

Then Cappararo remarked it had been so long since Bill McGuire's death, that many things would have been forgotten.

"Be honest," he asked, "who remembers?"

"I gotta tell you," said Melanie, "there's so much I don't remember. I'm not being coy. I, I don't."

Then in the middle of the call, Melanie got a call-waiting from Selene and spoke to her.

A few minutes later, she resumed the conversation with her stepfather. Selene had now spoken to Detective Joraskie, she told him, who was giving her a hard time for not being able to meet him Saturday.

"She [said] he was much nicer the first time he called," Melanie explained. "I said, you know, 'cause I told her . . . he's really aggressive."

She then speculated that if there had been "some big-time lead," the attorney general's office or "somebody a little more savvy," would be dealing with it, and not the Woodbridge Police Department.

"Did you tell Mommy?" asked Cappararo.

"No, not yet," she said. "I figured I'd tell you first."

At the end of the five-minute conversation, Melanie said Detective Joraskie's call to Selene could not have come at a worse time, with Jack's diagnosis, the new house in Brick and a party she was attending on the weekend.

"This is the last fucking thing I need right now," she snapped.

Then Michael Cappararo pointed out the last newspaper article, about setting up the task force, was more than two months earlier.

"Nothing happens," he said mournfully, saying he had to go, as there were customers in the shop.

A few minutes later, Melanie's cousin Leslie called, saying the state police had just left her parents' house, making inquiries about a gun.

"They were looking for you," said Leslie. "Apparently there was a gun store in Palmerton that was robbed . . . and your name was on a receipt from having purchased a gun about a year ago."

"OK," replied Melanie coolly.

"My mom and dad didn't know what to say, so my mom said, 'Oh, she hasn't lived here in over a year.' You know, my mom didn't know what to say."

"Right," said Melanie.

"She was kind of really caught off guard," continued her cousin. "'Cause they were gonna wait. You know, they wanted to know what time you got home from work."

"Right."

Leslie told Melanie that the officers said they had only wanted to contact her, so she could fill out some paperwork indicating whether or not she had purchased a gun.

"I don't really know the truth behind it," said Leslie, "but that's what they told my mother."

"OK."

"So I felt I should contact you, and let you know that they were gonna probably be contacting you."

And, she warned, her mother had given the police Melanie's home address.

"Is there anything I should know?" she asked.

"Mmmmm," replied Melanie. "Not particularly. I mean, you know, not over the phone."

Melanie then asked if a local gun store had been robbed.

"I think it was a story they were telling my parents," said her cousin.

And they both agreed it didn't make sense, as police wouldn't be going through receipts after a robbery.

"Yeah," said Melanie. "Well, another Bill McGuire special."

After putting down the phone with her cousin, she immediately contacted Michael Cappararo.

"Leslie just called," she told him. "And the state police in Pennsylvania went to Aunt Barbara's house and wanted to know if I was there. Some cockamamie story about a gun shop being broken into."

She told Cappararo that Aunt Barbara had given them the Constitution Drive address, saying Melanie hadn't lived at the house for a very long time.

Melanie then asked if she should tell her mother about the police having the address.

"I don't want Leslie to say something to Mom at the party this weekend," she said. "Maybe I should let a day go by, though."

"Yeah," agreed her stepfather, "because you gave her too much already, right? Did you tell your mom already about it?"

When Melanie said she had told her mother about the police visiting Aunt Barbara, Cappararo asked what his wife's reaction had been.

"She was shaking, like we were," replied Melanie. "But you know she was."

"But you know it is inevitable that something like that was going to happen," said Cappararo. "And I was surprised that they didn't catch that Pennsylvania thing, they didn't go there before."

Melanie then told him that her cousin Leslie had asked if there was anything Melanie wanted to tell her.

"And you said no," said Cappararo.

"I said, 'No. I'm not going to talk to you on the phone, anyway.'"

"Right," said her stepfather. "But I'm just saying, you know, hopefully Selene's the same way. I mean . . . Selene knows more than most people."

Melanie said the police would probably visit the Cappararos next with "the knock on the door."

"Yeah, and it's fine," he said. "What? I have got nothing to say. I really don't, OK? And if they knock on the door . . . we have that guy in Toms River."

"Right."

"Just give him a buzz, OK?"

Then Melanie said she had to go to collect her boys from day care.

A few minutes later, Melanie telephoned her mother, Linda Cappararo.

"This shit has to pop up now," said her mother.

"Exactly," said Melanie. "The gift that keeps on giving. He fucks me again."

Melanie said there must be a reason why they wanted to question Selene again.

"It's interesting that they keep coming back to that," said Melanie. [It] makes me wonder. I have no idea what's in Alex's [Selene's husband's] past."

They then discussed whether her cousin Leslie would come to the weekend party, as it was a two-hour drive each way.

"We don't need her with her big mouth either," snapped Linda Cappararo.

Later on in the half-hour conversation, Melanie discussed her use of Xanax, to help her get through her ordeal.

"I'm, like, wandering around back and forth," she related. "I can't even get my head out of my ass. It's funny, though, on the meds. It's bad, but nowhere near . . ."

"I know," replied Linda. "But that's scary, too. It's like a false sense of . . ."

"No," replied Melanie. "It just gives us the ability to say, 'Well, they're gonna do what they're gonna do . . .' and not start picking the flesh off our bones."

At the end of the conversation, Linda mentioned the last newspaper story in December, revealing that an assistant attorney general from the Division of Criminal Justice would be leading the investigation.

"What the hell shit is that about?" she asked her daughter.

"It's not that unusual," replied Melanie. "If they do that though, that means that the prosecutor has questions. Yeah, like it got tossed on his desk. And if this is a new guy, like Armen seems to think it is, that's who you hand it off to. You're not gonna hand it off to a veteran, unless you got something smoking."

"I guess," said her mother.

At 8:00 p.m. that night, Melanie called Selene Trevizas from her home phone in Brick, urging her to get an attorney. She described how detectives had visited her aunt in Pennsylvania, checking up on receipts after a gun store robbery.

"It's bullshit, obviously," said Melanie.

"Yeah, definitely," agreed Selene.

"But," said Melanie, "so I think that seals the deal about you not talking with a lawyer."

Selene expressed surprise that New Jersey police had contacted her, when the ones from Virginia Beach had never followed up on the June interview. Melanie asked why police had visited her Aunt Barbara, giving her "the heads-up" and "that much advance notice."

Selene said it looked like the New Jersey detectives were doing a fresh investigation, covering new ground.

"Yep," agreed Melanie. "In some ways I'm trying to tell myself [at] least when they go through this, then it will be done. And I won't have to sit there and worry, 'Are they gonna call?' Like once they go through this, there's nothing more to go through. It's hard not to fucking die all over again."

Later that night, Melanie McGuire called Dr. Brad Miller, advising him to get a lawyer. The doctor took his lover's advice, hiring an attorney named Mike Rogers, who was recommended by her lawyer Michael Pappa.

"I met with him," remembered Dr. Miller. "I told him the situation. He said, 'Be assured, they are going to meet with you. They're going to want to speak to you, and when they do, just give me a call and we'll meet with them.' I said 'Fine.'"

At 8:12 the following evening, Regina Knowles called Melanie McGuire on her cell phone. Little Jack and Jason could be heard playing in the background, and during the conversation Melanie told them to be quieter.

First Melanie updated Knowles on the situation, saying that Woodbridge police wanted to question Selene and Alex Trevizas, speculating that it was because they had organized her move out of 2902 Plaza Drive. And at the same time, New Jersey State Police had visited her aunt's house in Pennsylvania, asking questions about her.

She mentioned that her attorney had advised Selene to get legal representation.

"You gotta be kidding me," said Knowles. "For what? Why do they have to pay an attorney because they're your friends? For what?"

"Because when a detective and a prosecutor want to come talk to you," replied Melanie, "you should not talk without an attorney."

"That is bullshit," said Knowles. "They're not the suspected or anything, are they?"

"Dude," said Melanie, "I'm sure I'm prime suspect number one, so by her being my best friend . . ."

"Well, that's insane that she should have to get an attorney and pay those ridiculous rates. Haven't gotten around to the rest of us yet, huh?"

Melanie said she had seen Selene several times after Bill's disappearance.

"Selene came down to help me look at apartments," Melanie said. "[She] saw me at least twice during those first few days before they found the first part of him, if you will. So she kind of helps put me there."

Melanie also said that Alex Trevizas had mentioned Bill McGuire being shot at his June 2004 interview with Detective Ray Pickell.

"And the cop said, 'I didn't say he had been shot,'" she told Knowles. "That was before they had told any of us how he had died. And Alex was just like, 'I assumed.' You know, so I'm sure that stuck with them."

When David Dalrymple reviewed Melanie McGuire's wire-tapped conversations, he was most interested in her responses.

"There were immediate and extreme reactions," he said. "If a family member of mine was murdered, and I had nothing to do with it, and I found out that the police were going to be investigating . . . I'd be the first one at their door. I wouldn't be scared to death, and worried about one of my peripheral friends being interviewed.

"It's just not the proper reaction that you'd expect from somebody who had no involvement. It was very unusual."

THIRTY-TWO

Into the Open

By the next morning, Melanie McGuire was definitely feeling the pressure. A detective had contacted her divorce attorney Risa Kleiner, asking about Melanie's HP Pavilion laptop computer, which was in Kleiner's office for safekeeping.

"My God," Melanie told Selene Trevizas, calling her in Brooklyn on her cell phone at 1:20 p.m. "So they called my divorce lawyer about my computer. So they're definitely doing their stuff."

Then Selene asked if the police knew how to contact her directly or were deliberately not doing so.

"I think they're just not," replied Melanie, saying she was going to talk to her lawyer again over the weekend.

When Selene asked if she would be at the party that night, Melanie changed gears, becoming self-piteous and portraying herself as an innocent conspiracy victim.

"[I'm] trying to keep my head on straight," she said. "I was doing okay for a couple of days and then when Armen [McOmber] called me this morning and he was like, 'Oh, your divorce attorney called me,' I was like, 'Oh, all right. I'm going to go home and get sick now. And then I'll take a Xanax and I'll be okay after that.'"

The wiretapping phase of the task force's investigation lasted forty days. During that time, investigators played a cat-and-mouse game with Melanie McGuire and those closest to her, taping around 500 hours of conversations.

"Stimulation is like anything good," said David Dalrymple. "You want to use it in doses."

And from the very beginning, Melanie McGuire's conversations put her relationships in context, including the fact that she was having a passionate affair with her boss, Dr. Bradley Miller.

"The stimulation resulted in immediate conversations, which helped us," Dalrymple would later explain. "It provided evidence [and] statements that can steer us. It also establishes and reinforces relationships, which is huge."

In mid-March, the murder investigation moved into a new overt phase, as detectives began face-to-face interviews with those closest to Melanie McGuire. The task force was particularly interested in Dr. Bradley Miller, who the wiretapping had revealed to be Melanie's secret lover. The millionaire married father of two, and partner in RMA, now also became a murder suspect.

"Dr. Miller is her boss," said Detective Sergeant Dalrymple. "We know he's helped her move out of the apartment, which is unusual. But we really didn't know the extent of the relationship until we hit that point. We suspected, but we didn't know."

At 7:00 p.m. on Saturday, March 12, Dr. Miller was leaving his RMA office, when he was cornered by four homicide detectives in the stairwell—two coming up from the first floor and two descending from the second. They asked him to follow them in his car to the New Jersey State Police's Somerville Barracks in Somerset County. En route they briefly stopped at a party store in a strip mall to ensure that they were not being followed.

Once they arrived at the barracks, Dr. Miller was brought into an interview room with David Dalrymple, immediately invoking his right to have an attorney present. When the doctor couldn't remember his new lawyer Mike Rogers' phone number, Detective Dalrymple tracked it down, even making the call.

"His advice was not to speak with the police," said Dr. Miller. "That I have him present for questioning."

Dr. Miller was then handed a subpoena to appear before a grand jury, before being allowed to leave. A shaken Dr. Miller drove home, knowing that his life was tumbling down around him.

Arriving home, Dr. Miller acted as if everything was normal, helping his wife get the children ready for bed. Once they were asleep, he said he had something important to discuss with her.

"Then I had to tell Charla," he would later testify. "I didn't know how her reaction was going to be."

He told her about his three-year affair with Melanie McGuire. And also that he was now a suspect in the brutal murder of Melanie's husband Bill.

"In one evening, my whole life turned upside down," he would later testify. "I was looking at losing my job, losing my wife, losing my kids and being involved in a murder investigation."

But even after his emotional confession, Dr. Miller was still highly conflicted about his wife and children, and his obsessive love for Melanie McGuire.

"I was still very much in love with her," he explained. "And I still believed that she had nothing to do with [Bill's murder]."

The next day, Dr. Brad Miller and his attorney Mike Rogers met with detectives. During the four-hour conference, Detective Sergeant David Dalrymple laid out all the evidence, tying Melanie McGuire into her husband's murder.

"He was resistant to the idea that she could be involved," remembered Dalrymple. "He did not want to believe that this woman had done this."

Finally, Miller agreed to cooperate with the investigation. His attorney negotiated a proffer agreement, whereby the New Jersey Attorney General would recommend Miller's immunity from any subsequent prosecution, as long as he supplied truthful information against Melanie McGuire.

On Thursday, March 17, Dr. Miller signed the first of two proffer agreements with the State of New Jersey. The next day, the doctor had the first of three meetings with Patti Prezioso and David Dalrymple, to debrief him and prepare him for his scheduled grand jury testimony at the end of the month.

Detective Sergeant Dalrymple, who spent hours questioning him, says Dr. Miller never displayed any "malice" or "pleasure," when secretly providing incriminating evidence against his lover. But although he told detectives he had ended the affair, Miller continued having sexual relations with her for several more months, even as he betrayed her to law enforcement.

At 4:20 p.m. on Saturday, March 19, Melanie McGuire called Selene Trevizas on her cell phone. Selene had seen an attorney, who wanted a $7,000 retainer, warning that she would have to tell police everything, or risk perjuring herself.

"Why in the hell should I pay seven thousand dollars for a lawyer?" Selene asked. "They were like, 'We just want to make sure you're not implicated.' So I was like, 'If I'm telling them everything I know, then obviously I'm not implicated.'"

She and Alex had discussed it, she told Melanie, and decided that if they were going to tell everything anyway, what did they need an attorney for?

"But then I said, 'Let me ask Melanie . . . Is there something that we don't see?' 'Cause they're telling me that I have to say everything."

Selene said the attorney had warned her that at some point police would ask if there was anything else they should know.

"You have to tell them, or you are committing perjury," said Selene.

She had kept asking if she could "just skip this part," but the attorney was adamant, saying she had to tell everything. Also, her attorney needed to be present at the interview to ensure that she and Alex were not "implicated."

"I'm not implicated," said Selene. "Then I started thinking . . . this doesn't make sense."

"All right," said Melanie, "Let me talk to my lawyer."

The next morning, Michael Cappararo telephoned his step-daughter, for a very cryptic forty-six-second conversation. By now it was obvious they suspected their phones were being tapped, as they appeared to use a code.

"I spoke to aah, aah, what's-his-name, about shipping," said Cappararo.

"Alex?" asked Melanie.

"Ah, I didn't want to say names, yeah," said Cappararo. "And the shipping is whatever happened to the practice that they didn't want, really, you to know. They didn't want to worry you, happened to, aah, them."

"OK," said Melanie.

"You understand what I'm saying?"

"Yep."

"The same thing that happened to everybody there happened to them. OK?"

"OK."

"OK sweetie, bye."

"All right, thanks, bye."

Selene Trevizas would later admit that Melanie had told her certain things she did not want the detectives to know.

"She did confide in me," said Selene. "We had nothing to hide, but she told me things that I would prefer not to tell cops."

A few days after the conversation with Melanie, Selene and Alex were interviewed at their home in Brooklyn by task force detectives.

"Cops came to my house and there was a surveillance guy there," she said. "We knew our phones were tapped. We knew we were pretty much watched, so we were careful what we said on the phone. Not that we had anything to hide. We just didn't want anything to be misconstrued."

The task force was also busy, working on the trash bags that had packaged Bill McGuire's body parts. When they finally came back to Trenton, forensic scientist Tom Lesniak spent weeks physically examining them.

It was painstaking work. He would lay them out, counting the number of chads—the tiny perforation marks at the tops and bottoms of the bags—where they had been pulled apart.

He then placed them side-by-side with the six bags found at Justin Marrero's house in Brooklyn containing Bill McGuire's clothes. Using a light box, he examined the swirling striations embedded in the black dye of the plastic.

"It's kind of like a fingerprint of the extrusion," he explained.

And he discovered a distinct pattern of swirls and lines in the industrial-sized bags, showing that both sets of bags had been made in the same factory, by the same machine, and in the same production line.

"Every piece matched," he said, adding that the "chads" were in "perfect orientation," with a tiny bump on the upper edge of each bag, proving they were all sliced by the same slightly warped blade.

"The bags were cut almost sequentially," explained Dr. Thomas Brettell, director of the Office of Forensic Sciences, saying they very likely came out of the same box.

THIRTY-THREE

"Could I Have Killed Him?"

On March 28, 2005, Melanie McGuire signed the contracts on her new house, at 753 Constitution Drive in Brick Township. Because she would now be spending so much time commuting to her job in Morristown, she gave Regina Knowles a set of keys for emergencies.

Three days later, New Jersey State Police forensic scientist Thomas Lesniak led a team of task force investigators to thoroughly search Melanie and Bill McGuire's old Woodbridge apartment, looking for any signs of blood.

The forensic team arrived early in the morning, and literally began taking the master bathroom apart, using a hammer and chisel.

"There was an awful lot of work done," explained Lesniak. "We were looking for any type of blood evidence."

The experienced crime-scene investigator swabbed the bathroom tiles, the caulking around the bathtub and the floor. Then the unit sprayed luminol throughout the master bedroom, looking for any signs of blood or other bodily materials. They failed to find any.

At 3:30 p.m., investigators left the apartment carrying several boxes of evidence.

The next morning, the *Home News Tribune* ran a front-page story with the headline, "Body in 3 Suitcases: Cops Comb Apartment of Victim." The story, by staff writer Ken Serrano, reported that the present occupants of the old McGuire town-house had been moved, so the forensic team could thoroughly investigate. Before going in, the Division of Criminal Justice had relocated the new occupants, a mother and her two adult daughters, paying all their expenses.

After the search, Melanie McGuire and those close to her went into lockdown. From now on they would be guarded in all telephone conversations, and she would even joke about be-ing under surveillance to her colleagues at RMA.

"She knew that they were taping her phone conversations," remembered Lori Thomas. "As a joke, she would pick up the phone and say, 'Oh, hi, it's the three-to-eleven shift.'"

"She knew an investigation was going on," said Jim Finn, "and she was probably the target of it. If you said anything even remotely incriminating, you said, 'Aahh, three-to-eleven's going to write that one down.'"

Eventually Melanie told Finn about her long-term affair with her boss Dr. Brad Miller. Although Finn felt betrayed, he continued pursuing her.

On April 6, Melanie made a late-night call to Finn at his home, after discovering that Assistant Attorney General Patti Prezioso, from the New Jersey Division of Criminal Justice, was leading the investigation. He began teasing her about go-ing on a double-date with Dr. Miller and a woman Finn was seeing.

"So I'm going to hell," Finn joked.

"Well, I'll save you a barstool," Melanie wise-cracked.

"We'll have a couple of drinks."

"Exactly. Tell Brad and Theresa to meet us there."

"We'll have a foursome," said Finn sarcastically.

"Nice, nice," said Melanie. "Oh Christ. Did you just say that?"

Later in the conversation, they were apparently discussing the investigation when Melanie suddenly said, "Maybe the deputy attorney general has the answer. Maybe we should ask her."

"Let's give her a call," suggested Finn.

"'Patti,'" joked Melanie. "'Can I call you Patti?'"

" 'How you doing? . . . What's up?' "

"Can't we just give her the respect that as Madam Deputy Attorney she deserves, and move on?" said Melanie, laughing.

A week later, two New Jersey State Police detectives arrived at the hospital where Finn worked, bringing him to the Howell Police Department for questioning. Initially when Detective Sergeant Jeffrey Kronenfeld asked about Melanie McGuire, Finn claimed not to have been in touch with her from 1998, when they'd graduated, until September 2004. He told the detectives he had first learned of Bill McGuire's death through media reports. In September 2004 he'd begun e-mailing her, offering support.

At one point in the eight-hour interview, Detective Sergeant Kronenfeld accused Finn of being in love with Melanie.

"I denied that," Finn would later testify. "I didn't want the police to think that I was in love with a girl that murdered somebody. I told them no, but eventually I told them I was."

Then Detective Sergeant Kronenfeld asked if he knew Melanie had bought a gun, just two days before the murder. This was the first time Finn—who had advised her to get a firearm for protection, and then told her how to do it—had ever heard she had actually done so.

"[That was the] deal breaker," he explained. "By the end of the meeting I was pretty well turned around. I walked into that meeting believing in [Melanie's] innocence and walked out believing [she was] guilty. [She] bought a gun, and she had always told me she never did."

Then Finn agreed to cooperate with the task force investigation, signing a proffer agreement as Dr. Miller had done.

Two days later, on Friday, April 15, Jim Finn participated in a consensual wiretap of Melanie McGuire. Its purpose was for Finn to try to get her to incriminate herself, by getting her to discuss the gun and where she had hidden it.

At midday, he went into an office with Detective Sergeant Kronenfeld, who would monitor the conversation, while feeding him questions on a notepad.

"It is April fifteenth, 2005," said Kronenfeld, as he turned on the recording device. "We will attempt to call Melanie McGuire. The time is now twelve three p.m."

Melanie immediately answered the phone, asking Finn how he was. As previously arranged, he said things were "Not good," as he had to be at the Howell police station for an interview in two hours' time.

"I thought I was Mr. Tough Guy," he told her. "But these guys scare the shit out of me. They're all tall, so tall. You know I'm not used to looking up at people. Dude, I'm a gun owner."

"Where'd they come to you, work?" asked Melanie sounding calm and collected.

"Yeah, I'm in Howell," he said. "Surprised they didn't haul my ass out of here. Uh, Mel, I'm really scared, dude. What do I say to these people? You know we talked about buying a gun? I mean, what if they ask me about that?"

"You have to tell them the truth," replied Melanie. "You know, we— Most of our conversations about that after the fact— You know?"

"Yeah, I did tell you before though, 'cause you told me he was acting like a nut, and I was worried about you. I mean, what should I tell them?"

Then Melanie, suddenly sounding cautious, asked if there was a number she could call him back on, saying she'd be right back on a landline. A couple of minutes later she called, telling him to calm down. She would be on her guard throughout the long, emotional conversation. It was as if she knew she was talking directly to the detectives through Finn, instead of the other way around.

Finn asked if she had obtained the gun legally, and Melanie said she'd gotten it in Pennsylvania, by showing proof of residency. She said she only did it for Bill, who, as a convicted felon, was unable to buy a firearm.

"You tell them that I asked you to buy a gun, absolutely," Melanie told him. "You didn't do anything wrong."

"Of course I didn't do anything wrong," he replied.

"Believe me when I tell you," she said, "they're going to have you convinced that I killed him six days, six ways to Sunday."

She said investigators had already told Selene that Melanie had murdered Bill, and now they just had to figure out how it had been done, and with whom.

"What's their evidence?" asked Finn.

"Their evidence is that I bought a gun," replied Melanie.

Then, prompted by Detective Sergeant Kronenfeld, Finn asked what she wanted him to tell the police during his upcoming interview.

"I can't coach you," she replied. "It's better you did nothing. You have no knowledge of anything, it is better for you that you don't. The more you know, the more you're going to get dragged in—take it from Brad and Selene."

"So you're trying to protect me," said Finn. "I appreciate that."

"It's got nothing to do with protecting you," she said. "It's the truth, Jim."

"Oh, man," said Finn. "What about the suitcases?"

"No. I don't even remember what I fucking said to you about the suitcases. Believe me when I tell you, what they're going to try and do is corner you into a story, and then get you to change that story. The key is just to be honest."

Then Finn asked why she had never mentioned her affair with Dr. Brad Miller, saying he felt "a little betrayed."

"I know you're angry," she replied. "I was instructed [by my lawyer] not to tell anybody anything."

Then Finn asked if she thought Dr. Miller had murdered Bill.

"No!" said Melanie. "Get the fuck out of here! He didn't do it any more than I fucking did it."

Detective Kronenfeld upped the ante, with a note to ask her if she was lying.

"Look," said Finn, "don't hate my guts for this. You didn't tell me about him. Is there anything else you're not telling me?"

"Like what? Like I killed my husband?"

"Did you?"

"No," said Melanie, laughing, "but thanks for asking."

"Mel, can you blame me?"

"I think having an affair is a little different than murder. You should know. Aren't you seeing a married woman?"

"Yeah, well, I told you."

"Right," said Melanie. "Were you a suspect in a murder investigation at the time?"

"No, but maybe I am now," he replied. "Look, dude, I don't want to get roped in. I mean, we got to be straight with each other right now, and be on the same page. What are you not telling me?"

"What I am not telling you is that night that he left I went to AC to look for him. [I] found his car and moved his car 'cause I figured he was there at some shitty hotel . . . with somebody. And just out of spite, 'cause honestly, I looked in my car for a screwdriver to pop his tires, and I didn't have one. I moved his car out of spite, and so the video that they have is me moving his car."

"I think you're lying," replied Finn.

"Excuse me?" said Melanie, sounding offended.

"Honey, I'm sorry. I think you're lying to me, your voice just got real low."

"Because I'm in my office."

"No. If you did it, just tell me what to say. I'll do anything for you. Just tell me."

"Jim, I didn't do it."

Then Finn told her his "ass is on the fucking line," and Melanie asked him why, if he didn't do anything.

"Honey, I love you," he said, becoming emotional. "I'll do anything for you."

"Jim."

"Help me."

"Jim, I didn't fucking do it. Does it make sense that I would do it? If I had an affair with Brad for three years, do you think I would fucking pop my husband?"

"I'm gonna be blunt," said Finn, "but it happens every day. Mel, what's going on?"

"I don't believe this," she said angrily.

"Honey . . . I've been loyal to you. I want to help. You got to step up here."

"So you want me to tell you I did it when I didn't?"

"I want you to tell me the truth. I don't want to hear that you did it, but if you did, I gotta know."

"I'm telling you the fucking truth. I said it was circumstantial evidence. Circumstantial evidence. Think, think, think. And you know you're like, what, 'Hello, I bought a fucking gun.' 'Hello, I'm on videotape moving a fucking car.'"

Then Finn challenged her, saying that she'd never told him about buying a gun, and that when she'd first mentioned the video, she'd said it was so "grainy" they didn't know if it was a man or woman getting out of the car.

He then accused her of lying, asking what exactly had happened to the gun.

"What about the fucking gun?" she snapped. "I don't have it."

"Well, who does?"

"I don't know. I don't know."

Then Finn pleaded for something to give the police, saying he was going into a "lions' den," and they would "rip [his] guts out."

"You're going to tell them the truth, Jim," she replied calmly. "Tell them I asked you about buying it and you mentioned . . . you've lived in Pennsylvania. That's how you bought it, period. You didn't do anything else."

When Finn asked why she had never mentioned buying a gun before, Melanie said her divorce lawyer told her not to tell anyone.

"Weren't you happier not knowing?" she asked him, telling him to calm down.

"Easy for you to say," he said.

"Oh, it is? I've been living my life this way for a fucking year, pal."

Then, apparently prompted by a note to change tack, Finn began asking for more information on the gun.

"Mel," he began. "Getting a little nervous here. What kind of gun was it?"

Melanie said it was a .38, but knew little else about it.

Then Finn said their friendship was over, unless she gave him something to tell the police at the interview.

"I don't believe you're doing this," said Melanie, sounding exasperated.

"I don't believe *you're* doing this," he replied. "Dude, the clock's ticking. I gotta go soon."

"Jim, on my kids, I'm telling you. On my kids. Now do you believe me?"

"No, I don't. There, I said it. All right, look, if you didn't do it, and I hope to God you didn't, who did?"

"I don't know. I didn't hire anybody. I didn't ask anybody. I didn't involve anybody. 'Cause I didn't do anything."

Now, ratcheting up his questions, presumably at the prompting of Detective Sergeant Kronenfeld, Finn said he was beginning to put two and two together.

"I know about the gun. I know about the suitcase. I know about the affair. What if they make me take a lie detector test? You talk to me, now."

"You need to understand something," she told him. "My parents know the whole story. Brad knows the whole story. Selene knows the whole story. Those are the people who are physically around me in the days following him leaving, OK? They all believe me."

"How come I can't know the whole story?" he asked. "You trust me? Throw me a bone. Where's the gun? Make me believe. I really need you to believe in me."

"First and last time," she replied. "The gun was in a lockbox. When he first left I picked up the lockbox, which had something inside it. I didn't stop to take inventory, and I packed everything up and put it into the storage unit. I was told by my attorney not to go look to see if the gun was in there, OK? Of course I went later and I looked and it's not in there. It's not in there. They don't have the gun, because they were asking Selene where the gun is. They were asking Selene, did I give her something to hold? Like I'd say, 'Oh, yeah, hold this.'"

"Yeah, but if you did it," said Finn, "you wouldn't keep it."

"If anybody did it, they wouldn't keep it," said Melanie. "That's just asinine."

"Well if you have it, then, I know you didn't do it. And if you don't have it . . ."

"Then I absolutely did it. He didn't take the gun with him. He was the one who wanted it. Why do you think he wanted it?"

"Well, I don't know. All I know is, he's the one who got shot."

"Yeah, OK, so I shot him in my apartment. All right with me. Like, six neighbors around me. Nobody heard anything?"

"Did you?"

"And I cut him up with what—a butter knife? And carried him out by myself?"

"Well . . ."

"Does that make sense to you?" she asked.

"I don't know what makes sense anymore. I don't know what's going on here, Mel, and now you're telling me all these other people know, and suddenly I'm out of the loop."

Once more Melanie tells him to calm down.

"Mel," he replied, "now's the time. You need to be straight with me."

"I'm being straight with you. And if swearing on my kids isn't enough to convince you of that, then . . ."

"Then, what?"

"I don't know what to fucking tell you," she said, losing patience.

"Then what? Fuck me?"

"No, not 'Fuck you.' You're breaking my heart."

"You're breaking mine. Look, you know I'll cover for you."

For the next few minutes, Finn pressed Melanie to tell him where the gun was, promising "to take care of this," if she told him. But she refused to move an inch, insisting she had no idea where the gun was now.

She then became very emotional, after he repeated that if she was innocent she would have the gun, and know exactly where it was.

"Well, then, you know what?" she sobbed. "I guess you go into your interview and tell them that. And you tell my sons they don't have a mother."

Then, Finn changed the subject, asking about her affair with Miller and what her parents thought about it.

"My parents think I was married to a monster," she said. "And that they're not perfect. They're not OK with it, but that's how my parents got together. They can't exactly . . ."

"Do you love him?" he asked, saying he wanted to know the truth, even if it was something he didn't want to hear.

"Yes," she replied.

"Do you want to marry him?"

"Not really a possibility," she replied. " 'Cause he's kind of married to somebody else."

"Does he love you?" he asked.

"I don't know anymore," she said sadly.

"Did he help you in all this?"

"He did nothing . . . And now he's lost his partnership, he's lost millions of dollars. He's lost peace."

Then Finn asked if Dr. Miller knew about the gun, and she suddenly started sobbing.

"Yes, he does. I didn't tell him. I was ashamed. How stupid I am."

"Honey, sweetheart," said Finn, trying to comfort her.

"I'm going to sit in jail for the rest of my life for something I didn't do."

"If you didn't do it, you're not going to jail. Come on."

"Do you understand that they went back into my old apartment?" she asked him. "I didn't sleep there for the three nights after he left. I stayed in a hotel 'cause I was afraid."

Then Melanie speculated that some "rabid" guys may have come into the apartment when she was away, planting incriminating evidence. And she even suggested maybe Bill had brought somebody back to the apartment, who then killed him there.

"I didn't sleep in the apartment," she said, her voice breaking. "I didn't know that he didn't come home with somebody, or looking for me. I don't know something didn't happen there. You know I'm so fucking scared to stay. You know how scared I am, Jim? All I want to do is raise my kids, and I betrayed so many people. [I] lied and withheld stuff from so many people, not because I was looking to deceive anybody, but because I was embarrassed and ashamed. I didn't want anybody to be any more disappointed in me than they [already] are."

Then she told Finn she had always known he was in love with her, and had tried not to hurt him.

"Jim," she said, "I have tried for years to close my eyes to how I know you feel about me. 'Cause I know it's going to hurt you."

Finn told her he didn't care anymore, and just wanted her to tell him the truth.

"I don't think you trust me," he told her.

"I do trust you," she replied.

Then, apparently at Detective Kronenfeld's urging, he returned to the gun.

"Look, I'm confused about the gun," he said. "You would still have it, if you didn't do it, right?"

"When he left that morning," said Melanie matter-of-factly, "I was not downstairs. I didn't see what he took, see what he left with. I was on the floor with my baby crying, 'cause he locked me outside the door.

"Could I have killed him? I would be lying if I said I didn't think about it. Do you think I have the strength and wherewithal to shoot somebody, carve them up, carry them out of the house? Do you honestly think that I'm capable? I can't believe that you're saying these things to me, and I know why you are. And I wouldn't be hurt, and I wouldn't be angry, and I don't have any right to be, because why would you believe me?"

Finn then asked her about the hotel she had stayed at after Bill left.

"A place in Metuchen," she answered. "My parents said they would take the kids. They wanted me to stay up there, so I could pull money out of the bank accounts, find an apartment and do what I have to do without worrying about the kids. I mean, the hotel is no secret, it's right there in the fucking register."

"Who was with you?" he demanded.

"My friend Armen, who's my general attorney," she replied. "We talked about divorce. He was with me—not at the hotel, but we met for dinner down the road from [there]."

"Were you with anyone else at the hotel?" asked Finn. "Make me believe."

"One of those mornings Brad had to be at work," she told him. "And he rang my cell phone at four thirty. He just was worried about me. [He] came in, just laid down next to me and watched me sleep, 'til he had to get up and go to work."

"So Brad was with you at the hotel," said Finn, accusingly.

"Oh, that sounds great," she replied. "Not like that. For an hour. For an hour. Yeah the cops know that already."

At 7:45 that night, Jim Finn telephoned Melanie McGuire on the pretext of telling her how his interview with investigators had gone. This time, although he had no detectives with him, he had been given a list of subjects to ask her about.

"So how was it?" asked Melanie, who was at her new Brick house, with her two boys, watching television.

"Not fun," replied Finn. "They were pushing that gun thing."

Finn told Melanie the detectives thought he had supplied the gun.

"So who was it," she asked, "my girlfriend, the deputy attorney general?"

Finn said that Patti Prezioso had not been there, and it was seven-feet-tall men in expensive suits.

"They said that they are going to arrest you, Mel."

"Of course," she replied coolly. "They've been saying that for a month."

"I believe them," he said. "They really believe you have the gun. They say you bought it, and if they come calling and you can't produce it, that's gonna look really bad."

"Well, actually, from what my defense attorney says, and just playing out the different scenarios . . . the worst thing that could happen is, you produce the gun, they do ballistic testing and . . . they can't tell if it was the murder weapon or not."

Then Finn told her the police were now asking him about a second video, and also about whether she took Bill's phones out of his car.

"Yeah, I did," she said. "When I found the car, I found two phones in it. I didn't recognize either one. One looked like one of those pre-paid jobbies and the other one was a Nextel."

Melanie said she realized it was not his Nextel, so she went into the phone book where she saw all his contact numbers.

"But what struck me at that point," she said, "was, he tells me he's leaving . . . never coming back. And I know my husband. I know how he left his first wife, and you know, he already had Plan B all lined up. I'm looking at it and I'm like, 'Oh, got another phone?' [He's] got his friends' numbers programmed into it like he's ready for Plan B. And I was so pissed off, I junked them. I threw them in a garbage can someplace."

Finn told her the detectives thought he had accompanied her to Delaware.

"I didn't go to Delaware with anyone," she said. "I went to Delaware to look for furniture, and I was in Manhattan that afternoon. So unless I'm, like, driving at a hundred and twenty miles an hour, or I took the Concorde. . . ."

"I wasn't piloting that, by the way," quipped Finn.

Melanie said she had gone over the Delaware Memorial Bridge, furniture shopping.

"I was selling all my shit," she explained. "I was getting divorced in my head. My husband wasn't dead. Now, looking back, it looks strange that I did X, that I did Y, that I did Z. That's knowing he's dead. At the time, not knowing he was dead, you're doing different things."

"That makes sense," agreed Finn. "You're not thinking that somebody's going to scrutinize your every [move] to see where you were."

Melanie said the police knew she had gone shopping in Delaware, because Selene had told them.

Then Finn pressed her again whether there had been anyone else with her in Atlantic City, when she moved Bill's car to the Flamingo Motel.

"Yeah," she replied. "What is this, Team Kill Bill? I don't think so. On my children's life, I got out of that car alone. There was nobody with me."

Melanie said the police had already accused Brad and Selene's father of being with her in the car.

"Who's next," she asked, "the guy who took me to the high school prom? They got it in their heads for whatever reason, good, bad or indifferent, that I did this. And they are going to do anything they can to force those pieces into the puzzle to make them fit. And that may sound paranoid, but it's not."

Six weeks later, after Melanie McGuire sent him an e-mail accusing him of tricking her, Jim Finn sent her a bouquet of flowers, inviting her out on a dinner date.

"Ambivalence," would be the word he would later use to describe his striking change of heart. In an e-mail, he wrote:

Finally, you got the flowers. I wanted to give you orchids, but they didn't have them, so I left it to the florist's discretion.

Then in a P.S. he added:

If you like I work with a guy who writes for the *Asbury Park Press* part time, and would probably write an article, highlighting your side of the story and shed light on the fact that an abused woman and mother of 2 special needs children is being terribly persecuted by the Attorney General's office. I figure you won't go for it but it couldn't hurt to bounce it off your lawyer. My friend is a good guy and I see him being very fair with this. Just an option.

THIRTY-FOUR

"On My Kids' Lives"

On Tuesday, May 31, just before Dr. Brad Miller was due to make his second appearance before a state grand jury hearing investigating William McGuire's murder, detectives asked him to participate in a consensual wiretap of Melanie McGuire.

"I had a lot of qualms about it," he would later admit. "My thought process is that if she's truly innocent—and I wanted her to be innocent—this would be the best piece of evidence that you could have."

So at 11:30 a.m., after his testimony, Dr. Miller was driving home with homicide detectives, when he called his lover at the RMA Morristown office.

When she answered, he asked her to call him back on a different phone, somewhere private.

"What's up?" asked Melanie when she called back.

Dr. Miller told her he had just spent two hours with investigators, and they wanted him to come back again.

"You're joking," said Melanie.

"No," said Dr. Miller. "I don't know how much more I can take of this. They really think I'm involved."

The doctor said police had asked why they had been on the phone together for one hundred minutes the day she bought the gun. And they were also "hammering" him about the trip to Delaware.

"They believe you went there with your father," he told her, saying they were particularly interested in what furniture stores she visited.

"So it's nothing new," said Melanie. "It's the same old shit over and over and over."

Dr. Miller agreed, saying the detectives were implying that he knew more than he was telling, and was somehow involved.

"Well, they can imply that 'til the cows come home," she said.

He asked if she stopped at any stores during her trip to Delaware, and if anyone saw her there. Melanie said she had already given a "lengthy" list of furniture stores and warehouses to her attorney.

Dr. Miller asked about the gun, saying that police thought she had "stashed" it somewhere.

"Which is asinine," said Melanie.

She then brought up the question of there being a second person in Atlantic City with her in the car, saying it was "crazy."

"There was nobody else in that fucking car with me," she told him. "On my kids' lives. It's fucking shit."

The doctor then warned her that the investigators would either come down on him, or her stepfather, as her murder accomplice.

"I just want this to stop," she said.

"It's not going to," said Dr. Miller. "They're just going to keep going. They don't care who they take down, whether it's me or the partner or the practice. They're gonna keep coming."

At 2:30 p.m., Dr. Brad Miller made a second twenty-six-minute wiretapped telephone call to Melanie McGuire. This time he was sitting in his RMA office in Somerset with New Jersey State Police Detective Sergeant Jeffrey Kronenfeld, in yet another attempt to get Melanie to incriminate herself.

"How are you?" he asked, after getting her to call him back on a more private phone. "Are you doing all right?"

"Pretty much sick to my stomach all night," she replied.

Dr. Miller said he'd been told she had disputed an E-ZPass charge, and then he had called on her behalf, something his wife Charla had confirmed.

"That's a lie," snapped Melanie. "Can they lie to the grand jury?"

Dr. Miller said he had told them he knew nothing about her disputing any E-ZPass charge.

"Mel, I don't know how much more of this I can take," he said. "They were drilling me on the gun again and the trip to Delaware."

He then became emotional, saying that detectives were closing in on him. They'd said he didn't have a good alibi for the night of Bill's disappearance, and they found it "unbelievable" he didn't know she was buying a gun.

Then he asked her to swear on her children's lives that she'd had nothing to do with her husband's murder.

"Yes," she said without hesitation.

"I will lose everything—my kids, my job."

"Why are you saying that?" she asked.

"Just because of some of the things that are going to become public," he said, close to tears. "I'm just gonna get everything taken away, and I'm going to lose you in the process."

He then said that if they "make it through this," he would take whatever money was left and start again somewhere else.

"I don't know what else to do," he said. "I'm at my wits' end. Are all the things you told me today a bunch of bullshit too?"

If she wanted them to "stick together," he said, she had to tell him everything before it went any further.

"What do you mean, you have to know everything now?" she asked indignantly.

"I mean, there's no other secrets between us, right?"

"None that I can think of."

"I mean, it wouldn't be easy," he told her. "But we could probably make it, you know. After the divorce and she gets half the money, I mean, it's still something to live on."

"Why are you talking about this all of a sudden?" she asked.

"I just feel like I want to know . . . what's going to happen to us," he said.

"I'm thinking I'm confused," she told him, "because you've been the one who stressed to me that we have to wait and see how everything plays out. I mean, why are you talking about a divorce all of a sudden, when you weren't before?"

" 'Cause I'm tired of living this way," he said.

"Fairness to her, you could probably attribute a fair amount of your misery to knowing me."

Finally, Melanie said she just did not understand why the prosecutors were "slinging all their shit" at her.

"Just fucking indict me," she snapped. "Let's just do it."

THIRTY-FIVE

The Arrest

Two days later, exactly one year to the day after Melanie McGuire had first been interviewed by Virginia Beach detectives, the task force finally made its move.

"We came up with the arrest plan," said case manager David Dalrymple. "We were surveilling her, so we knew her pattern. We wanted to minimize the impact on her family."

The three-pronged plan consisted of first arresting McGuire before executing search warrants on her parents' house in Barnegat and her Brick residence. The stage was set, after Middlesex Superior Court Judge Linda Feinberg signed a warrant to arrest her for "purposely and/or knowingly" causing the death of William T. McGuire on or about April 29, 2004.

At 5:00 a.m. on Thursday, June 2, Detective John Pizzuro took up position in an unmarked car outside 753 Constitution Drive in Brick Township, waiting for Melanie to come out to take her two little boys to day care. Another state police officer waited nearby, also in an unmarked car.

"I was only able to observe the driveway portion of the residence," said Detective Pizzuro. "It was the only way to leave, and she would have to go past me."

A couple of hours later, Melanie's black Nissan Pathfinder drove out of the parking lot, heading out onto Constitution Drive.

"It passed me," said Detective Pizzuro. "I followed her several miles south."

Then Melanie pulled up outside a café and went in, leaving Jack and Jason in the back seat. Another detective discreetly checked the Pathfinder, while Detective Pizzuro entered the café, where Melanie was waiting for service.

"Well, good," she said, as he walked in. "Now there's two of us, maybe they'll open the door."

After buying coffee, and candies for the children, she walked out and got into her SUV, driving north along the Garden State Parkway.

Detective Pizurro followed her at a safe distance, and when she got off at the Metuchen Exit at about 9:00 a.m., another officer took over. She then drove into Metuchen, dropping off 5-year-old Jack at the gates of the ABZ Academy on Hillside Avenue.

She then drove three blocks to Kinder Kastle on Middlesex Avenue, to drop off Jason.

"We had it all set up," said Detective Sergeant Dalrymple, who was already waiting outside the day care center, with another surveillance team.

At precisely 9:30 a.m., Melanie McGuire came out of Kinder Kastle and Dalrymple and several other detectives approached her, escorting her to tree-lined Factory Street, on the south side of the building.

She was then formally arrested for the murder of Bill McGuire, and read her Miranda rights.

"Melanie was very calm," said Dalrymple. "She didn't make any comments and [it] was without incident."

She was then placed in the back of a police car and driven to Somerville State Police Station, to be processed and officially charged.

Straight after making the arrest, Detective Sergeant Dalrymple executed the next stage of the plan. He made two calls: one to Detective John Pizurro, who would search McGuire's Constitution Drive residence; and the other to Detective William Scull, in charge of searching her parents' home in Barnegat.

Then, after getting keys to Melanie's Brick residence, Pizurro and a small forensic team drove back there and entered.

"It was very well-organized and clean," said Pizzuro. "Everything had a purpose. The spice rack was in alphabetical order."

The detective took nine items into evidence, including a home computer, DVDs and a circular saw, which were brought to the state police laboratory for analysis.

As Detective Pizzuro searched Constitution Drive, Detective Bill Scull and his forensic team arrived at 22 Aqua View Lane, with a search warrant. Linda and Michael Cappararo answered the door, and Detective Scull explained that their daughter had been arrested for murder and he needed to search their home.

"They expressed concern over some valuables they had in the house," remembered Detective Scull. "Currency and jewelry. And that the policemen were going to be looking through their items. I walked with Mr. Cappararo through his residence, so he could identify the valuables he was concerned about."

First Cappararo took the detective to a closet in his master bedroom, retrieving $480 in cash from a suit pocket. He then went to some shelves in the closet, bringing out a further $14,600 in cash. Then he brought Detective Scull to the attic, where there was $13,000 in bank notes, hidden under a bag of insulation.

Later during the search, detectives recovered Bill McGuire's Taj Mahal comp card.

At 3:30 that afternoon, a visibly shaken Melanie McGuire was led into Middlesex County Superior Court in handcuffs, wearing a black knit top and pink cotton slacks. During the brief hearing she stood silently, staring blankly at the floor.

After pleading not guilty to the first-degree murder of William McGuire, she was formally arraigned in front of Judge Deborah J. Venezia, who set bail at the maximum—$750,000—remanding Melanie to the Middlesex County Adult Correction Center.

"She has been orchestrating her defense," Assistant Attorney General Patti Prezioso, opposing bail, told the judge, "creating excuses to her friends and family. She was not expecting the forensic evidence would be this clear. The forensic evidence is overwhelming."

Her attorney, Mike Pappa, argued that the 32-year-old mother of two autistic children did not pose a flight risk.

After the hearing he told reporters that he had been representing Melanie since her husband's death, and she was now "in a state of shock."

"We knew she was a target of the investigation," said Pappa, "because the spouse is always a suspect. But the arrest came as a complete surprise. This is like an out-of-body experience for her."

Later that day, at a hastily called press conference in Trenton, Attorney General Peter Harvey said he had still not decided whether to seek the death penalty. He said that Melanie faced a minimum of 30 years to life if convicted, pending indictment by the ongoing state grand jury.

"This intensive 'cold case' investigation utilized the latest criminal forensic investigative techniques," said Harvey. "And is an example of what can be accomplished by a veteran homicide prosecutor, detectives, investigators and forensic scientists doggedly pursuing justice."

He revealed that Melanie McGuire had made "deliberate attempts" to thwart the investigation, steering it away from the principal subjects.

"There is nothing in our investigation that suggests he met his death in Atlantic City, where his abandoned car was found," said Harvey, "and no evidence that a battered-wife situation, gambling or nefarious characters in Atlantic City were involved."

The attorney general also said that the diminutive Melanie McGuire must have had an accomplice, as she could not have carried her 200-pound husband alone, or lifted the three suitcases over the Chesapeake Bay Bridge-Tunnel railings. He also noted that the fertility nurse was unlikely to have had the skill or equipment needed for "the very particular method and kind of cuts" used to dismember her husband.

"She did not act alone," he said. "It's pretty clear to us that she had help. It's not easy to cut up a body that way. It was cut up very carefully."

New Jersey State Police Superintendent Colonel Joseph "Rick" Fuentes also told reporters that Melanie's arrest gave a "very loud and somewhat vengeful voice" to her murdered husband.

"The investigation over the past nine months," he said, "has woven a very strange tale of lies, deceit, infidelity and murder."

At 5:00 that afternoon, Michael Cappararo collected his grandsons from Kinder Kastle and ABZ Academy day care, driving them back to Barnegat. Then he began to arrange to put up his home as collateral for the $75,000 bond needed to free his stepdaughter.

Cindy Ligosh had been eating breakfast alone that morning when she received a call from victims' advocate Gail Faille, informing her of her sister-in-law's imminent arrest.

"I'd been waiting a year for her to be arrested," she remembered. "It was a great weight lifted off me."

Then Cindy telephoned her sister Nancy, and other relatives and friends, to give them the news.

"I always believed Melanie killed my brother," said Nancy. "She had no remorse whatsoever. She's a horrible person."

Sue Rice was on a business trip in Providence, Rhode Island, when she heard from Investigator Don Macciocca.

"I just remember these tears just rolling down," she said. "And again, that sickening feeling, because we didn't only lose Bill, now we lost Melanie. He told me that she had had an affair and that she had purchased a gun. I was speechless."

When her husband Jon heard, he was delighted.

"I gave Bill a high five," he said. "I thought it was about time."

That afternoon, all the nurses at RMA were called to a meeting, where the nurse manager gave them the news of Melanie's arrest.

"There was just silence," remembered Lori Thomas. "Then one of the nurses, who was close to Melanie, burst into tears."

Within minutes of the meeting, reporters and photographers started arriving at the RMA headquarters in Morristown, and were barred entry by security.

A spokesman for RMA refused to answer any questions, putting out a statement that the clinic "will continue to support any ongoing efforts to gather information related to this situation."

Although she had long suspected Melanie and Dr. Miller of having an affair, when Christine Richie, who had worked so closely with them on the Gestational Carrier Program, heard it confirmed, she was shocked.

"I always thought Dr. Miller had a very good moral character," she said. "I was absolutely shocked, because that's how he portrayed himself."

And when Nurse Melanie McGuire's fertility patients learned of her arrest for murdering and dismembering her husband, there was shock and disbelief.

"I was floored," said surrogate Melissa Coulter. "I just thought, 'This has got to be some sort of mistake.' Melanie was all about family. I mean, obviously her job was about making families. I still don't believe she did it. That's not our Melanie."

THIRTY-SIX

"Whores Don't Deserve to Live"

On Friday morning, news of Melanie McGuire's arrest for the murder/dismemberment of her husband made headlines across America.

"Year After Dismembered Body Was Found, Wife Is Charged in Killing," read the headline in *The New York Times*. And *The Washington Post* ran the story: "Wife Charged in Man's Death: Dismembered Body Was Recovered in Va. Waters."

The *Home News Tribune* carried a front-page story, headlined: "Victim's Wife Had Affair With Man From Bridgewater."

Quoting an anonymous source from local law enforcement, staff reporter Ken Serrano's story revealed Melanie McGuire's three-year affair with her married RMA boss Dr. Bradley Miller. The source claimed that Dr. Miller had "disposed" of "love lines"—two family-plan cell phones—in an attempt to hide the affair.

Serrano also interviewed Bill McGuire's first wife Marci Paulk, who had nothing good to say about him.

"If she did it," said Paulk, "she probably did it in self-defense. If I can help Melanie in any way, I will."

That morning, task force investigators descended on Barnegat, questioning Michael and Linda Cappararo's neighbors, while their grandsons stayed with them behind closed doors. They had told Jack and Jason that their mother had a new out-of-town job, and had to sleep there.

After reading about Melanie McGuire's arrest, a day care worker from the ABZ Academy telephoned New Jersey's Division of Youth and Family Services (DYFS), saying she was concerned for little Jason's welfare. Under its mandate, DYFS is responsible for investigating any allegations of child abuse and neglect, and if necessary arranging for an endangered child's protection.

A few hours later, after Cindy Ligosh and Nancy Taylor both telephoned DYFS, expressing concern for their nephews, the agency decided to take action.

At 11:00 Friday night, a DYFS team arrived at the Cappararos' home, with an order to remove Jack and Jason for their own protection. They were then taken away in a DYFS van.

Soon afterwards, Cindy Ligosh received a telephone call from DYFS, asking if she was prepared to take her nephews, and she instantly agreed.

But first the traumatized little boys were taken to a nearby hospital to be checked out by a doctor, before being brought to Cindy's new house in Wyckoff at 4:00 a.m.

"I put them in the smallest bedroom in one full bed together," remembered Cindy. "And I just sat there all night until they woke up in the morning."

Cindy had not seen her nephews since before her brother's murder, so she was concerned they might have forgotten her and be scared.

"When they woke up," said Cindy, "before they could see me, I put my head under the blanket at the bottom of the bed. And I came through there and made it a game and fun. And Jack remembered me, but Jason did not."

Over the next few weeks, as the boys adjusted to their new life with Cindy and her husband Bill, she kept up the pretense that their mother had a new job and couldn't come home.

"But they adjusted well," said Cindy. "They really did."

On Tuesday, June 7, Melanie McGuire was released from Middlesex County jail in New Brunswick on $750,000 bail.

Although her parents had posted the 10 percent bond necessary to free her the previous Friday, she had to remain in jail until the State Department could confirm whether or not she had a valid passport.

She walked out of the jail wearing the same pink tee shirt and black slacks she had been arrested in, and was met by her parents. Then they drove straight to the Family Court building in Toms River, where Melanie unsuccessfully attempted to regain custody of her sons.

After the brief hearing, Melanie's mother Linda told *The Star-Ledger*'s Suleman Din that the media had not "portrayed my daughter fairly. My only concern right now is for my daughter."

That night, Attorney General Peter Harvey appeared on the *Nancy Grace* show on CNN, where he appealed to the public for any information on Bill McGuire's murder.

"[It's an] ongoing investigation," he told Grace. "It's subject to grand jury proceedings right now. We know people saw things, and we're urging people to come forward and share with us information. We know that there's information out there that could be had."

After Melanie McGuire's arrest, the task force investigation continued. Over the next eighteen months, detectives would continue to uncover compelling new evidence linking her to her husband's murder.

A couple of weeks later, the New Jersey State Police CSI Unit searched and processed Melanie McGuire's Nissan Pathfinder at its Hamilton headquarters. Inside they found a Pennsylvania driver's license in her name, as well as a change of address form. And they also found a notebook and a two-page typewritten document, all of which tested negative for fingerprints.

On July 2, Detective John Pizzuro searched Melanie's two lockers at Arthur's Self Storage again, after learning she had tried to access them. He first examined #3161, which was empty, before searching the smaller #3162. Inside, he found a black lockbox, and called in a local locksmith, who opened it.

"It contained a hollowed-out wooden container," Detective Pizzuro would later testify. "I opened it to find two packets of Panasonic batteries. I observed a wallet . . . which I seized as evidence. It had Bill McGuire's Social Security card, medical card and pictures of Melanie and the children, and business cards of several associates."

The weekend after Melanie McGuire was released on bail, she went to RMA in Morristown to collect her belongings. While she was in her office, Dr. Brad Miller suddenly came in and locked the door. It was the first time they had seen each other in several weeks, and they immediately fell into each other's arms, making passionate love on the floor.

"I still loved her at the time," the doctor would later explain.

After her release, Melanie McGuire moved back in with her parents in Barnegat, trying to get on with her life. She knew she was being watched, and that everyone close to her was under suspicion. And investigators kept up the pressure on her close friends.

"I was supposedly her accomplice for a while," said Selene Trevizas, who now visited her regularly in Barnegat. "Then my husband was her accomplice, and we knew something that we weren't telling them. They were playing games. That they knew that I was with Melanie on certain days. They have pictures. They have proof. They were trying to find an accomplice somewhere."

Nurse Lori Thomas was questioned three times by police, including one marathon five-hour session. After walking in thinking her friend was innocent, she came out convinced Melanie was a murderess.

But when the investigators interviewed Regina Knowles, she insisted Melanie was innocent.

"Quite frankly they considered me a hostile witness," she said. "They came to me and they said, 'Your friend Melanie killed her husband.' I said, 'Prove it.'"

The first week of July, Regina Knowles made a series of

anonymous calls, attempting to have Jack and Jason taken away from Cindy Ligosh. Over a period of several days, she called the New Jersey Board of Pharmacy, Crime Stoppers and the Teaneck Police Department, claiming the two special needs children were in danger.

"There is a family in town that owns a pharmacy," she told the Teaneck dispatcher on July 7 at 2:30 p.m. "And it has come to my attention that the wife in the family is self-medicating with Valium, which was provided to her by her husband."

She told the female dispatcher that the two boys had been placed with Cindy Ligosh by DFYS, after their father's death. She claimed they were both autistic, and that someone under the influence of Valium would not have the "energy and attention" needed to look after them.

"Part of the problem with Mrs. Ligosh," said Knowles, "is that there's been a significant history between the family of hostility, ever since her brother died."

She claimed that Cindy Ligosh had "made a huge number of false accusations" against the children's mother, in order to get custody.

"I assure you this is not vindictive," she told the dispatcher. "I'm not trying to play a game. I'm not trying to get back at her for something."

After receiving the call, the dispatcher contacted the Wyckoff Police Department, reporting possible drug use at the Ligosh residence. Detective Daniel Kellogg went to investigate.

"I spoke to Bill and Cindy Ligosh," he remembered. "I said the purpose I was there was to check on the welfare of the two children."

Then, without hesitation, they agreed for Detective Kellogg to search their house for any evidence of drugs.

"I found no evidence of any narcotics," said Detective Kellogg. "In my opinion as a fourteen-year police officer, Bill and Cindy Ligosh were not under the influence of narcotics."

Investigators believe that Melanie McGuire—or someone close to her—had sneaked into Cindy Ligosh's garden late at night, planting a Chock full O'Nuts can among two beds of wild black-eyed Susans growing by the side of the house. Inside were prescription pills, a small quantity of marijuana, $80 in cash, several Thomas the Tank-Engine stickers and a pair of rubber gloves—a clumsy attempt to create the impression that the garden was a drop-off point for children to buy drugs.

There was also a note left in the can, reading:

Whores don't deserve their children. Whores don't deserve to be presumed innocent, whether they did it or not. Whores don't deserve to live.

At midday on Friday, August 5, Wyckoff Police Department dispatcher Mike Rose received a forty-five-second anonymous call from a man who would later be identified as Michael Cappararo.

Dispatcher:	"Wyckoff Police Department."
Caller:	"How are you doing? . . . I got this kid, always bragging about that the cops—his name is Max Ligosh—the cops can't find his stash, that his mother and him have. And it's buried outside someplace by the bushes or the flowers. I mean, all he does is brag, brag, brag that he got away with it."
Dispatcher:	"What's his name?"
Caller:	"Ligosh."
Dispatcher:	"What town is this in?"
Caller:	"Wyckoff."
Dispatcher:	"What's your name?"
Caller:	"Pardon me?"

Dispatcher:	"What's your name?"
Caller:	"I'd rather not say, because I know him, OK? But I mean, all he does is brag. He's just a braggart. A little braggart."
Dispatcher:	"What's your name?"
Caller:	"I'd rather not say—like I say, because I know him . . . OK? I'm sorry. Maybe I shouldn't have called, OK?"

After listening to a tape of the anonymous call, Detective Kellogg called Cindy Ligosh, asking her to come to the station to see if she could identify the caller. Later she would recognize it as Michael Cappararo's voice.

Then Detective Kellogg accompanied Cindy back to her home to thoroughly search the garden for any evidence of drug usage.

"I was doing a counter-clockwise search of the property," he said. "I looked in the bushes, in the grass, under the deck and even in the woods behind the home."

Detective Kellogg spent almost half an hour searching, without finding anything. It would be another three months, when all the summer blooms had gone, before Bill Ligosh would accidentally discover the Chock full O'Nuts can.

That summer, RMA founder Dr. Richard Scott fired Dr. Brad Miller as a partner in the practice for violating his agreement. He was then exiled to Detroit as a humble employee, to start a new Michigan satellite branch of the fertility clinic.

And although Melanie McGuire had been forced to quit after her arrest for murder, Dr. Scott rehired her as a consultant, while she was free on bail.

"With all the things that happened, she could no longer remain within our practice," explained Dr. Scott. "But her experience and knowledge . . . was something we wanted to pass on to the next employees."

And the accused murderess also found a summer job as a hostess at Buckalew's, a bar on Long Beach Island, favored by surfers.

All through the summer the custody battle for Jack and Jason continued under the radar in Family Court. In the weeks after her release, a judge had awarded Melanie supervised visitations of her sons, although Michael and Linda Cappararo had unsupervised overnight ones.

Under court order, the grandparents would have to bring the boys to a private DYFS-approved facility, where they could only see their mother in the presence of a social worker.

"A lot of games were being played," said Cindy Ligosh. "The Family Court did not understand. I have a judge there that's saying, 'I don't understand the animosity.' You don't?"

THIRTY-SEVEN

Red Herrings

On Tuesday, August 9, 2005, prosecutors believe, Melanie McGuire wrote a four-page single-spaced letter, in a desperate attempt to misdirect the investigation, shifting the focus away from herself. The anonymous rambling letter, reading like a bad *Sopranos* script, was mailed from Monmouth County, New Jersey, to Attorney General Peter Harvey. (Copies were also sent to Melanie McGuire's Brick address, with the attached note, "Melanie, I tried to right the wrongs of the past. Keep your legs closed and everything will be all right"; to Dr. Brad Miller, with the note, "Help her you poor son of a bitch"; to her new criminal attorney Henry Klingeman; and to the *Trentonian* newspaper.)

Prosecutors believed that certain key facts toward the end of the rambling letter could only have been known by Bill McGuire's murderer.

Mr. Harvey,

Your office and the media have reflected on the life and death of William T. McGuire, and you've made it obvious that you intend to prosecute his wife. You and the media have exalted him as a decent person and a victim. He was a victim, all right. Of his greed, his big ego, and his even bigger mouth. I first met McGuire because we knew a lot of the same people. He was friendly enough at first, and loved to talk about himself along with anything and everything else he could claim to know everything about. He talked about work. He talked about AC. He talked about a house. About Virginia. About his wife. His sister. His ex-wife. You couldn't shut the guy up, which was part of his own undoing.

McGuire bragged often about his position at NJIT. Said he had the placed [sic] wired and that the boss man had no idea what he was up to, which is how I imagine he got out and got away as much as he did. He talked of his connections at the local and state level, in various departments of state. How they could and would play into his consulting business. He talked of corruption at the health departments, and how it was given a pretty face by NJIT. He bragged about how he once worked two full time jobs, at NJIT and at a local health office, and how even doing that he still had enough time to get in all his side action and get home without the wife being any wiser. He talked about all his scams at work, the anonymity the access to some of the technologies could give him, to do almost anything he wanted at work or outside of it. He talked of blackmailing some of the higher ups at the state level who were doling out grant work to people collecting unemployment. He seemed to be unfazed by the stink his confrontations could raise in the office, stating it was their own fault for putting themselves in a compromised position to begin with. He talked of overthrowing his boss at the college, and about overthrowing the state level boss with the help of a guy named Ray. Did your office bother to note any of that during their thorough investigation? I think not.

He also loved to gamble, loved to flash cash. I'd see him in AC, and at some private games to [sic]. The funny part is that he was a pretty good player but his ego wouldn't let him lose. He won a lot, but when he lost, he lost big and chased the money as hard as he chased some of the tail that hangs around those places. He blamed everyone when he lost, the other players, the house, the dealer, even his wife, if you can imagine that. I personally find your observation that his death could have nothing to do with gambling one of the more hilarious things you've said publicly. Have you ever BEEN to AC?

Don't believe me? Ask his wife about the Steakhouse in North Jersey, and about an unfortunate accident coming home from work there late one night. What he didn't tell her was that he wasn't working, and he had lost a bundle. I heard him talk about getting pulled over on top of it that night, and how it was her fault. I laughed. You can't be serious, man. She takes that from you? That and more. She likes it, is what he said and that put me off. You want to screw around on your old lady? Fine. You want to gamble away the family nut? That's fine to [sic]. But saying she likes it and seeing that he believed it blew me away. No wonder she ended up in bed with some doctor. Of course, you could say it was her own fault for marrying him, more her fault for staying.

More laughter from me when you leaked to the papers that this doctor friend of the wife's turned "state's evidence." There was nothing that man could of [sic] said that would hurt her for the simple reason that she didn't kill him. So that either makes you a liar, or him a coward who makes up stories to save his own sorry skin. Either way. I guess she never learned her lesson about choosing men.

Also, if you haven't figured out yet that his sister knew more of what he was up to than what she ever let on, you have your head further into the sand than I imagined. He talked about her a lot, and I think they had a weird relationship, those two. The guys used to joke about it a lot. She did something with real estate—he bitched about paying for her license, and he got her to give him access to one of those agent only sites. He would plug away on there for days at a time, looking up houses, looking up tax records of people he knew. She had a husband who owned some kind of pharmacy, and he talked a lot about all the scams there, and cash to be had. But in the same breath he would complain about how selfish she was to not want to put her own ass on the line, whatever that meant. I tuned out a lot after I figured out he lacked a certain amount of follow through with some ideas. He shrugged it off, saying there are all kinds of stings that get set up around stuff like that. He wanted the cash, but didn't want to get his hands dirty where anyone could see, was more what I thought. As for the other sister, I guess the apple didn't fall far. He played us a phone message she left him, laughing at what a crazy she was. The message had said she would sue him and he wouldn't get his house he was buying. Christmas must have been something at their house.

We kept McGuire close because he was good for certain things—obviously things you'll never find out about. But in time he developed a drug habit. He even tried dealing. Then he decided he wanted a piece to [sic]. We privately agreed against putting one in his hands. He tried in Camden, Trenton, even Newark, but his problem was that he looked like a cop. No surprise the wife bought it, even if she was a damn fool for not knowing better. He always complained about how stupid she had gotten. I even asked him, wasn't she stupid when you married her? He said no way, his first wife was stupid but good in bed. The second he said was a lousy lay, but pretty. He claimed she had been smart but let herself go to hell after having kids. Which is why he felt completely justified in sticking it in anything that walked. Personally, I thought he was either gay or sexually bent. He said his wife was so stupid he came home high one night, and when she asked him why his eyes were blood shot he told her he had taken viagara [sic]. When she asked why he got pissed and told her even that couldn't help him get it up for her. Nice guy. My point being that Billy Mac liked an altered state of mind. I'll bet you twice your pension that the toxicology report showed more than a little viagara [sic]. How about H? Do you believe yet that I'm more than some random psycho writing to harass you? If not, you will.

Here's a question for you, Mr. Harvey. McGuire was talking about the life insurance he was going to get. A mill on the wife. Two on him. He talked about Virginia, and how that was where he was going once he made his money here. How the wife hated it. When I asked how he was planning on convincing her to move, he smiled and said he would be rid of her by then. Did it dawn on you that Mrs. McGuire, in her 'selfish' plot to kill her husband, didn't bother to wait for him to actually purchase the insurance? Oh, she's got the boyfriend with money, she didn't need it. First, I don't know anybody who would pass on two mill, money or not. Second, even if she coaxed that boyfriend away from his happy home, how much do you think it would leave for her after he paid out his old lady? I'm telling you that I don't know what he meant when he said he'd be "rid" of her by then, but I have a couple of thoughts. And two mill on him and one on her casts a little doubt on his motivation should something tragic happen. Did any of you in the midst of your "dogged detective work" even ask her about it? Or are you going to sit there with a straight face and tell me McGuire meant he wanted a divorce?

Don't get me wrong, I'm not going for sainthood myself. But what got to us about him was that he eventually turned on everyone. He talked about going to the press a lot about the money the college spent on equipment for a terrorism database that no one bothered to use. He talked about getting "rid" of his old lady. He talked about turning in the sister's husband to the pharmacy board. Even blood wasn't thicker than water with this guy. And he wouldn't shut up. Didn't matter if he liked you or didn't or even if he owed you. He feared no payback from anyone. I don't even think he wanted the piece out of fear. Not a guy like that. He wanted to intimidate people with it. What intimidated people more was his running mouth.

You shouldn't care that the wife bought a gun. You shouldn't care that the suitcases were hers. You shouldn't care that the garbage bags match. I'm telling you that you shouldn't care if there's video footage of her smiling and waving from the docks at Virginia Beach. Know why? Obviously you don't, so I'll make it simple. And it's not because she couldn't physically have done what it took two—and at one point three men to do. It's because Billy Mac brought everything that was needed to do him, and more. Not on purpose of course, but it was easier than anyone could believe. And the fight with his old lady? Probably he saved her life leaving her that morning, even if all he was doing was looking to get the hell out of dodge for a few days. I'm guessing you didn't find any of his cell phones—the ones that weren't traceable, anyway. Point is if it was necessary, if she was with him, she would have been done same as him. Probably worse, if you catch my drift, even if she was a lousy lay like he said. She ended up helping us, but not in any way you or your dogged detectives think. Her bad luck was our good fortune. And Billy Mac left the door wide open.

So why write this? Well, I can tell you now to abandon the print analysis, and even analysis of the type. This will be photocopied and handled in a manner you couldn't trace even if you did your job. So it's not hurting me any. And I've got nothing for the wife, or against her. But I read about those kids. The father they're better off without, but they don't need a Ma on death row. So now it's up to you to figure it out. She can't help you much, but did you ever even ask her? I know, you think this is a hoax. Well, allow me to part with some facts that should finally convince you otherwise:

1. *I'm taking the liberty of sending this to the media, in case you want to close your eyes to this same as you have everything else in this case.*
2. *I'm sending it to the wife's lawyer.*
3. *The way the articles read last year, it made it seem like his arms were cut off. They weren't.*
4. *He was wearing nothing but purple briefs when you found him.*
5. *Ever figure out where the weights came from?*

NOW DO YOU BELIEVE ME????

When the letter was received by the attorney general's office, a secretary opened it, before throwing away the envelope.

But *The Trentonian* had kept theirs, giving it to Division of Criminal Justice investigators to test for saliva.

Straight after the letter was received, Melanie McGuire was ordered back to Middlesex Superior Court, to provide hair and DNA samples. Prosecutors deliberately kept the letter secret, never mentioning it during the hearing—for it contained three significant facts only the killer and the police knew: that Bill McGuire's torso had been wearing a pair of underpants, the body had been weighted down and both arms were attached.

Making her first appearance in court since getting bail, Melanie arrived with her mother and stepfather, wearing an autism ribbon pendant pinned to her white button-down shirt. In the public gallery were her sister-in-law Cindy Ligosh, and her son Max.

"We recovered hair from the suitcases," Assistant Attorney General Patti Prezioso told Judge Frederick DeVesa, now assigned to the murder case, "and we'd like a sample of the defendant's hair for comparison."

Judge DeVesa then ordered McGuire to provide DNA, and she was taken to a nearby conference room, where New Jersey State Police Detective James Ryan swabbed the inside of her cheek and took a hair sample.

A week later, *The Trentonian* ran a front-page story, congratulating itself for having the foresight not to throw away the envelope, which could contain vital clues:

> *The Trentonian* may be helping solve one of the most grisly murders in New Jersey history. Detectives from the N.J. state police rushed to this newspaper Thursday to retrieve what may be significant evidence in the case.

McGuire's new attorney Henry Klingeman said the letter appeared to put his client in the clear.

"[It was written by] someone," said Klingeman, "who wants us to believe that he knows who was responsible, if he wasn't responsible himself, for the murder. The attorney general should conduct a very thorough investigation to find the author, and thus the killer. Exonerate Melanie and let her get back with her kids."

Bill McGuire's sister Cindy had no doubt who had written the letter.

"It was just obvious it was Melanie," she said. "Obvious."

On Thursday, September 8, task force investigators Don Macciocca and George Delgrosso brought two computers seized during the McGuire investigation to be processed by forensic computer analyst Jennifer Seymour of the New Jersey State Police Digital Technology Investigations Unit. Ultimately she would forensically search a total of eight desktop computers, three laptops, eight cell phones and a BlackBerry.

Seymour, who now works for the Department of Defense, concentrated on the HP Pavilion recovered from Melanie McGuire's divorce attorney Risa Kleiner, and a Dell Dimension XPS taken from her parents' home.

"The investigators gave me screen names that they felt were important to the case," said the attractive blonde forensic analyst, "and some other key words and names of individuals that they would like me to search on."

When she examined the HP Pavilion, Seymour discovered a series of deleted e-mails from two Hotmail accounts.

"The names on the Hotmail accounts were Brad Miller and Melanie McGuire," said Seymour. "The e-mail messages appeared to be some conversations between people who may have been having an intimate or loving relationship. There were some expressions such as 'I miss you,' and 'I love you.'"

Investigators had briefed Seymour to focus on any Internet activity on and around April 26, 2004.

"There were several searches that involved things like names of chemicals and poisons," she said. "There were searches that involved guns and gun laws."

Using the state-of-the-art EnCase Forensic investigation software, Seymour actually searched on the word "search," bringing up any web pages or Internet activity investigated during the relevant time period.

"And then I can look through that," she explained, "and draw some conclusions, based on the Internet activity of the computer."

Among the suspicious searches she found were: "how to commit murder," "undetectable poisons," "where to purchase a gun without a permit," "instant poison," "how to purchase a gun in Pennsylvania," "fatal insulin doses," "instant undetectable poisons," and "chloral hydrate."

And straight after the search for chloral hydrate on April 26, 2004—the day Melanie McGuire bought the gun—was a search for a Walgreens store locator.

On Sunday, October 9, prosecutors believe, Melanie McGuire made one final desperate attempt to save herself, by framing Cindy Ligosh for the murder. Two days earlier Patti Prezioso had made a courtesy call to attorney Henry Klingeman, informing him that the grand jury would be voting Tuesday on whether or not to indict his client for first-degree murder. After learning that, they believe, Melanie McGuire panicked.

Then she or an accomplice raided her sister-in-law's garbage, taking the September page from the calendar of a local school that Jack and Jason now attended, a diaper bag and other items to try to set her up with.

Then at 3:48 Sunday afternoon, she walked into a Rite Aid in a strip mall on Main Street, Passaic, buying a $50 American Express gift card. Three minutes before the purchase, she was photographed by a surveillance camera in the car lot.

Previously, she had filled out a FedEx air bill, addressing it to Assistant Attorney General Patricia Prezioso. She listed Cindy's employer, Weichert Realtors, as the sender, mistakenly writing down the address as "Franklin Road" instead of "Franklin Avenue," as well as giving an incorrect telephone number.

She then drove 5.7 miles to a FedEx drop-off at the Styertowne Shopping Center on Bloomfield Avenue in Clifton, using the gift card to pay for the $8 mailing of the package, which was picked up at 8:00 Monday morning for overnight delivery.

On Tuesday morning, the FedEx package arrived at the Division of Criminal Justice at the Hughes Justice Complex in

Trenton, as Assistant Attorney General Patti Prezioso was in the grand jury chamber, questioning her final witness, Detective Sergeant David Dalrymple.

Suddenly, with Prezioso in full flow, Deputy Attorney General John Higgins walked in, saying he needed to talk to her urgently.

"It was quite the *Perry Mason* moment," remembered Detective Sergeant Dalrymple. "We were about to wrap up, and it was quite dramatic."

Irritated at being interrupted in the middle of an examination, Prezioso asked Higgins, in a whisper, what was going on.

"You just received a Federal Express package from somebody saying Melanie is not the killer," he told her. "And Bill's wedding ring is also in the package."

"At that point I stood up," said Prezioso. "The look on Detective Dalrymple's face was priceless, because he didn't know what was going on. [Then] I asked the grand jury if we could take a recess."

After the grand jurors left the chamber, Investigator Don Macciocca opened the Federal Express package, carefully laying out the contents on a sheet of brown paper on a conference table.

"It included a letter addressed to me," said Prezioso. "And then a list purportedly written by the deceased's sister, setting up [Melanie] to be the killer."

There were other items inside the package, including an empty bullet box of Ultramax wadcutter .38-caliber bullets, the exact same ones purchased by McGuire when she'd bought the Taurus handgun.

"It's huge," said Detective Sergeant Dalrymple. "And in addition to that is the condition of the box. And again, smart work by whoever sent it, presumably Ms. McGuire. For they tore the flaps off the box . . . with the only information that I can use to track it back."

Also inside was a silver bracelet, a wedding ring, rubber gloves, a Nissan car key and a key from a lockbox, a key holder, a plastic boy's diaper bag, a calendar from Ligosh's school district with a "Set her up" note on the back, a small amount of marijuana in silver foil and a clear plastic bag, containing prescription medication, including amphetamine sulfate, Ambien, Alprazolam, and Temazepam.

Then Investigator George Delgrosso photographed all the items, before sealing them into evidence envelopes.

"That package was just explosive," said Detective Dalrymple. "And it turned into a lot of work for us that day."

Within minutes of receiving the FedEx package, Detective Jeffery Kronenfeld took copies of the three notes to Weichert Realtors in Franklin Lakes, NJ.

"A very tall state trooper came in," remembered Weichert manager Tamar Joffe, who is Cindy Ligosh's boss. "I brought him into my office and he showed me some paperwork."

Then Joffe took out Cindy's personnel file and some of her sales, comparing her handwriting to the letter inside the FedEx package.

"I'm not a handwriting expert," said Joffe. "It did not look like Cindy's handwriting at all."

She then told Detective Kronenfeld that Weichert no longer used Federal Express, and pointed out several other glaring errors that jumped out at her.

"I saw some incongruities," she would later testify. "It was not our phone number in the right-hand corner. And anyone who works for me, I hope, knows that we are at 784 Franklin Avenue—there is no Franklin Road in Franklin Lakes."

Cindy Ligosh had just dropped Jack off at kindergarten when Deputy Chief State Investigator Joseph Buttich called her cell. He informed her that a package had just been received, telling her to come straight to the Division of Criminal Justice in Trenton.

"I remember the fear in my heart," said Ligosh. "And I'm thinking it's body parts."

She then backed onto the school driveway, grabbed Jack and drove him home, less than a block away. She had decided to take Jack and Jason with her to Trenton, in case they were in danger.

"The two of them were still in diapers," she said. "I thought we needed the juice boxes and snacks and things to keep them busy. So I ran into the house like a madwoman, grabbed just what I needed for the children."

On the way to Trenton, Cindy "frantically" phoned her daughter Laura, who was in Boston, and son Max.

"I'm thinking, 'It's the body part[s] of my children now,'" she said. "Neither of them were answering the phone, so I just kept redialing and redialing."

Finally Max answered, saying that he was safe, and Laura was in a five-hour college class.

When Cindy Ligosh arrived at the Justice Complex, she was brought straight into a conference room, where Patti Prezioso was waiting. The deputy attorney general first showed Ligosh the wedding ring and the bracelet that had been inside the package. Ligosh said they looked similar to the ones Bill had worn, but could not positively identify them.

She was then shown a handwritten letter with a clumsily photocopied Weichert logo on the top, and asked if she had written it or ever seen it before.

"I was never allowed to read anything," she said. "I was shown the diaper bag, the school calendar that had the 'Set her up' thing written on it. And they questioned me about that."

Then the grand jury was reconvened for one unexpected last witness—Cindy Ligosh.

"They whisked me next door into the grand jury room," remembered Cindy. "I was sworn in on the stand, and I was asked, 'Did you write this? Tell us about your relationship with [Melanie].'"

Dear Madame Assistant Att General—
This package contains items I found when searching for something I had lost in the trash at work. The only reason I paid attention was because of the words "Sale File" on the folder. I only know of this case what I read in the papers and seen on TV, so I hope you are the correct person to send this to. If not, kindly pass it on to the appropriate individual. Please understand that I do not in any way wish to involve myself in

this situation, but the contents of the ziplock bag frighten me. I placed what I found as best I could, as I found it, into the zip-lock bag which was my own. I did have gloves on as I was going into the trash, so I'm hoping I succeeded in preserving the integrity of what I found. I recognize the handwriting as belonging to one of my colleagues—a Ms Ligosh. You are ob-viously more qualified to make sense of the rest, but what I read here scares and disgusts me. May God bless you & assist you in your endeavor for the truth, as I fear it may not be as obvious as we all assumed.

final stages

- *bring bullets if no need to plant at her dad's*
- *indictment*
- *termination of her parental rights*
- *public statement against prosecution if no indictment of her family*
- *speak to publisher re story rights*
- *estate for boys*
- *taunt her with not seeing kids*
- *we are their parents*

Set her up

1 - deny that we knew about firearm or that he made her get one

2 - deny that he would move her car when they fought sometimes

3- call prosecutors with mafia allegations to implicate her family!

\

Dyfs

\

Adoption yields stipend for adoption thru division

4 - secondary beneficiary on his state life insurance

5 - have kids say they saw her do it &/or dispose of his body

Later that afternoon, the New Jersey State grand jury handed down a four-count indictment, charging Melanie McGuire with the first-degree murder of her husband. She was also charged with the second-degree possession of a weapon for unlawful purpose; desecrating William McGuire's human remains, a second-degree offense; and third-degree perjury, for making "false material statements" to Family Court that her husband was "a threat to her health and safety," and that he had left home "by his own volition."

At 1:30 p.m. on Wednesday, October 12, Melanie McGuire and her parents were in Courtroom 506 at the Middlesex County Superior Court for her arraignment. Earlier that morning the New Jersey Office of the Attorney General had issued a press advisory, announcing that the Division of Criminal Justice would be making a major announcement regarding the McGuire murder investigation.

In the public gallery to observe were Michael and Linda Cappararo, Selene Trevizas and Cindy Ligosh.

After reading out the four-count grand jury indictment, Assistant Attorney General Patti Prezioso asked Judge Frederick DeVesa to raise bail to $3 million. And then she dramatically revealed how she had received the Federal Express package yesterday, calling it a "laughable" attempt by McGuire to divert the course of justice.

"This is a sign of the defendant disintegrating," she told the judge. "[The acts] of a desperate woman."

The accused sat impassively next to her attorney Klingeman, as the deputy attorney general told the judge that her investigators now had more than 8,000 pages of "inescapable circumstantial evidence" linking her to her husband's murder. Yesterday's FedEx package, she said, was only the latest in a series of attempts by McGuire to make "a mockery" of the investigation.

"This package [sic] is allegedly written by a co-worker of Cindy Ligosh," Prezioso told the judge, "saying [he] found these items in the garbage, and was so afraid that he felt he needed to get it to me."

She said the package had contained notes, allegedly written by Ligosh, setting up Melanie McGuire for the murder of her husband.

"As of yesterday the entire world of who could have killed William McGuire," she said, "is narrowed down to two people—Melanie McGuire or Cindy Ligosh. And the State submits, Your Honor, it is not Cindy Ligosh. There's no evidence of that."

Judge DeVesa said he found the recent developments in the case "extremely troubling." And calling the circumstantial evidence "compelling" with "a likelihood of conviction," he raised bail to $2 million.

"Bail must be increased to ensure [your] continued presence," he told her, rejecting Klingeman's request for forty-eight hours' freedom in her mother's custody.

Then, looking distraught, Melanie McGuire removed her earrings and wristwatch, as armed sheriff's officers handcuffed her and led her away. Outside the courtroom, her attorney told reporters his client was innocent.

"We are going to mount a vigorous defense," he said, vowing to first get her out of jail.

PART FOUR

The Trial

THIRTY-EIGHT

Joe Tacopina

As Melanie McGuire was being taken back to Middlesex County Adult Correction Center in New Brunswick, Selene Trevizas promised the Cappararos she'd soon have Melanie free again. And a couple of days later, Selene heard about high-profile New York attorney Joe Tacopina.

"I hired him," said Selene. "We spoke to him, and felt this guy knew what he was doing. He may cost a lot more than everybody else, but at this point, it's her life on the line. Her parents and I both financed it."

The New York Times dubbed him "the 'Donald Trump' of New York's defense bar," while *Women's Wear Daily* viewed him as "The Devil's Advocate," but the 41-year-old celebrity attorney, who bills $750 an hour, is always larger-than-life.

He'd grown up in blue-collar Flatbush and Sheepshead Bay, Brooklyn. While at Skidmore on a hockey scholarship, he had an epiphany when he read true-crime writer Joe McGinniss's 1983 bestseller *Fatal Vision.* The book is a riveting account of the murder trial of Green Beret Captain Jeffrey MacDonald, M.D., who was convicted in 1979 of slaughtering his wife and two young daughters in Fort Bragg, North Carolina.

"The book told the legal drama that developed," he told his alma mater newspaper, the Skidmore *Scope* in 2003. "I was just glued to it."

Deciding that his future vocation lay in law, Tacopina found a summer job in New York City, working for the attorney then representing the murdered Gambino family Mafia boss Paul Castellano. And ironically, in 1991, after graduating from the University of Bridgeport School of Law, his introduction to the courtroom was as the second chair on the defense team for the man who'd ordered the Castellano hit, John Gotti.

The ambitious young lawyer then got a job in the Brooklyn district attorney's office, gaining swift promotion as Patti Prezioso was taking a similar legal path across the river in Manhattan.

A self-confessed "hockey madman," who holds the single season NCAA penalty minute mark, Tacopina has become something of a celebrity since opening a "virtual office" on Madison Avenue, holding client meetings in local diners. A natural self-publicist, he is a regular on *Imus in the Morning*, where he has taken his licks from Don Imus for defending Melanie McGuire, as well as being a regular legal correspondent for MSNBC and ABC's *20/20*.

Over the years the happily married father of five's famous clients have included rapper Foxy Brown, former New York Police Chief Bernie Kerik, controversial publisher Judith Regan, and a co-conspirator in the Michael Jackson child-molestation trial.

Immaculately groomed, Tacopina looks and acts like a movie star, wearing a $6,500 Panerai watch and dressing in expensive Italian suits, which he buys on frequent trips to Milan, where he runs a second office for corporate clients including Ferrari. He also proudly sports a Roman eagle tattooed on his right hip, which he enjoys showing off.

But despite all the glitz, Joe Tacopina is all business once he enters a courtroom for one of his celebrated cross-examinations.

"I smell blood a mile away," he told *Westport Magazine*, in a profile he reprinted in his press kit. "And I will bring you right there. And I will do it slowly and methodically. And I will make sure the jury sees your innards coming out of you.

"Some people go to Las Vegas and gamble. I'm up there taking a shot with a witness. I have some guy's life literally in my hands. This is the scary part, but it's also the part I sort of get off on."

The Melanie McGuire murder case—featured in a two-page *People* magazine article on November 14, 2005, entitled "Gruesome Discovery," was already attracting heavy media interest from CBS's *48 Hours*, ABC's *Primetime* and *Dateline NBC*. It seemed to have everything, with a beautiful accused husband-killer and what *People* called "a grisly denouement."

And after meeting with the Cappararos and Selene Trevizas, Joe Tacopina agreed to represent Melanie McGuire.

"I've spent a few days with Melanie," Tacopina told Ken Serrano of the *Home News Tribune* in mid-November, "and there's no question in my mind she's innocent. This case has not been accurately portrayed in the media."

Paradoxically, Patti Prezioso was one of the few people who had never heard of Joe Tacopina.

"I never read any of the articles that talked about Joe," she said. "And I don't watch TV, and I had never heard him on the radio. So I did the research that I would do on any person."

There was one hurdle to get over, though, as the New York–based attorney was not licensed to practice law in New Jersey. So with Melanie's old attorney Henry Klingeman stepping down, it was agreed his former law partner Stephen Turano, based in Newark, would come onboard as Tacopina's co-counsel. But first Judge Frederick DeVesa had to agree.

On Friday, November 18, there was a special hearing, where Melanie McGuire sat forlornly at the defense table in hand-cuffs, wearing a regulation green inmate's uniform. Attorney Klingeman said she now wished to change her legal team, confirming that he had already received 18,000 pages of discovery from prosecutors.

After setting October 1, 2006, as a tentative trial date, Judge DeVesa questioned if Tacopina and Turano could prepare a defense in time, with so much discovery to review.

"I understand the defendant is of somewhat modest means," he told them. "Don't think I'm ready to say, 'Okay, we'll change attorneys and see what happens.'"

He then rejected the motion, saying it was "incomplete," ordering Tacopina and Turano to file new applications for another hearing on December 1.

As she was led out of the court, Melanie McGuire sadly mouthed the words "I love you" to her parents, sitting in the front row of the public gallery with Selene Trevizas.

Outside the courtroom, Tacopina refused to discuss who was paying for her defense, only saying that she had a lot of supporters in her time of need.

"I would not have come into the case if I did not have one hundred percent confidence in her innocence," he declared, "and one hundred percent confidence in my ability to represent her."

On November 2, the State Police Office of Forensic Sciences positively matched Melanie McGuire's DNA to DNA found on the floor of Bill McGuire's Nissan Maxima, abandoned at the Flamingo Motel in Atlantic City. A subsequent police report said that the DNA profile occurred in just one in 210 trillion Caucasians. Also found on the car's front-seat carpet were minute particles of Bill McGuire's human bone and tissue, labeled "human sawdust" in the report.

Task force investigators were now working even harder, gathering concrete evidence against Melanie McGuire. In mid-September, Division of Criminal Justice Civil Investigator John Janowiak, known to everyone as JJ, started investigating local taxi companies for any record of a fare from Woodbridge Station to Atlantic City on April 29 or 30, 2004.

"I was unable to locate them making a pick-up anywhere where they are licensed to Atlantic City," he said.

The task force had also enlisted the services of Dr. Steven Symes, an anthropologist and professor at Pennsylvania's Mercyhurst College, and a leading expert on bone injuries. After examining pieces of Bill McGuire's bones, he determined that a reciprocating saw had been used in the dismemberment. He was also certain that a beveled knife had sliced through the soft flesh.

Detective George Delgrosso, a decorated former New York City homicide detective who had come out of retirement to work for the attorney general's office, was assigned to find the saw, as well as any green-colored furniture that had been in the Plaza Drive apartment, as investigators were trying to match the green strand of material found on one of the bullets removed from the victim's body.

On November 5, he asked Cindy Ligosh for a detailed description of furniture in her brother's apartment.

"I gave them a list of the furniture," said Ligosh. "I tried to draw a floor diagram of where the furniture was—the rugs and things like that."

On the Sunday afternoon of November 27, Bill Ligosh was raking leaves in his garden, when he discovered a rusty Chock full o'Nuts can among two beds of wild black-eyed Susans growing by the side of the house. Inside was about $80 in cash, some marijuana, prescription pills, latex gloves, several Thomas the Tank Engine stickers and a typed note, reading:

> *Whores don't deserve their children. Whores don't deserve to be presumed innocent, whether they did it or not. Whores don't deserve to live.*

Immediately, Cindy Ligosh called the Wyckoff Police Department, prompting a third visit by Detective Dan Kellogg. When he arrived, Cindy gave him the one-pound can and without opening it, he brought it back to the police station to be logged into evidence.

The next morning, Investigator George Delgrosso collected it for forensic analysis and Detective Kellogg returned to the Ligosh residence for another search.

"I was looking for any additional contraband," he later testified. "Evidence of drug use of what we felt may have been planted evidence. I found nothing else whatsoever."

Cindy Ligosh, who'd suspected her sister-in-law had been secretly watching her property while out on bail, had little doubt she was responsible.

"Did she think drug addicts would come and dig up the can and leave money for the honor system?" asked Ligosh. "What would have happened if the children had found it and taken them?"

Three days later, after Judge Frederick DeVesa ruled that Joe Tacopina and Stephen Turano could defend Melanie McGuire, Assistant Attorney General Patti Prezioso stood up, dramatically revealing how the rusty coffee can had been found in the Ligoshes' garden.

But after she'd listed the contents, reading out the "Whores" note, the angry judge ordered her to stop, saying it wasn't necessary for her to "continually recite all the facts of the case," explaining that it would make jury selection more difficult.

"We do believe it relates to a phone call," she told the judge. "It is rather unique."

Then, as McGuire sat impassively at the defense bench, Joe Tacopina stood up to address the court for the first time.

"This can," he said. "It is not known who put it there, and Mrs. McGuire has been in custody since October."

Judge DeVesa then adjourned the hearing, ordering the defendant to submit samples of her handwriting in the next couple of weeks.

On Saturday night, Melanie McGuire was released from jail, after posting a $2 million bail bond. Joe Tacopina welcomed her release, saying it would be far easier to prepare her defense with her out of jail.

"Without getting into the specific details," he told a reporter, "Melanie McGuire spent a good portion of her adult life helping people as a nurse. Some of these people are now rallying around her and stepping up to the plate. All Melanie wants to do is to get back to her children and defend herself against these charges."

On Christmas morning, a Family Court judge allowed Melanie McGuire to spend three hours with Jack and Jason, under the supervision of her parents.

"Let the fox guard the henhouse," quipped Cindy Ligosh later.

After Melanie's release, her two boys were given unsupervised visits to their grandparents' Barnegat home. But most of the time was spent in the Cappararos' car, driving up and down the Garden State Parkway between Wyckoff and Barnegat.

"It seemed to be very important for them to have the children," said Cindy Ligosh, who was now going for full custody. "I'm sure they didn't enjoy being in the car for five or six hours, during their visitation with Grammy and Pop Pop."

THIRTY-NINE

"Melanie Is Not Capable of Such Evil"

In early 2006, Melanie McGuire's supporters launched a website to raise money for her defense, with gushing testimonials from friends and family. On the biography page of www.Melaniemcguire.com was a graduation photograph of her wearing a collegiate black gown and mortarboard. The site also carried media stories, including some negative ones.

> Melanie is innocent of the crimes she is accused of committing. This website is here to provide some background information on Melanie, and to keep her many avid supporters apprised of the court case and the situation as it evolves. This site was created by friends of Melanie in response to the overwhelming number of inquiries into the case and into Melanie's well-being during this incredibly trying time for her and her family.
>
> It is also here so that the many individuals who are looking for a way to help Melanie through this overwhelmingly stressful time can do so through a contribution to the Friends of Melanie Legal Defense Fund.

Among the emotional testimonials on her behalf were some from her RMA patients, writing how she had changed their lives.

One anonymous patient, who had known her ten years, wrote:

> We met when I was an egg donor . . . not only has Melanie proven to be a great, loyal, and true friend. She is also a loving compassionate human being. She dedicated her life to help bring life into this world. I love her and trust her unconditionally. I feel, no, I know, she has been wrongfully accused. Melanie is not capable of such evil. She is not at all what the media and prosecution has portrayed of her.

At 1:30 p.m. on Valentine's Day, a small band of Melanie McGuire supporters turned up at the Middlesex County Superior Court, for a routine status hearing. Melanie, arriving early with her parents, seemed confident as she chatted with her friends, the drab green jail garb now replaced by designer clothes. Cindy Ligosh sat quietly in the back row of the public gallery, staring straight ahead.

Also in the public gallery were field producers from *48 Hours*, *Primetime* and *Dateline*, laying the groundwork for interviews with all the main players at a later date.

At the short hearing, the defense had a minor victory, when Judge DeVesa agreed to allow McGuire to travel to Manhattan to work on her case at Joe Tacopina's swank law offices at 40th Street and Madison Avenue. Assistant Attorney General Patti Prezioso had objected, citing "citizen safety." But the judge overruled her, warning Melanie that if she violated his order for any reason, he would immediately revoke bail.

After the hearing, the defendant and her attorney appeared upbeat.

"Her state of mind is good," Joe Tacopina told Rick Malwitz, of the *Home News Tribune*. "She has a legion of fans who love and support her. Her support is a window into who she is."

Two days later, Judge DeVesa released a series of prosecution motions, revealing some of the forensic results of the investigation. And although heavily redacted, one January 31 state motion created a sensation:

> Laboratory results received after the grand jury presentation concluded found what laboratory personnel describe as "human sawdust," in the vacuuming of the front drivers' side and passenger side carpet of William McGuire's car, recovered at the Flamingo Motel. DNA tests confirm that these bits of human tissue came from William McGuire.

But Joe Tacopina was unfazed when asked about it.

"We would hope there would be his DNA in his car," he told reporters, questioning the meaning of "human sawdust."

"I haven't found that term in a medical book yet. It's human tissue. It's his. No kidding."

Within days of the report, New Jersey State Police forensic scientist Tom Lesniak led another search of 2902 Plaza Drive. This time they were looking for any green fibers that might match the one wrapped around the wadcutter bullet found with Bill McGuire's body.

Lesniak spent almost a day searching the McGuire apartment, helped by Deputy Chief State Investigator Joseph Buttich and Dan Dietrick, a former FBI expert on microscopic analysis, now working for the DC Metro Police Department.

"We did a complete vacuuming and search," Lesniak would later testify. "We vacuumed out air vents, crevices along the woodwork. I took a paint control from . . . the wall."

They even removed the return vent to the furnace, and vacuumed it out for any traces of green fiber. But they came up empty-handed.

On Monday, March 13, Melanie McGuire's defense team moved to have all charges dismissed, saying that the State had no evidence against her.

Arguing against the motion, Assistant Attorney General

Patti Prezioso conceded that the state did not know the exact circumstances of Bill McGuire's murder.

"There are things we don't know," she admitted. "Do we have evidence that William McGuire was killed in the Woodbridge apartment? No."

Prezioso allowed that there was no direct evidence that Melanie McGuire had fired the gun that killed her husband, although there was plenty of circumstantial evidence linking her to the crime.

"She doesn't get the benefit of doing a good job of killing," Prezioso declared.

Judge DeVesa refused to dismiss the charges, saying that although elements of the case covered four states, the majority of them had happened in New Jersey, where it should be tried.

"I am satisfied the State has met its burden," he told the court. "It appears [Melanie McGuire] was the last person to see the victim alive in Woodbridge, in Middlesex County."

And then the judge added that the petite defendant must have had an accomplice.

"There is an abundance of evidence that the defendant did not act alone," he said. "Given the small size of the defendant and the manner of desecration and separation [of the body], one could not engage in that behavior alone."

The following week, Judge DeVesa dealt another blow to the defense, denying a motion to suppress the secretly recorded wiretaps from being heard at trial. He ruled that the state had sufficient probable cause when it had obtained a court order to tape Melanie McGuire's phone calls.

Outside the courtroom, Joe Tacopina told reporters that although he was disappointed with the judge's decision, he did not feel the recorded conversations were in any way prejudicial to his client.

"We're not concerned about the substance of the wiretaps at all," he declared.

At the end of April, Dr. Brad Miller contacted Investigator George Delgrosso, saying he had purchased a Ryobi combination kit with a reciprocating saw from Home Depot around the time of Bill McGuire's disappearance. He said he had forgotten to tell detectives about it at the time and now wanted to.

And in August, he flew to New Jersey to meet with detectives, giving the $113 receipt to Investigator Delgrosso.

"I always thought I was a suspect," explained Dr. Miller. "I didn't know what this combination kit was [so] I turned it over to them. I said I did buy a combination kit that had a drill, a circular saw, a reciprocating saw and a flashlight. The detective took the receipt and he checked it out. He told me that it was an air compressor that I had bought."

Soon afterwards, detectives went to Dr. Miller's house, where he gave them his reciprocating saw and two blades. They were later analyzed and found to have had nothing to do with Bill McGuire's murder.

Soon after Melanie McGuire's arrest, her old Rutgers friend Anthony Sclafani read about the case online, and got in touch with her. It had been twelve years since they had last spoken, and he was now living in New Mexico, working as a prosecutor. But Sclafani had never forgotten the beautiful girl he credited with preventing him from committing suicide.

In June 2006, Sclafani moved back to Brick, New Jersey, and called Melanie, now staying with her parents in Barnegat.

"We saw each other three times over the summer," he said. "We sent a ton of e-mails, some telephone calls."

As an ex-prosecutor, Sclafani warned her not to trust him, although he was "confident" in her innocence.

On their first date, they spent a day at the beach at Point Pleasant.

"Then we went to a bar and got dinner and drinks," he said. "I told her, 'Look, assume your conversations with me are being taped.' Because she already knew that the person who said he loved her had taped her. Honestly, I tried to make her paranoid, because I've seen how prosecutors can take things on tape out of context."

A couple of weeks later they went out again, going to a T.G.I. Friday's for dinner.

"We talked for a long time," he remembered. "I got the impression she was innocent and they really didn't know who had done it."

Sclafani was living in a friend's condominium in Brick, and Melanie suggested he rent her small house nearby, which was empty.

"I was going to move into that house and pay rent to help her with her legal fees," he said. "But I didn't know where I was going to be working, so I decided not to."

Then, feeling guilty, he gave her $5,000 anyway.

"It was a gift," he said. "She didn't really personally request it."

From the beginning of the investigation, Patti Prezioso had always been convinced Melanie McGuire had somehow disabled Bill before murdering him. The smoking gun, she thought, was finding out what drug he had been given.

"We pushed and pushed," she explained. "Because there was something with the prescription medicine. There were no defense wounds, and I knew that Billy had to have been incapacitated. I knew it. We all felt it, because it didn't make sense without it."

One of the big mysteries of the case was the vial of pinkish liquid and syringes found in Bill McGuire's car, which Melanie had admitted parking at the Flamingo Motel. Although investigators had ordered a barrage of toxicology tests to identify it, without knowing what they were looking for, it was like finding the needle in a haystack.

"There is no machine that can tell you what it is," said Prezioso. "A toxicologist has to know what they're testing for. If you have an unknown liquid with no clue, it's a difficult proposition. And we couldn't figure out what the hell that stuff was."

Then months into the investigation, after learning that Melanie McGuire had been allowed to write RMA prescriptions on behalf of Dr. Brad Miller, Prezioso asked investigators to isolate all his prescriptions written around the time of Bill McGuire's murder.

And in early October, they came up with one for RMA

patient Tiffany Bain for 500 mgs of liquid chloral hydrate, dated April 28, 2004—the morning of the closing.

On October 13, Investigator JJ Janowiak went to the Walgreens pharmacy in Edison to collect the prescription for chloral hydrate.

"And I remember getting a call from [him] in Walgreens," said Prezioso. "And he's sitting there with the pharmacist and I said, 'Ask, "Does it come in a liquid?" ' And he said yes. And I started to shake. I said, 'Ask her what color it is.' And she said, 'Light red.'

"And my eyes filled with tears, because I knew we had it. That was pivotal."

A few days later, Patti Prezioso and Detective Sergeant Dalrymple flew to Detroit to show Dr. Brad Miller the prescription. He told them he had never seen it before and would never prescribe chloral hydrate for fertility patients.

And when the pinkish liquid was finally tested by a toxicologist, using the correct protocol, it was found to be chloral hydrate.

"Patti's very, very driven," said Dalrymple, "and she stuck with that until the very end. And it's such an oddball substance. There's only one use for it, and it's certainly not anything in reproductive medicine."

That July, task force investigators subpoenaed water records for the McGuires' Woodbridge apartment, to see if there had been any excessive water usage around the time of Bill McGuire's disappearance. Once again they found nothing.

Two months later, forensic scientist Tom Lesniak returned to the apartment for yet another search.

"I was looking for any type of scraping," explained Lesniak. "Maybe violent movement that had chipped the porcelain [in the tub or shower area] or made lines in it. I was looking for a sawing motion. But I found nothing."

On July 27, at a status conference, Judge Frederick DeVesa delayed the trial until January 15, 2007, due to numerous legal issues still to be worked out between the two sides. The main problem was whittling down the five hundred hours of recorded wiretaps and determining what would be admissible at trial.

"That's the monster staring us in the face," said Joe Tacopina, adding that he planned to lodge "a host of objections" to the wiretaps.

Judge DeVesa observed that many of the wiretaps contained "long, rambling conversations," asking prosecutors to highlight the parts they wished to present for their case.

After the hearing, Tacopina announced he would be setting up a "war room" in New Brunswick, for the duration of the trial.

"This is a mission," he declared. "The objective is to get justice for Melanie."

FORTY

"The Game Is Over"

On Thursday, October 26, a state grand jury returned a further eight-count indictment against Melanie McGuire. It was sealed until the following Monday's scheduled status hearing, when prosecutors intended to serve it and then re-arrest her. It charged her with evidence-tampering, obstruction of justice and four drug offenses, relating to the anonymous letters sent to Peter Harvey, Patti Prezioso and the Chock Full o'Nuts can found in Cindy Ligosh's garden.

When Melanie arrived at Middlesex County Superior Court for the routine status hearing, she had no idea what was about to happen. At the beginning of the ninety-minute hearing, when Prezioso officially served the new indictment on McGuire, she looked stunned.

The prosecutor asked Judge DeVesa to increase bail by a million dollars, declaring, "At this point the game is over."

Prezioso then outlined sensational new evidence against the defendant, saying that a forensic examination of the McGuire home computer had revealed Google searches on subjects like "undetectable poisons," "how to purchase an illegal weapon," and "how to commit a murder."

"And eventually, Judge," said the assistant attorney general, "her research in poisons came up with 'chloral hydrate,' a substance that is traditionally referred to when you slip someone a 'Mickey.' The next search she did was 'availability,' and it pointed to Walgreens."

She said investigators had recovered a prescription filled on April 28, 2004—the morning of the fateful house closing—at a Walgreens close to her son's kindergarten.

"It is likely," said the prosecutor, "she used this later on her husband. The state submits that this was a planned homicide, a planned murder, executed in a planned, controlled way."

She then revealed "detailed new evidence" against McGuire, pertaining to the stream of anonymous correspondence, proclaiming her innocence. The first letter, Prezioso told the judge, was sent in July 2005 to the attorney general, with copies to the *Trentonian* newspaper, Dr. Brad Miller, her former attorney and McGuire herself.

"That letter was written in a tone," said Prezioso, "to make the reader believe that the writer was a member of organized crime."

The second communication, she said, was a FedEx package addressed to her, received the same day the grand jury was scheduled to vote on her murder indictment.

"This letter was written supposedly by an anonymous person," said the prosecutor, "a co-worker of Cindy Ligosh, who is the sister of the deceased. And the writer alleged he had found other items in the package at work, when he was looking for a sales file."

As Ligosh listened intently in the public gallery, Prezioso said the package contained a "list on how to set up the defendant, Melanie McGuire, for the murder of her brother."

She said the letters had been examined by the same FBI linguistics experts who had worked the Unabomber investigation, and, on comparing them with examples of percent McGuire's handwriting, had determined with an 85 to 95 percent certainty that she had written them.

Defender Joe Tacopina labeled the state's new claims "laughable" and "rank speculation," calling them "a desperate attempt by the attorney general's office to salvage a failing case."

At the end of the hearing, Judge DeVesa increased bail by $100,000. Then Melanie McGuire, who pleaded not guilty on all counts, was handcuffed and taken back into custody until the new bond could be posted.

Less than twenty-four hours later, she walked out of Middlesex County Adult Correction Center with her parents, after posting the additional $100,000 bail. And she wouldn't have had to spend the night in a cell if the $10,000 bond check hadn't been made out to the wrong payee.

"I spoke with her," her attorney Stephen Turano told Jim O'Neill of *The Star-Ledger.* "And she's certainly glad to be home."

But Cindy Ligosh was worried that her sister-in-law was free, after the campaign she had allegedly waged against her.

"I'm scared," she said. "Now she's facing fifty years and she's desperate. You don't know what she might do, and she still has the gun."

On November 10, Judge Frederick DeVesa again delayed the start of the trial, to February 26, 2007, giving defense attorneys time to prepare for the new indictments.

"We're dealing with thirty-two thousand pages of discovery, and counting," Stephen Turano told the judge.

At another status hearing, five days before Christmas, Judge DeVesa cracked the whip, instructing attorneys on both sides to provide a complete witness list by January 19. He also earmarked three days in late January to hear various defense motions, including an attempt to keep the telephone wiretaps out of the trial.

At the end of the hearing, Judge DeVesa announced that jury selection would begin February 2. The trial, still on course for February 26, was expected to last five weeks.

On Monday, January 22, 2007, at the start of the motion hearings, Judge Frederick DeVesa consolidated Melanie McGuire's two grand jury indictments, allowing the State to use the anonymous correspondence as evidence in the murder case. Then Assistant Attorney General Patti Prezioso argued that a "grainy" videotape, allegedly showing the defendant in a Passaic strip mall shortly before buying an American Express gift card, should be admissible evidence.

"We're really lucky to have this," she told Judge DeVesa.

But defender Joe Tacopina disagreed, saying it was "impossible" to identify the woman on the three frames of videotape, as it was such bad quality.

"It calls for rank speculation," he declared. "It could be anyone."

After reviewing the videotape himself, the judge ruled that it could be shown to the jury.

The hearing then moved on to the wiretaps of McGuire's calls to her close friends and family, and the consensual ones made by Dr. Brad Miller and Jim Finn. Although the audiotapes were not played in court, Judge DeVesa and attorneys from both sides read the transcripts in silence. Then they discussed them, providing reporters with enticing snippets like "cutting up the little pieces," "dead weight," and "floating in his luggage."

On the second day of hearings, Prezioso revealed that the state contended one of the reasons Melanie McGuire had murdered her husband was to be with Dr. Brad Miller. She asked Judge DeVesa to allow recorded conversations where McGuire discusses her affair with a close friend, to be played to the jury.

But defender Steve Turano disagreed that her extramarital affair was a motive for murder.

"I think [it] is a tremendous leap," he told the judge, "and suggests to me a real absence of motive."

Later Judge DeVesa ruled that references to the affair in the wiretaps could be used at trial.

On the third day of motion hearings, the defense won a major victory when the judge ruled there was insufficient scientific evidence to show that the black trash bags found with Bill McGuire's body had come from the same batch as the ones recovered with his clothes in Brooklyn. At an earlier hearing, Prezioso had told Judge DeVesa that both sets of bags had been compared by New Jersey State Police forensic scientist Thomas Lesniak, who had found that they were from the same manufacturer, were the same size, shape and type and were fewer than twenty bags apart in the production run.

But at Thursday's hearing, Lesniak told the court that there were roughly one thousand American trash bag producers, and that he could not identify the manufacturer. After hearing his testimony, Judge DeVesa ruled that Lesniak could testify at trial about the similarity of the bags, without claiming they had come from the same plant or extrusion line, or been manufactured during the same time frame.

The prosecution's mainly circumstantial case took another hit when Judge DeVesa ruled that FBI linguistics expert James Fitzgerald could only tell the jury about comparing the anonymous letters to samples of Melanie McGuire's handwriting. But the judge refused to let Fitzgerald illustrate his findings with the same statistical analysis system he'd employed on the Unabomber case, saying it would be "misleading" or "confusing" to the jury.

Five days later, Judge DeVesa reversed his decision on the trash bags, now allowing Lesniak to testify that both sets of bags were produced on the same machine. This was after convincing testimony from Frank Ruiz, the prosecution's expert witness on trash bags, who'd told the judge that he had tested both sets of bags, using chemical and infrared analysis, concluding they had been made from the same raw materials at the same time.

The judge also postponed the trial by a week until March 5, allowing more time to whittle down the 289 potential jurors to 16.

On February 5, 2007, Detective William Scull, the supervisor of the south squad of the New Jersey State Police Major Crimes Unit, called Lieutenant Bruce DeShields of the Atlantic City Major Crimes Unit. He had been asked by Patti Prezioso to check on the status of the Flamingo Motel's video surveillance system, to see if it warranted further investigation.

During their conversation, Lieutenant DeShields mentioned how a man, staying at the Flamingo in October 2005, had later been murdered in Egg Harbor City. When Detective Scull casually asked if Atlantic City Homicide had made any connections between the two murders, DeShields said absolutely none.

After the conversation, Detective Scull, who is known for his thoroughness, e-mailed a brief report of it to Patti Prezioso, who then forwarded it to Joe Tacopina, as a courtesy.

Later, in his closing statement, Tacopina would make much of Detective Scull's innocent query, moving the date of the conversation forward two weeks, apparently to suit his agenda.

On the final day of motions on February 16, Judge DeVesa had the grim task of deciding which gruesome photographs of Bill McGuire's body would be shown to the jury. While arguing for the jury to see the graphic color pictures of the body parts, Patti Prezioso revealed that the State now contended that Melanie McGuire had dismembered her husband in the bathroom of their Woodbridge apartment.

Defender Joe Tacopina said the grisly photos were unnecessary, only serving to prejudice the jury. Finally Judge DeVesa ruled that the jury could see an image of the victim's severed legs, reserving his decision as to whether the State could introduce a second one, showing Bill McGuire's head and torso wrapped in a blue hospital blanket.

At 9:00 a.m. on Monday, February 26, 2007, 150 potential jurors arrived at Middlesex County Superior Court for the start of jury selection. They had been weeded out from the original 397 prospective jurors, who had completed a sixteen-page questionnaire comprising sixty-five different questions about background and experience.

Of the first thirty people questioned in the jury box by Judge Frederick DeVesa, seven admitted having some knowledge of the case. It was a long, arduous process on the first day, as the judge and attorneys from both sides studied the prospective jurors' answers to a specially prepared questionnaire, before interviewing them.

"I'm sorry this process has to be undertaken," Judge DeVesa

told the remaining jury candidates at the end of the day, telling them to return tomorrow for more questions.

But by Tuesday afternoon, a sixteen-person jury had been picked, comprising twelve women and four men, and including four alternates. Among the jurors who would decide Melanie McGuire's fate was a divorced banker, a truck driver and a female letter carrier.

FORTY-ONE

State of New Jersey v. Melanie Mcguire

On Monday, March 5, 2007, two years and ten months after the first suitcase had washed up in the Chesapeake Bay, Melanie McGuire went on trial for her husband's first-degree murder and dismemberment. The trial, now expected to last six weeks, had around one thousand exhibits and four hundred possible witnesses from both sides.

The entire trial from gavel to gavel would be broadcast live on Court TV, which had spent the weekend setting up a white satellite truck, complete with an interview stage, to the side of the superior court.

At 8:15 a.m. a team of video and audio engineers arrived at the courthouse, where they transformed a small office adjoining Judge Frederick DeVesa's courtroom into a studio, handling feeds to all three television networks.

There was huge media interest in the trial, and by 8.30 a.m. producers and reporters from CBS's *48 Hours*, NBC's *Dateline* and ABC's *Primetime*, were milling around the fifth-floor corridor outside the courtroom. The prize everyone was vying for was an exclusive interview with Melanie McGuire, who faced 30 years to life in prison if convicted.

True to his word, lead defender Joe Tacopina had moved into a $450-a-night suite at the luxurious Heldrich hotel in downtown New Brunswick for the duration of the trial, commuting back to his wife and five kids in Connecticut on weekends.

Ironically, the weekend before the trial, the March edition of *GQ*, with a six-page profile of Joe Tacopina, went on sale.

The fawning profile in the "Power" section carried the headline "1-800-SAVE-MY-ASS." It made much of how TV makeup artists called him "Joe-too-bad-he's-married-Tacopina," and his obsession with Julius Caesar.

"Caesar was the greatest strategist of all time," he told *GQ* writer Lisa DePaulo.

Patti Prezioso, the oldest of the four case attorneys, knew that when it came to looks and glamour, Tacopina would win hands down. So the doggedly determined New Jersey State employee decided to take another approach.

"Joe was certainly the pretty one, and the funny one," she said. "I needed just to try and keep everybody focused on the evidence, and not make it a media circus . . . so when the jury were looking at me, they saw some[one] very well-grounded."

Prezioso, wearing a sober black business suit, arrived soon after 9:00 a.m. with co-prosecutor Deputy Attorney General Chris Romanyshyn, who would partner her for the trial. A former civil litigator, Romanyshyn had joined the Division of Criminal Justice in 1999, bringing extensive experience in forensic science and electronic surveillance. The tall, immaculately dressed prosecutor would play a key role in the trial, and was the perfect foil for Prezioso.

A few minutes later, Melanie McGuire arrived at court with her parents, walking past the television camera crews stationed outside without a word. Then, after going through the metal detector, they rode the elevator up to the fifth floor, turning right into Courtroom 506, and taking their place with Tacopina by the defense table.

The defendant, who had visibly aged since her arrest, was wearing a sage-colored jacket and skirt with high heels, her heavily moussed black hair, curling around her shoulders. She was sporting an autism pin and ribbon on her jacket, reading "Mom to Jack and J.T."

There was an air of excitement in the courtroom. The second and third rows of the public gallery were packed with the local and national press. The *Home News Tribune* had the crack investigative team of Ken Serrano and Rick Malwitz, while *The Star-Ledger* had veteran court reporter Jim O'Neill and Suleman Din providing up-to-the-minute coverage through his BlackBerry to the paper's website. At the end of the press row was Kathy Chang, a dogged young reporter from the *Sentinel*, who would file comprehensive weekly reports on the trial.

In the front row, directly behind their daughter, Linda and Michael Cappararo had just taken their seats when a sheriff's officer politely asked them to leave the courtroom, as they were on the witness list. For the rest of the trial, Melanie McGuire's parents would have to wait outside in the hallway, while the fight for her life played out behind closed doors.

At 9:24 a.m. Judge Frederick DeVesa entered the courtroom. After reminding everyone to turn off cell phones, he called in the jury for the prosecution's opening statement.

"It took William McGuire nearly until his fortieth birthday to purchase his first home," Patti Prezioso told the jury. "It was a lovely house in Warren County, a long commute for him—but it would be a decent commute for his wife Melanie, who was commuting to Morristown, New Jersey, where she worked as a nurse.

"William and Melanie, or as his family referred to him as *Billy*, closed on that house on April twenty-eighth, 2004. They never moved in, though. You see, the defendant seated at that table was having an affair, and she was actually very much in love with someone else.

"The evidence will show that while Bill was engrossed in purchasing the house and all the closing details that go along with such a purchase, the defendant was very busy planning his death. She planned for her husband to disappear, and disappear he did."

As the jury listened intently, Prezioso told them how the first of three suitcases was recovered in the Chesapeake Bay, a week after the closing. Two more suitcases surfaced a few days later.

"It was their matching luggage," said the prosecutor. "Within these three suitcases were the deceased's cut-up body."

She then described how Bill McGuire had been shot at least twice, in the head and chest, with a .38-caliber handgun consistent with one that Melanie had purchased two days earlier. He had then been cut up into three pieces, his body parts wrapped in plastic bags, like garbage.

She said the jury would hear evidence that McGuire had carefully planned the murder of the father of her two children, including Google searches on the home computer for "undetectable poisons" and "how to commit murder." She also described McGuire's "poor and transparent" attempts to implicate Cindy Ligosh or the mob in the murder, with letters to the attorney general and the newspapers.

Preempting any attempt by the defense to portray Bill McGuire as an inveterate gambler, she told the jury that he was a hard-working family man.

"Did everyone love him?" she asked. "I'm sure not, because few people are loved by everyone. But he was a regular guy [who] loved and adored his two young sons. He enjoyed red wine. He had a good sense of humor. He liked to gamble in Atlantic City. He was a regular guy."

She also conceded that, under the prosecution's theory of the murder, the 5-foot, 4-inch, 110-pound nurse would have needed an accomplice.

"It is likely she had help with certain parts of this horrible crime," Prezioso told the jury. "Whether she pulled the trigger herself, or helped or commissioned for it to be done, it doesn't matter. She is guilty just the same. The ugly truth in this case is that Melanie McGuire killed her husband William."

Then, after almost an hour on her feet, Prezioso sat down and Judge DeVesa called the mid-morning recess.

Twenty minutes later, it was defender Stephen Turano's turn to address the jury. He immediately attacked the prosecution for rushing to judgment.

"This is something that was thrown together," he told the jury. "This is a three-year investigation . . . there's not even a murder weapon. From the beginning, the prosecution, as stated, have presumed Ms. McGuire was guilty. And you can do that in certain walks of life; you can't do it in an investigation. Because you know why? It leads to a bad investigation. It leads to an incomplete investigation. It leads to injustice."

He accused the state of "flip-flopping" with a "sloppy" investigation that ignored any evidence—direct or circumstantial— pointing to his client's innocence.

"What do they do?" he asked. "They just chalk it up to her being cunning, her being smart, her being able to concoct this great story. They go both ways on that. She can't be stealth-like and cunning in one instance and downright stupid in another."

Turano said Melanie McGuire loved her children with "every fiber of her being," and never would have murdered their father while they were in the apartment.

"Miss McGuire wasn't perfect," he said. "You're going to hear about extramarital affairs. And this was absolutely a failing marriage. There's no hiding that. There's no mistaking that. This was a marriage permeated with extramarital affairs. And not just Miss McGuire."

He also speculated that Bill McGuire's gambling had led to his demise.

"He was more than a regular guy who liked to go to Atlantic City," he told the jury. "He was a big gambler who gambled beyond his means. On the streets, when you owe money and you are not making payments, you know what happens? You get shot here and you get shot here," said Turano, pointing a cocked finger to his head and chest.

He questioned what possible motive McGuire would have for killing her husband, saying the fact that she had filed for divorce after Bill went missing proved that getting out of the marriage was an option in her mind.

"Ladies and gentlemen, this is a tragedy," he told the jury. "Absolutely a tragedy. Mr. McGuire was brutally murdered, and Melanie stands falsely accused."

After a lunch recess, the prosecution called its first witness, Police Officer John Runge of Virginia Beach's Special Operations

Marine Patrol. Under Patti Prezioso's questioning, he explained how he had inspected the first suitcase, containing a pair of legs.

"At first, all you could see was black plastic bags," said Runge. "At that point I moved the bags back, and you could see the legs."

Then Chris Romanyshyn went into a small room behind the jurors, bringing out the first green Kenneth Cole suitcase and laying it down in front of them.

"It wasn't very heavy," said Officer Runge. "Twenty to twenty-five pounds. I stayed with it until the medical examiner arrived."

Prezioso also had him narrate a short video of the Chesapeake Bay Bridge-Tunnel, pointing out emergency pull-offs with help phones.

The State's next witness was Virginia Beach Homicide Detective Janine Hall. Under direct examination by Chris Romanyshyn, Detective Hall identified the suitcase on the floor in front of the jury as the same one in which Bill McGuire's legs had been found.

While she was speaking, a grisly color photograph of the bloody limbs was projected onto a large screen. At first Melanie stared at them, before tightly closing her eyes.

In his cross-examination, Joe Tacopina asked if she had noticed any "decoloration or decomposition."

"The legs appeared fresh," she replied. "There was no smell. I didn't see any decomposition."

Then the State called Virginia Beach Crime Forensic Supervisor Elizabeth Dunton. As Melanie McGuire took studious notes at the defense table, Dunton told how she had examined the trash bags found with the legs in her laboratory, finding no latent fingerprints.

Deputy Attorney General Chris Romanyshyn then asked about the second suitcase, which had been found May 11, 2004, on Fisherman Island. As a photograph of the largest of the cases was displayed for the jury, Dunton explained how the medical examiner, Dr. Turner Gray, had removed the plastic bags.

"We discovered it was the upper torso of a white male," she said, as a female juror looked away. "At that point we sealed it up and placed it in a body bag."

Then, as the thirty-inch Kenneth Cole suitcase was brought out and placed by the jury box, Dunton described searching it and finding a 5.5-pound Weider barbell weight in the top outside pocket.

At 4:45 p.m. Judge DeVesa recessed for the day, telling Dunton to return the next morning to complete her testimony.

The next morning, the Melanie McGuire trial made sensational headlines around the world.

"Nurse 'Sawed Up' Her Hubby," screamed the *New York Post*, "Nurse Cut up Body of Husband," was the headline in *The Australian*.

The *New York Post* story breathlessly reported:

A highly respected nurse shot her husband in cold blood, then surgically sawed his body into pieces and stuffed them into suitcases, because she was having a torrid affair with a doctor at the clinic where she worked, a New Jersey prosecutor charged yesterday.

It was just 17 degrees with strong winds when Melanie McGuire and her parents arrived at Middlesex County Superior Court, rushing past several news crews waiting on the steps.

At 9:15 a.m. Judge DeVesa entered the courtroom and took his seat, resembling a middle-aged Eddie Munster with his slicked-back hair. He then called in the jury, who entered through a side door left of the defense table, filing past Melanie McGuire.

Beth Dunton then returned to the stand to continue her testimony about the second suitcase.

"Did it smell?" asked prosecutor Chris Romanyshyn.

"Yes," replied the forensic scientist. "Like decomposing flesh, rotten fish and actual bay water."

She then graphically described how she and Norfolk Medical

Examiner Dr. Turner Gray had, with some difficulty, separated the bags.

"It was a torso from the head to the waist down," she said. "It was severed at the waist."

Several jurors appeared shaken, when she matter-of-factly described the state of the decomposed torso, saying that there were body organs visible on the waistline, where it had been cut.

Then prosecutor Romanyshyn had her unseal two manila evidence envelopes containing the two bullets recovered with the body.

"The first bullet was found in the chest cavity area," she told the jury. "A small lead projectile, smaller than an inch in length. It was fairly clean. The second bullet was found loose on the gurney, close to the waist area. A lot of the inside came out, and the bullet was under that. There were a lot of greenish-colored fibers around the bullet."

Romanyshyn then projected a color photograph of Bill McGuire's Fruit of the Loom men's briefs, stained with blood and bodily fluids, and the defendant showed her first trace of emotion, lowering her head to her hands and dabbing her eyes with a tissue.

Then Romanyshyn moved on to the third suitcase found in the bay, containing the victim's mid-section, in an even worse condition than the others.

"This was probably the most potent of all the suitcases," she told the jury. "By the time you hit the dock, you knew exactly what you had."

The next witness was Detective Ray Pickell, who had led the original Virginia Beach investigation. Under Prosecutor Patti Prezioso's direct questioning, the softly spoken homicide detective described how Chesapeake resident Jon Rice had recognized a police sketch as his best friend Bill McGuire.

Detective Pickell told the jury he had then spent five days in New Jersey, meeting the victim's widow Melanie McGuire, in her divorce attorney's office.

"She made facial expressions that she may be crying," said the detective. "But I didn't see any tears."

He said that the defendant was unusually bitter about the murdered father of her children, spending most of the fifteen-minute interview belittling him.

"She said it wasn't a very happy marriage," said Pickell. "That her husband had a knack for pissing people off."

She told the detective that her husband had a "big" mouth and often made people angry.

The last time she had seen Bill, the defendant said, they'd had a violent argument and he'd stuffed a dryer sheet in her mouth. Then, he'd left their apartment, saying she would never see him again and she would be the reason the children would not have a father."

Detective Pickell said the only question she'd asked during the brief interview was if they had found her husband's car. When told they had not, she suggested they start looking in Atlantic City, saying he was a frequent visitor to several casinos there.

On intense cross-examination, Joe Tacopina attempted to pick holes in Detective Pickell's investigation, first asking how he could possibly know if McGuire's grief was genuine, as they had never met before.

"So you made summary conclusions?" said Tacopina accusingly. "She appeared to be crying and no tears?"

"I watched her actions for fifteen to twenty minutes," replied the detective, unfazed. "She would bring her hands up to her face, and I watched her eyes, and never a tear came to her eyes."

Under Tacopina's tough questioning, the detective admitted not canvassing the McGuire neighbors to see if anyone had heard gunshots or the sound of a power saw.

"That would be an important piece of information, wouldn't it?" asked Tacopina.

"Yes," agreed Detective Pickell.

Getting into his stride, Tacopina chipped away, asking why the laptop, BlackBerry and credit card records found in the victim's Maxima had never been checked; why a brochure for an Atlantic City hotel also found in the car had never been followed up.

Tacopina also drew the jury's attention to the fact that Detective Pickell's luminol testing for blood at the Woodbridge apartment had found nothing.

"And the end result of that," said the defender, "is that there was no evidence, no indication that there was blood there?"

"Right," said Pickell.

Late Tuesday afternoon, the State called John Coscia, the elderly Pennsylvania gun shop owner who had sold Melanie the .38-caliber Taurus revolver and wadcutter bullets two days before Bill was last seen.

"She was very well-dressed," he said. "In all the years I worked here, she was the first registered nurse to buy a handgun."

On Wednesday morning—day three of the trial—Dr. Wendy Gunther, the assistant chief medical examiner for Virginia Beach, was due to take the stand. But before she was called, Judge DeVesa had to rule on the prosecution's request to show the jury gruesome color photographs of the autopsy.

"Your Honor," said Prosecutor Patti Prezioso. "We live in a visual society. We need photographs to illustrate marbling, rigor mortis and washerwoman's syndrome."

Not surprisingly, defender Joe Tacopina argued that they should not be shown to the jury, as they would be highly prejudicial to his client.

Judge DeVesa agreed, saying the photographs were "rather unpleasant and gruesome," and would "do much to inflame the passions of the jury."

Dressed in a white medical gown, Dr. Gunther then took the stand, telling the jury that Bill McGuire's remains had been drained of blood when he was dismembered.

"This makes me feel he was cut up long after he was killed," she said.

As she described the three autopsies on the body parts over a two-week period, as each of the suitcases was recovered, Melanie McGuire took notes.

The first suitcase, she told the jury, had been found on May 5, 2004, and contained a pair of legs from the knees down.

"They looked like they had been sawn off," she recalled.

"[And] fresh to me, like the legs of people who come from the hospital the day before."

She said everyone had been "anxiously awaiting . . . the rest of the body," when the second suitcase with the victim's badly decomposed upper body was discovered six days later on Fisherman Island.

At the autopsy, a close examination of the torso, head and arms had provided the crucial clues, making her conclude that Bill McGuire had died from gunshot wounds. One bullet had entered the left side of his forehead, passing through his skull and brain.

"So I say with complete confidence," she told the jury, "this is the fatal gunshot wound."

The third suitcase, found on May 16, had contained the final body part.

"This one was from below the belly button to above the knees," she said. "It was also badly decomposed, but not as bad as the torso."

Finally, Prezioso asked if Bill McGuire's body had been cut before or after he had died.

"It is extremely likely he was cut after death," said the assistant chief medical examiner. "You can't bruise a dead body. There's no blood pressure."

In his cross-examination, Joe Tacopina closely queried her about the "fresh" condition the legs had been found in. And under his questioning, Dr. Gunther described them as being "like people who died in the hospital the day before."

This timing would be a vital element of the State's theory that Melanie McGuire had been in Virginia on May 4, 2004, one day before the first suitcase was found. Patti Prezioso believed the defendant may have put her husband's body on ice in the Woodbridge apartment, to prevent it from decomposing.

The last witness of the morning was John Ward, a ballistics expert from the Virginia Department of Forensic Science. He told the jury that the bullets recovered from Bill McGuire's body were flat-nosed lead wadcutter, mainly used for target practice.

He testified that he was able to identify six "lands and

grooves"—the indentations cut into the gun barrel during manufacture, making the bullet spin through the length of the barrel to stabilize in flight. From the unique "fingerprints" then created on the bullets, he used an FBI program to narrow down its origin to one of just six manufacturers, including Taurus, the brand of gun that the defendant had bought in Pennsylvania.

During the luncheon recess, Melanie McGuire and her parents ate at the Legal Grounds Cafe, one block away from the court.

"Be careful," Melanie told the Cappararos, "there's jurors in here."

For the duration of the trial, the defendant, who was free on $2.1 million bail, would come and go from the court as she pleased. She was staying with her parents in Barnegat, and each morning they would drive 70 miles to New Brunswick, always arriving early at the Middlesex Superior Court.

Once they passed through the metal detector, they went up to the fifth floor, where they would sit with their supporters, in a seated section in the hallway.

Every so often, a reporter or one of the young producers from the three network news magazine shows would come over and chat with Melanie and her parents, still competing for that elusive first interview everybody wanted. After several weeks of the trial, there was almost a chummy tea-party atmosphere in the corridor outside Judge DeVesa's Courtroom 506, with Melanie playing the part of hostess. Very soon, Melanie McGuire knew every reporter by name, making a point of chit-chatting with them on everything from cosmetics to the weather.

But when it was time for the trial to continue, the party would temporarily break up, as everyone returned to the courtroom—with the exception of the Cappararos, who would loyally wait outside until their daughter came back out at a recess.

That afternoon saw testimony highly damaging to the defense, from a stream of State witnesses. Timothy Lacek, an account executive with Allentown, Pennsylvania–based Hospital Central Services (HCSC), a medical supply company that distributed the white cotton blanket recovered in one of the suitcases, identified it as the same type he supplied to Reproductive Medicine Associates in April 2004.

He pointed out the distinctive four-arrow logo on the stained blanket found with the body, also marked, "Property of HCSC–Never Sold."

Under defender Steve Turano's cross-examination, Lacek admitted that his company supplied about one hundred other New Jersey medical facilities besides RMA.

The state then called Peter Burnejko, who testified that several hours after selling his $500,000 Halls Mill Road home to the McGuires, he'd telephoned Bill to congratulate him. Melanie had answered and been strangely quiet.

Then Detective Joseph Joraskie, recently retired from the Woodbridge police, testified how he had assisted Detective Ray Pickell's investigation in June 2004. He described Melanie McGuire's hostile demeanor at her first interview in her divorce lawyer's office.

"In reference to Bill's personal habits," he told Patti Prezioso on direct, "she said he was a 'jerk' . . . at work he was unliked, that his boss was looking to fire him. She seemed upset and angry. She seemed upset, but not emotionally upset, more like she didn't want to be in this situation."

In his cross-examination, Steve Turano asked if Joraskie had written up a police report for his work in the June 2004 investigation.

"I wouldn't really call it an investigation," he told the defender. "I call it an assist to the Virginia Beach investigation."

Under Turano's questioning, Joraskie said he had interviewed several of the McGuires' Plaza Drive neighbors, but no one had heard any gunshots coming from the apartment.

At 4:05 p.m., Judge DeVesa recessed for the day, telling the jury to be back on Monday morning. There would be no court for the following two days as there was a scheduled Family Court placement hearing, to decide who Jack and Jason McGuire should live with.

On Thursday morning, Melanie McGuire and her parents arrived at Ocean County Family Court in Toms River, New Jersey.

There were no satellite trucks, television cameras or reporters at the undistinguished office building, as all the DYFS proceedings are held in secret.

In the months before the trial, Cindy Ligosh had attended many of the hearings to decide custody issues for little Jack and Jason McGuire. She'd often had to wait for hours in a room with Melanie and her parents before being called into family Judge June Strelecki's chambers.

"The whole thing was surreal," said Ligosh. "I was left alone with these people, and it was extremely intimidating."

And with Michael and Linda Cappararo going for full custody of their grandsons, the Family Court part of the ongoing saga would far outlast the criminal one.

"This is the toughest part," Melanie McGuire told a *Star-Ledger* reporter in the freezing snow, as she smoked a cigarette after Thursday's two-hour hearing. "This is heartbreaking."

FORTY-TWO

"A Power User"

On Monday, March 12, the trial entered its second week, with the prosecution calling several witnesses to introduce the jury to Bill McGuire, anticipating the defense's negative portrayal.

"Bill is the best friend any person can have," said his NJIT colleague and business partner, Jaychandra Tandava on direct. "He's the best father and he's a very, very good brother, and I can give you a lot of examples."

Patti Prezioso asked Tandava if Bill McGuire "enjoyed" gambling.

"He used to gamble," he replied, "and go to Atlantic City with some cash and a set time frame. He said, 'I'm going to play for twenty minutes.' If he wins he'll go again, but if he loses he wouldn't go there for months."

Prezioso asked how he had been in April 2004, before buying the new home.

"Bill was very, very excited," testified Tandava, "because his dream was to give a new home to his kids and to his family. That was his dream house."

Tandava told the jury that as partners in their company, Jvista, they both had access to its business bank account. And in April 2004, with Tandava's full approval, Bill had taken a $10,000 loan for the closing of his new house, saying he would soon be getting money from his mother's estate settlement.

On cross-examination, Joe Tacopina asked if Tandava was

aware that the estate had been settled on April 8, three weeks before the closing.

"I didn't know that," he replied. "No one told me."

Going on the attack, Tacopina then fired off a series of questions about Bill McGuire's alleged "other side."

"You said he was friendly and nice," said the defender, as Melanie McGuire sat at the defense table making copious notes. "But he had a bad temper. He was temperamental, right?"

"I won't say 'temperamental,'" replied Tandava. "If there were some issues, he used to voice out his opinions."

"And he was easily excitable?" continued Tacopina.

"Yes," Tandava agreed, "but at the same time, if Bill had an argument . . . after a few minutes he used to go back and say, 'Sorry,' and try to make it up."

"Now this Bill McGuire, your friend, that you told this jury about. Did you know everything about him?" asked Tacopina, going on the offensive.

"Yes," replied Tandava.

"Did you know that he had a felony conviction?"

"No, I didn't know," said Tandava.

"Did you know whether he had a girlfriend or not on the side?"

"When, from 2003 to 2004?" asked Tandava.

"Did you ever know Bill McGuire to ever have an extra-marital affair?"

"No," he replied resolutely, "he never had an extramarital affair after the marriage. No. In 2003, 2004, I know Bill. He never had any girlfriend."

Then Judge DeVesa intervened, unhappy at the direction the defense was going.

"Excuse me, Mr. Tacopina," he said, in his understated schoolmasterly voice. "Can we go to sidebar?"

Following that, Tacopina questioned Bill McGuire's work ethic.

"Were you aware," he asked, "that Mr. McGuire had spent over ten days in Atlantic City when he was punched in as working at NJIT?"

Patti Prezioso stood up to object, but Judge DeVesa over-ruled her.

"No," said Tandava. "If he goes to Atlantic City, then he'll go only after work. That is, after three thirty to four o'clock."

"You can vouch for it?" questioned the defender. "So, if I was to produce you a gambling record to show he was at some slot machine when he's punched into the clock at NJIT, that would surprise you?"

"Yes," he replied.

"How much did William McGuire make at NJIT?" Tacopina demanded to know.

"Sixty-five thousand dollars a year," he replied.

"And for instance," said the defender, "on one of those three or four day trips, he would bring in the neighborhood of ten thousand dollar to twenty thousand dollar in cash?"

"Mr. Tacopina," interrupted the judge, "I can't imagine that this witness has personal knowledge of what we're talking about right now."

The next witness was Tom Terry, NJIT's associate vice president for information resource development.

"I was kind of a father figure," said Bill McGuire's boss, under Prezioso's direct questioning, "since his father had passed away."

Then Prezioso asked if Bill had been in danger of being fired in April of 2004. Terry said he had not.

Terry also told the jury how he had received a phone call from Melanie McGuire on May 17, 2004—the same day her husband was due to return to work after a two-week vacation—asking if he had seen him. And she had called again, asking about Bill's life insurance and how she could apply for it.

"I told her to call Human Resources," he said.

After lunch, NJIT senior progammer analyst Jason Stein-hauser, who'd shared a cubicle with Bill McGuire, took the stand. He told the jury that McGuire had run the help desk, fielding all the calls on their 1-800 number. He said McGuire had constantly talked to clients on his Nextel cell phone, while sending e-mails on his BlackBerry.

"He was a power user," declared Steinhauser. "He received a lot of e-mails to his BlackBerry device, and he had a working relationship with many people that relied on him for help on a regular basis."

Prosecutor Chris Romanyshyn then asked when McGuire had last communicated with the NJIT server.

"I remember specifically, after this whole thing happened," he said, "looking at the consul, [which] told me the last time his BlackBerry talked to the computer was April twenty-ninth in the evening. I thought that was something relative to tell the detectives."

Over the next few days, the prosecution would deftly weave its circumstantial case together, using numerous witnesses to each insert a different part of the puzzle. Although some testimony left questions for the jury, other witnesses would then be called to answer them and fill in the holes.

On Tuesday, March 13, Patti Prezioso called Jennifer Seymour to the stand. The State's forensic computer expert detailed for the jury her investigation of the McGuire home computer.

She explained how she had first uncovered some casual searches on Sunday, April 11, 2004, when the user had Googled topics like "undetectable poisons" and "suicide." A few days later subjects such as "instant poisons" and "gun laws in Pennsylvania" were checked.

Displaying records on a screen in front of the jury, Seymour said the searches increased over time, investigating various poisons like insulin and morphine. Then on Sunday, April 18, at 5:45, there was a Google for "how to commit murder."

Eight days later, a few hours after Melanie McGuire had bought the Taurus revolver, someone Googled the date rape drug "chloral hydrate," closely followed by a search on the Walgreens store locator.

Under Steve Turano's cross-examination, Seymour admitted that the HP Pavilion's clock was approximately thirty minutes off, and it had not been adjusted for daylight saving time. She also conceded that it was impossible to know exactly who had conducted the searches in question.

Earlier that day, Virginia forensic toxicologist David Barron had testified that McGuire's remains were never tested for chloral hydrate, and that his widow had had them cremated long before New Jersey had gotten the case.

"No, we don't look for chloral hydrate," he said, adding that there were no traces of any drugs in the body, and just a minute amount of ethanol, commonly produced by decomposition.

The jury also heard from the director of the Kinder Kastle preschool, Donna Todd, who testified that the defendant had dropped off her sons for class just twelve minutes before the chloral hydrate prescription was dispensed at Walgreens in Edison, a two-minute drive from the school.

Then Tiffany Bain—whose name was on the chloral hydrate prescription—testified that she had never been prescribed the drug. She also told the jury that whoever had written it had one digit of her phone number wrong.

The next morning, the jury heard an audiotape of a tearful Melanie McGuire telling a Family Court judge that her husband had slapped her during a violent argument after they closed on the house. As the defendant, wearing a fitted houndstooth suit and black stilettos, scrutinized a transcript of the temporary restraining order hearing, jurors heard her voice for the first time, through speakers placed around the courtroom.

"We argue pretty frequently, but this argument just became different," the jury heard her tell Judge Jessica Mayer. "He grabbed me by my shoulders and put me up against the wall."

"Did he hit you, ma'am?" asked the judge.

"Not until . . ." said the defendant, in a breaking voice. "Well, I don't mean to sound like I had absolutely no part in this. I said some not nice things, and at that point, yeah, he slapped me."

Finally, the judge asked if Melanie or her husband had any weapons.

"Not to my knowledge," she replied resolutely.

Then forensic anthropologist Dr. Steven Symes took the

stand, testifying how he had spent months studying five bone fragments recovered from the victim's remains. He had concluded that Bill McGuire's body had been dismembered with a thin-blade knife and a reciprocating power saw.

"It was a frustrating case," said Dr. Symes, whose expertise is in saw- and knife-mark analysis. "I didn't have a lot of bone to work with."

On Thursday, March 15—the seventh day of the trial—former RMA nurse Lori Thomas took the stand. The defendant's one-time friend and office mate did not look at her once during her testimony.

Prosecutor Prezioso first asked about her visit to 2902 Plaza Drive, a month after Bill McGuire's disappearance, to collect some furniture she'd bought.

"It was a nice apartment," said Thomas, who'd been fired by RMA in 2006 for being drunk at work. "The furniture was in place when you walked in the door."

Thomas testified that McGuire had given her some several HCSC medical blankets to wrap up the marble tabletops, which were part of the set.

"They were hospital blankets," she said. "They looked like the HCSC ones we use in the ward to keep patients warm and comfortable when they are going for their procedures."

Thomas said she had wanted to look around the apartment, going upstairs to a bedroom.

"And did you notice anything about upstairs," asked Prezioso, "and specifically the master bathroom?"

"I walked into the bathroom and there was just this horrible smell," she said. "Just a strong smell of bleach, musk, and cleaning supplies. It was just horrible."

"Let me ask it this way," said Prezioso. "Can you describe the smell better? Was it a typical bathroom smell or something else?"

"No," she replied. "It was a horrible strong smell."

"Are there any other words you can use to describe the smell to the jury?" pressed the prosecutor.

"Objection," cried Joe Tacopina, jumping to his feet. "She's asked it twice already and she gave all the words she could come up with. I object."

"I'll allow her to further explain if she can," said the judge. "Can you repeat the question, Ms. Prezioso?"

"Are there any other words you can use to describe the smell to the jury?"

"Again, it was bleach," said Thomas, starting to cough nervously. "I'm going to take some water. Sorry . . . Like a morgue."

"You just said, 'Like a morgue,' " said Prezioso, stressing it to the jury.

Later that day, the prosecution called New Jersey State Police Detective John Pizzuro of the Major Crimes Unit, who had been in charge of the wiretapping phase of the investigation. He explained to the jury how, as plant manager, he had organized the court-approved wiretaps of Melanie McGuire and those close to her.

Then the jury heard a series of secretly recorded telephone conversations between the defendant and her friends and family. In one conversation, she used the expression "cut him off at the knees," suggesting a way to stop police from questioning Selene Trevizas. In another conversation, she angrily complained that her dead husband's "hand reaches out from beyond the grave," making her life miserable.

But nowhere on the tapes does Melanie McGuire—who was well aware she was under investigation—make a single admission of guilt.

Later, after the court had recessed for the day, Liza Finley, a freelance producer for *48 Hours*, secretly gave Melanie McGuire a camcorder and videotapes. The idea was for her to record her thoughts and observations of the trial in the privacy of her parents' home. There were no strings attached and no guarantees that the popular primetime show would ever see it again.

But late that night in her bedroom, before going to bed, Melanie McGuire set up the camcorder to record the first installment of her video diary.

"So. This is, I guess, what is my first installment of my video diary, that I've been asked to prepare. And it is difficult not to feel a little self-conscious and narcissistic doing this, because I feel like, who would want to watch this? I am assured by many people that people want to get to know the real me, I guess.

"You know, one thing that has struck me about this process is that they bring in people that I haven't seen, in some cases, in years. And what they try to do is have them make sense of some sort of timeline, or testify to some fact. And it's really sort of bizarre to me, because it's like watching ghosts file into the room. Just these memories, these apparitions of the life that I once had. And it wasn't perfect—I don't even know that it was great—but it was mine. And more importantly it was my kids."

"And you know, I see these people come in, and the one thing that I'm struck by time and time again is that they talk about me like I'm dead. 'She was this.' 'She was that.' 'I liked her.' 'We did this.' 'We did that.' 'It's just all so past tense, and I mean, some of that, of course, is out of necessity, because of the situation they're testifying to, but some of it—'She was a good nurse.' 'I liked her.' 'Patients liked her . . .'"

On Monday, March 19, the trial entered its third week, with riveting testimony from Dr. Richard Scott, the founder and medical director of RMA. He told the jury for the first time about Nurse Melanie McGuire's three-year adulterous affair with Dr. Bradley Miller.

Dr. Scott said he'd suspected they were lovers, twice confronting Dr. Miller, whose partnership agreement explicitly forbade such an unprofessional relationship. On each occasion, Dr. Miller had denied having an affair with his nurse.

"I accepted it at the time at face value," Scott testified. "But if I hadn't been somewhat concerned about it, I never would have confronted him again."

Dr. Scott said that after the defendant's arrest, Dr. Miller had finally owned up to the affair, and was asked to leave the clinic.

Prosecutor Prezioso showed Dr. Scott two RMA prescriptions that the State alleged the defendant had forged Dr. Miller's signature on. One was for the sedative flurazepam, written in the name of Ruth McGuire, her late mother-in-law. The other one was for chloral hydrate, made out to Tiffany Bain.

Dr. Scott said it appeared to be a forgery, adding that his clinic would never prescribe that particular drug to a fertility patient.

"In April 2004 and the months preceding," asked the prosecutor, "were nurses permitted to write out prescriptions?"

"Yes," he replied. "When we wrote our orders on the electronic record, nurses were allowed to then transcribe those onto prescription pads for us."

"Would a nurse ever sign a prescription on behalf of a doctor?" asked Prezioso.

"I believe that did in fact happen at times," he replied.

Dr. Scott then described how the defendant had had access to all RMA's electronic medical records, containing patient information.

In his cross-examination, Joe Tacopina immediately honed in on his client's nursing talents.

"Melanie's character," he began. "Extraordinary work ethic?"

"She was a great nurse," replied Dr. Scott, turning to the defense table to smile at the defendant. "She *is* a great nurse. I'm sorry."

Late that night, before she went to bed, Melanie McGuire turned on the *48 Hours* camcorder.

"More poignant, and way more anxiety-provoking will be seeing Jim and seeing Brad, after almost two years. Jim, you know, whatever, I'll deal with it. Jim knows what went on, and I know what went on, and the truth will come out. Brad's another story. Not that I don't think the truth will come out, but I wish I could say that my feelings were that cut and dry. I would love to be able to just cross the board, despise what he did, write him off and be done. And I don't mean to intimate that it's not done with he and I. I think that's been pretty well established, but I guess I just wish I were more certain about

how I felt about it. I find myself making excuses for him. I guess it's what I do. Denial is not just a river in Egypt. And I've done it before. I did it with Bill. . . ."

On Tuesday, March 20—day nine of the trial—Melanie McGuire's old nursing school admirer Jim Finn took the stand to testify against her. As the stocky, gray-bearded blood-bank nurse mounted the witness stand, McGuire gave him a long, icy stare, as he nervously glanced towards her.

Under prosecutor Patti Prezioso's questioning, Finn told the jury how he had sat next to the defendant in class, falling "madly in love with her." At the time, she'd been dating Bill McGuire, and rejected his advances, saying she just wanted to be close friends.

"Was there ever a time when you were intimate with her?" asked the prosecutor.

"Never once," replied Finn.

He told the jury that after they graduated in 1996, they'd had little contact except for the odd e-mail or "rare" phone call once a year. But suddenly in February 2004, McGuire had renewed the friendship, with an increasing amount of e-mails.

Eventually they'd begun talking on the phone, and she told him her husband was drinking heavily and acting strangely. She'd reached out to him, saying she was becoming afraid for her safety.

Then, aware he was a gun enthusiast, she'd begun asking about how to buy a gun and get a permit. He'd told her that in New Jersey it took three months to obtain a permit, whereas in Pennsylvania you could walk into a gun store and buy one, as long as you could show proof of state residency.

Prezioso then had him read out loud a series of e-mails between him and the defendant in April 2004, when he'd advised her to get a gun to protect herself and the children.

"You're flirting?" asked Prezioso, after reading out one e-mail jokingly mentioning Condoleezza Rice.

"Oh, absolutely," he replied.

By the end of April, McGuire was getting more and more interested in the idea of buying a gun.

Finn had advised her to buy a lower caliber gun, as she was so petite, he felt a more powerful weapon would have too much recoil.

"I said a forty-caliber," he said, "or even a nine-millimeter. But I think I was focusing more on the forty, which would be, probably, more than someone her physical size could handle."

"At any time on April twenty-sixth," asked Prezioso, "did she tell you she went to Pennsylvania and purchased a gun?"

"No, ma'am, not at all," he replied.

At the end of April, said Finn, Melanie told him Bill had attacked her, before walking out. She told him she'd gotten a restraining order and filed for divorce. When he'd once again advised her to buy a gun for safety, she replied that she was not ready yet.

In September 2004, he had finally met Melanie in a diner, where she'd told him she was under suspicion.

Then, six months later, he had been approached by New York State police detectives, making a deal with them to secretly record conversations with her, in exchange for immunity.

During one of two recorded calls he'd made, with Detective Jeffrey Kronenfeld feeding him questions, McGuire had admitted buying a gun.

"She said her husband wanted her to buy a gun," said Finn, "because they were moving out into a rural area."

Then, after a short recess, the audiotapes of the wiretap conversations were played in court. The jury heard Melanie McGuire maintain her innocence, breaking down in sobs on one occasion, as Finn pressured her to tell him the truth.

But, although there was no confession, she did admit abandoning her husband's car in Atlantic City, saying she'd moved it in anger, believing he was with another woman. This was a vital part in the State's case, as it directly linked her to Bill's Nissan Maxima, containing damning evidence of the chloral hydrate and his "human sawdust."

After the two dramatic tapes were played for the jury, defender Joe Tacopina began his cross-examination. Under the defender's blistering questions, Finn admitted feeling betrayed when he'd learned about her affair with Dr. Brad Miller.

"You were angry," accused Tacopina.

"Yes, sure," he replied.

But throughout Tacopina's punishing cross-examination, Finn stayed calm, defending himself against the withering attacks on his character and credibility. If the experienced defense counselor smelled blood and was going for the kill, Finn doggedly refused to give an inch.

When Tacopina accused him of lying to detectives by initially claiming not to have been in love with the defendant, Finn agreed.

"I didn't want the police to think I was in love with a girl that murdered someone," he explained. "Eventually I told them I was."

"So you lied to them about that because you wanted to protect yourself," said Tacopina.

"Yes, sir."

"And you know that you're not allowed to lie to police during an investigation?"

"Yes," replied Finn, "but I also told them at the meeting that, yes, I was in love with Miss McGuire."

Then Tacopina accused Finn of secretly recording his client in return for law enforcement wiping the slate clean after he'd been caught lying.

"Stop right there," said Finn resolutely. "I was not caught in lies."

He then explained that he had agreed to cooperate with law enforcement and tape McGuire after Detective Sergeant Kronenfeld told him she had bought a gun without telling him.

"Mr. Finn," said Tacopina, staring him straight in the eyes, "I'm not asking you what Detective Sergeant Kronenfeld said about Melanie McGuire, and the information he fed you about her. My question to you, and I think you understand it, Mr. Finn, is, what did they tell you they thought you were lying about?"

"I don't recall walking out of that meeting with them saying, 'We think you're lying, and you better just watch out, buddy.' It was more along the lines of—we discussed all the things that I knew, they took that down in a recording or a transcript. By the end of that meeting, I was pretty well turned around. I walked into that meeting believing in your client's innocence, and I walked out believing that your client is guilty."

Then Tacopina asked Finn if he had "resumed" his friendship with the defendant after taping her twice for the police.

"When you believe your friend is a murderer," said Finn, "you're not their friend anymore. It really wasn't about the affair, it was about the gun."

"So, friend—murderer—friend. Switch back and forth on that one?" asked Tacopina.

"I think you're illustrating beautifully the ambivalence that was going through my mind at the time."

Then Tacopina asked if the police had been instrumental in him sending Melanie McGuire flowers, and asking her out on a dinner date two months after secretly recording her.

"No," said Finn. "That was strictly me. No one directed me to do anything."

Then Tacopina read the jury the postscript part of an e-mail that Jim Finn had sent McGuire after she'd received his flowers, offering to put her in touch with a reporter friend of his from the *Asbury Park Press*, to tell her story.

"That's a little offer you made to Miss McGuire in June 2005?" asked Tacopina sarcastically.

"Yes, that was me," said Finn.

"So, fair to say," continued the defender, "in June 2005 you thought it would be in her best interests to get her side of the story out. Correct?"

"Yes."

"No further questions, Mr. Finn."

In re-direct, Patti Prezioso asked if the defendant had kept the card he'd sent with the flowers out of love for him.

"I doubt it," said Finn.

FORTY-THREE

Dr. Brad Miller Testifies

The next morning—Wednesday, March 21—the State's highly anticipated star witness, Dr. Bradley Miller, took the stand. The courtroom was packed with many curiosity-seekers in the public gallery who had come to see the handsome doctor testify against his former lover.

When the bailiff called his name, Melanie McGuire looked away as he nervously entered from a side door. Throughout his day-and-a-half of testimony, she rarely looked at him, although he occasionally stole glances at her during recesses.

"Good morning," said Patti Prezioso, whose co-counsel Chris Romanyshyn sat next door in the press room, as his wife had once been a patient at Reproductive Medicine Associates.

Under Prezioso's questioning, the soft-spoken Dr. Miller, looking highly uncomfortable, told the jury he was married with three children. He said he had met Melanie McGuire at RMA's Morristown office.

"We started a Gestational Carrier Program," he said. "We also started a program called EGD, which required extra work. And she was always somebody who just rose to the challenge, and took on the extra responsibility."

"Did there come a time," asked the prosecutor, "when your relationship with Miss McGuire got more intimate?"

"Yes, it did," he replied.

"When did that begin, sir?"

"It was towards the end of her second pregnancy," said the

doctor, clearing his throat. "She was about thirty-eight weeks pregnant, and before she went on maternity leave, we had oral sex in the office."

"Which office?" asked Prezioso.

"My office," he replied.

When asked who had pursued whom, Dr. Miller said they were both at fault, adding that the defendant had bought him a birthday cake and a small Christmas present.

"I think we were always flirtatious," he said. "Both of us in the office."

The doctor said the affair had taken off after McGuire had returned from maternity leave. It had been hard, he said, with their busy work schedules and family demands, but they'd managed to squeeze romantic encounters into lunch hours, sometimes leaving work early or going to a hotel after evening meetings.

As he outlined their passionate affair, Melanie McGuire took careful notes, but when Prezioso asked if he had been in love with her, she stopped writing, looking up at him for the first time.

"Absolutely," he replied. "Yes, I was."

"And did she tell you she was in love with you?" Prezioso asked.

"Yes, she did," replied Dr. Miller.

He testified that they'd planned to leave their spouses eventually, so they could start a new life together and have children.

"She was going to divorce Bill," he explained. "Then a little later, I was going to divorce Charla. The two of us would get married, buy a house and have children."

But things did not go according to plan when Bill McGuire unexpectedly managed to raise enough money to close on 29 Halls Mill Road.

Dr. Miller admitted being angry when Melanie had told him that the deal had gone through, asking why she would possibly buy a $500,000 house if she eventually wanted to get a divorce.

Later that night she had called to reassure him that everything was going to be fine.

The next morning she'd telephoned, saying Bill had violently abused her and then walked out. She was so upset, he'd written her a prescription for the antidepressant Xanax.

Over the next few weeks, he testified, McGuire had withheld several vital pieces of information from him. She'd never told him at the time that she had purchased a gun, or taken a series of midnight trips to Atlantic City, directly following Bill's disappearance.

It was several months before she'd finally told him about the gun, saying it had been for her husband's protection. When she'd revealed making the first late-night trip to Atlantic City, she said it was to move Bill's car as a prank, and she had returned twice to see if he had collected it.

Although they spoke for hours on the phone every day, she'd also neglected to tell him about going furniture shopping in Delaware on May 4, 2004, until much later.

Finally, on March 12, 2005, he was cornered by four New Jersey State Police investigators as he was leaving work, and told he was a suspect in Bill McGuire's murder.

He had then agreed to secretly record telephone conversations with McGuire, hoping it would clear her.

"I was still very much in love with her," he testified. "And I still believed she had nothing to do with this."

The jury then heard two wiretap conversations between him and Melanie McGuire, where she vehemently proclaimed her innocence, ending in her swearing on her children's lives that she'd had nothing to do with the murder.

After lunch, Joe Tacopina began his cross-examination, relentlessly trying to destroy Dr. Miller's credibility. Within the first few minutes, the doctor had conceded that the future plans he and McGuire had made to be together were not as definite as he had previously told the jury.

"And before that closing in April 2004," said Tacopina, "you had made it clear to Melanie that you were not planning on leaving your wife any time soon?"

"That's correct," Miller confirmed.

"And you viewed your relationship with Melanie as long-term?" asked the defender.

"Yes, we did," replied the doctor. "I think that was in our minds, but nothing was written down in the time frame of two, three years—nothing like that."

"You were having an extramarital, secret affair, and there were no plans in place for a date you were going to get together?" asked Tacopina.

"There was no date certain," he said, "but I think we were both committed in our hearts that we wanted to be together."

Under Tacopina's tough questioning, Dr. Miller also admitted waiting more than a year before telling detectives about the affair. He acknowledged that he had lied to a grand jury, telling them the affair had ended in March 2005, when it had only finished after McGuire's arrest.

"You committed perjury in the grand jury," accused Tacopina, "because you wanted to conceal your ongoing relationship with Melanie. Correct?"

"I still loved her at the time," he replied. "Yes, sir."

But not everything went according to the defense plan, during Joe Tacopina's cross-examination. When asked about purchasing a reciprocating saw on May 2, 2004, the doctor said a Home Depot receipt from that day showed he had bought an air compressor and not a saw. He did admit owning a reciprocating saw, saying he had given it to investigators, along with a spare blade.

Then Tacopina asked Dr. Miller to compare two prescriptions—one for the chloral hydrate made out to Tiffany Bain, and the other, a legitimate prescription written out by the defendant.

"You don't know whose handwriting it is, do you?" asked the defender, referring to the Tiffany Bain one.

The doctor replied that, although he was not a handwriting expert, the chloral hydrate one looked like the defendant's penmanship.

It was late afternoon when Judge DeVesa recessed for the day, telling Dr. Miller, who had already been on the stand four hours, to come back tomorrow morning to continue.

On Thursday, March 22, Dr. Bradley Miller briefly returned to the witness stand to face Joe Tacopina again. Once again the defender went on the attack, asking the doctor why he had called a credit card company for receipts from Home Depot around the time of the murder.

"You were trying to re-create your whereabouts," he said. "Is that something that you did on your own initiative?"

"Yes, I did," said the doctor.

"Were just curious?" asked the defender.

"Yes, I was," said Dr. Miller.

Finally, Dr. Miller conceded that he felt he had to be able to prove where he was around the time of the murder.

In her re-direct, Patti Prezioso asked him to explain why he wanted receipts for that time period.

"Well, I certainly assumed that I would be looked at as a potential suspect," explained the doctor. "And I was doing my own due diligence to make sure I knew where I was."

On Monday, March 26, the trial moved into its fourth week with no end in sight. And at 9:00 a.m. a weary-looking Michael Cappararo was sitting in his usual spot outside the courtroom, while his wife Linda was reading the self-improvement book *Real Moments: Discover the Secret for True Happiness* by Barbara De Angelis.

"It's hard," Cappararo told a writer, when asked how he was doing. "I just wish it would be over. Yesterday Mel had to go into town to see her lawyer. It may be another two or three weeks. There's so many battles."

That morning, the prosecution introduced the anonymous FedEx package sent to Assistant Attorney General Patti Prezioso, and received hours before the grand jury was due to vote on an indictment.

New Jersey State Police Detective Sergeant Jeffrey Kronenfeld told the jury that the package had contained an anonymous letter and the "Set her up" memo, framing Cindy Ligosh for her brother's murder. Inside were also a wedding ring, a bracelet, keys and a quantity of marijuana.

Investigators had determined that the package had been sent two days earlier, and paid for with a $50 American Express gift card, purchased at a Rite Aid store in Passaic.

Kronenfeld said he'd later recovered a videotape from a surveillance camera, showing a woman the State said was the defendant, walking towards the store three minutes before the card had been purchased.

The video was then played several times for the jury, with Kronenfeld using a laser pointer to assist them. The prosecution argued that the figure in the video had the same distinctive "widow's peak" hairline as the defendant.

In cross-examination, Joe Tacopina maintained that it was impossible to positively identify the woman on the videotape. He objected to Prezioso showing the jury a comparison picture of the defendant in 2000, with her hair up, showing what the prosecution continually referred to as a "widow's peak."

In a rare light moment, the detective conceded that the defendant appeared "a little chunkier" in the 2000 photograph, compared with how she looked today, making the entire courtroom laugh, including Melanie McGuire.

Later that day, prosecutor Patti Prezioso read the four-page single-spaced typed "gangster letter," sent to then–New Jersey Attorney General Peter Harvey in August 2005.

On Tuesday afternoon, FBI Special Agent James Fitzgerald, a forensic linguist, testified that the gangster letter and the "Dear Madame Assistant Att General" one in the FedEx package, had punctuation similar to six known samples of Melanie McGuire's writing, and a taped conversation of hers.

The forensic linguist, who works for the FBI's legendary Behavioral Analysis Unit in Quantico, Virginia, found several common factors, including: the overuse of commas; the use of single quotation marks instead of double ones; the use of one dash to isolate a clause in a sentence, instead of the usual two; and the way the "+" was used instead of the word "and," and "w/" instead of "with."

On Wednesday morning, under defender Steve Turano's cross-examination, Fitzgerald conceded that his branch of forensics had "some level of subjectivity," and was nowhere near as accurate as fingerprint analysis.

But he maintained there were "distinctive" and "idiosyncratic" similarities between the anonymous letters and samples of the defendant's writings.

"In my experience, these are significant," said Special Agent Fitzgerald.

After the Wednesday morning recess, forensic scientist Thomas Lesniak of the state police crime laboratory, took the stand. The crime-scene expert, who was in charge of the overall scientific part of the task force investigation, testified that he had tested more than two hundred items of evidence.

He had spent more than three months examining the black garbage bags, telling the jury that ones removed from 2902 Plaza Drive containing Bill McGuire's clothes were identical to those found inside the suitcases with the body parts.

Under Assistant Attorney General Patti Prezioso's questions, Lesniak used a series of blown-up photographs of the trash bags to illustrate distinct patterns of pigment lines and waves, proving they had been made on the same machine in the same factory.

"It's kind of like a fingerprint of the extrusion," he told the jury, adding that the chads at either end of the bags, unique to the tool that punched them out, "matched perfectly."

At one point in his testimony, Lesniak used a light box to demonstrate to the jury the swirling dyelines in the industrial-sized 39 inch–by–39 inch bags. He testified that he had compared bags taken from the Cappararos' Barnegat home, also finding similarities.

He told the jury that he had removed an animal hair and a particle of nail polish from the adhesive side of the blue painter's tape used to secure the plastic bags in one of the suitcases.

"It was red-colored nail polish," he said.

Four pieces of blue painter's tape, recovered with the torso in the second suitcases, were tested for DNA, but none was found.

After the prosecution had finished questioning Lesniak at 4:00 p.m., Judge DeVesa dismissed the jury for the day, in-

structing them to return the next morning, when Joe Tacopina
would get his chance to cross-examine.

Although the jury went home when court was recessed for the
day, attorneys on both sides were only just starting their work.
Joe Tacopina, Stephen Turano and their defense team would
wheel the heavy cases of defense papers to their "war room"
suite at the Heldrich to strategize. The prosecution team, including investigators Don Macciocca, JJ Janowiak and George
Delgrosso, had an office on the second floor of the Middlesex
County Prosecutor's Office, across the street from the courthouse.

"We were there until midnight almost every night of that
trial," said case manager David Dalrymple. "We would carry
everything between us, and then it went back again the next
morning. We worked our butts off."

Patti Prezioso had not had a day off since Thanksgiving. "I
lost eleven pounds during the trial," she said. "And it wasn't
fat, it was dehydration. I worked every single day, and for
about three-and-a-half-months. The only time I saw my family
was for about fifteen minutes on Sunday."

Her co-counsel Chris Romanyshyn was so rarely home that
one day when he appeared on Court TV's coverage, his little
son ran over to the television screen and kissed it.

On Thursday, March 29, day 15 of the trial, Joe Tacopina began his cross-examination of Thomas Lesniak, trying to dis-
mantle the state's case against his client.

"The nail polish chip," he began. "It did not compare to
ones received for Melanie and her mother?"

Lesniak confirmed that it didn't, also conceding that the red
chip found was "a nail polish–type item," and could not say for
certain it was nail polish.

Tacopina intimated to the jury that if it was nail polish, it
could have come from Lesniak's Virginia Beach CSI counter-
part Beth Dunton, who had first analyzed the suitcases and
their contents in May 2004.

Under Tacopina's intense questioning, Lesniak also acknowledged that the five searches of 2902 Plaza Drive had failed to recover any blood or DNA evidence.

"You looked through thoroughly?" asked the defender.

"Yes," replied Lesniak.

"And you came up with no evidence?"

"That is correct," replied the forensic scientist.

When Tacopina pointed out that blood is very hard to wash away, Lesniak disagreed, saying it was not that hard if you do a thorough job.

"We do it in the lab every day with our tables," he said. "If there's blood on there, we clean it. You clean it up properly, we're not going to detect it."

Tacopina also pressed him on the mysterious green fibers found inside the garbage bags, and also wrapped around one of the bullets that had killed Bill McGuire. The scientist said he had compared the fibers to the McGuires' olive green couch and love seat, but they had not matched. Other tests comparing them to a carpet, rugs and the upholstery of the victim's car had also come up negative.

Late Thursday afternoon, Zhongxue Hua, chief of the state's regional medical examiner's office in Newark, testified about the "human sawdust" found on the floor mats of Bill McGuire's Nissan Maxima. Hua identified the flesh as "fibrous connective tissues," found in the deepest layers of the skin. He testified that his microscopic analysis had shown it was not of the type of dead cells that routinely rub off the skin surface, but far deeper tissue, only separated from the body by disease or trauma.

In his cross-examination, Joe Tacopina turned to the jury, twisting the wristband of his expensive Panerai watch, asking Hua if it could cut deeply, pull out a hair or leave a trace of the deep-layer connective tissue.

"That's a possibility," acknowledged the medical examiner, adding that it would not account for all the particles recovered from the car.

Over that weekend, Melanie McGuire made another entry in her video diary.

"Nobody knows what to say in a situation like this, and I don't know that there is anything to say. I mean, hell, I go to my psychiatrist and he's wonderful, but the guy pretty much throws up his hands and says, 'There's no guidebook for this. You do what you've got to do, and whatever works.' "

"It's hard, and it's not that I don't react or that I don't emote. I do. I've spent the last two or three years dealing with this, and I've learned how to live with it, because I haven't had a choice. So when people remark that, 'Oh, she's got cold eyes.' I love that one. That's my favorite—'cold eyes.' Or when people say I'm just sort of reticent, I'm just sitting there. Again, first time as a murder defendant and I don't quite know what the etiquette is, but I'm reasonably certain I shouldn't be sitting there with a grin on my face."

FORTY-FOUR

"Absolutely Mortified"

On Monday, April 2, the Melanie McGuire trial entered its fifth week. Concerned it was falling behind schedule, Judge Frederick DeVesa asked Patti Prezioso when the State expected to conclude its case.

"Thursday's a safe bet," she told him.

Joe Tacopina said he expected the defense case to last four days or longer, depending on whether or not Melanie McGuire took the stand.

"She'll decide later," he said. "We're trying to pin it down."

The state then called Leon Sarao, the casino supervisor for the Trump Taj Mahal, to testify about Bill McGuire's gambling prowess.

The casino expert testified that McGuire had been a rated player and a high roller who won big. He testified that in 2003, the $65,000-a-year computer analyst had changed $97,000 into playing chips, walking away with a $30,000 profit. McGuire's average bet in 2003 had been $293, ten times the casino's average.

Prosecutor Patti Prezioso had Sarao review the victim's gambling records from his "comps"—a loyalty card that allows customers to earn points that can be cashed in for free hotel rooms, meals and drinks. He said the records showed McGuire had visited Atlantic City twelve times in 2003, staying for a three-day period when he met the Rices that October.

But in the three months before his murder in 2004, he'd gone just once, losing $4,100.

Under Prezioso's questioning, Sarao said that Bill McGuire had not been to the Taj Mahal between April 29 and May 5, 2004, between the time the defendant claimed she'd last seen him and when the first suitcase had washed up.

On Steve Turano's cross-examination, Sarao agreed that Bill McGuire could have gambled in other casinos over that period, and conceded that his gambling activity would not be recorded if he wasn't using his comp card to be rated.

Later that night, a tearful Melanie McGuire recorded this entry in her video diary:

"And I don't want to cry. And I don't want to keep living with this loss over and over and over again between the loss of my family, of my husband for better or for worse—the father of my kids. For Brad. My whole life. And now it sounds like what he was saying up on the stand, which is whining. You know—'My life, my life.' And I really don't do that very often, but I feel like it today. And I couldn't cry, not because I didn't want to or because I physically couldn't, but because I was told I couldn't and I shouldn't and I know why. And I wonder about his kids. And he was so good to my kids. And it's done. It's over. It'll never be again. Never be . . . I can't keep up the momentum. I can't keep up the pace. I can't separate myself effectively enough any more to function appropriately in all these venues. And I just, when people call and friends call and they want to know how I'm doing, and I just—but I feel better when I talk to them, but until I get to that point I don't want to talk to anybody. Everybody keeps saying, 'Well, the worst is over, the worst is over.' Is it? Or is the worst living the rest of my life either, I don't know . . . All right. I think that's about enough for tonight. Talk to you tomorrow."

On Tuesday morning, Cindy Ligosh took the stand to testify against her brother's accused killer. Sitting in the second row of the public gallery, where she had been every day of the trial, representing the family, was her daughter Laura. Melanie McGuire looked highly uncomfortable during Ligosh's testimony, picking her cuticles until they bled.

"My brother and I were very, very close," she told prosecutor Patti Prezioso. "We spoke almost every single day. We were best friends."

Ligosh testified that before Bill's death, she and Melanie had had a very good relationship, saying she thought they were the perfect couple. But she had become suspicious of Melanie after Bill disappeared, with the allegations that he had been violent, walking out on her and the children.

Ligosh told the jury how she had asked the defendant for her brother's license plate number, so she could go to Atlantic City and search for him.

"She told me she couldn't remember it," said Ligosh.

Prezioso asked about the FedEx package sent to her, which appeared to incriminate her. Ligosh said she had never seen it before, calling the "Set her up" note inside it a lie.

"It's not my writing," she said. "I saw that for the first time when I testified at the grand jury."

When Prezioso showed her the wedding ring and bracelet found inside, asking if it had belonged to Bill, Cindy broke down in tears, taking several minutes to compose herself.

Prezioso showed her an RMA prescription for Xanax, written out in the name of her mother, Ruth McGuire. Ligosh said it had the wrong date of birth, and the Edison address on it was Bill and Melanie's first apartment.

During cross-examination, Joe Tacopina asked about the last time she'd seen her brother alive, a month before his murder. He showed her a list she had written with Bill about various ways to persecute their sister Nancy, who was giving them a hard time over their mother's estate.

"It was a joke," said Ligosh, referring to it as "doodling," after a couple of glasses of wine.

"It was just sibling, brother-sister, immature stuff," she explained.

She said one of the notes, "Letters from psychos in prison," related to Nancy's habit of meeting strangers in Internet chat rooms. Another note, "Burnt ashes of letter from nurse," had to do with Nancy allegedly being molested as a child by her father, and Bill making up a deathbed confession, to give her some closure.

She also acknowledged telling investigators that her brother may have had a brief "fling" with a part-time opera singer, around the time Jason was born.

"He came into my husband's store one day," she said. "He had a rash over his upper torso and thought it was some sort of poison ivy. He told me that he had been in the park with a woman from work, an opera singer. I took it to mean that they had relations, or whatever."

In her redirect, Patti Prezioso asked if she had ever intended anyone besides Bill to see the note with her doodles on it, and whether she had asked the defendant to save it.

"Absolutely not," she replied.

"What did you expect would happen to that paper after Bill read it?" asked Prezioso.

"I would imagine it would just be thrown in the garbage," she replied.

"Miss Ligosh," asked the prosecutor, "how do you feel about the fact that this jury is looking at that note now?"

"Absolutely mortified," she replied.

"No further questions."

The next morning, Wednesday, April 4, the State called its final two witnesses. At 10:00 a.m. an emotional Jon Rice took the stand, as his wife Sue waited outside, unsure if she would be called to testify.

Immediately, Jon broke down in tears when prosecutor Prezioso asked him to describe his relationship with Bill McGuire.

"I was best man at his wedding," said Rice, turning red, as he bent forward and pinched his nose. "We took the honeymoon with them, and he was my best friend."

At the defense bench, Melanie McGuire showed a rare

display of emotion, dabbing her eyes with a tissue as a picture Rice had taken of her and Bill in October 2003, at the Borgata Hotel in Atlantic City, was displayed.

In a breaking voice, Rice told the jury that it was on the way back from that trip, stopping over at the McGuires' Woodbridge apartment, that he had seen the Weider free weights in the basement, similar to the 5.5-pound one found in a pocket of the second suitcase.

He also testified that he had last spoken to Bill at about 6:00 p.m., the day he'd called to announce he had closed on the new house.

"He was very excited," said Rice. "He was asking me to come up and help him move in."

Rice testified that he had received a call from the victim's phone on April 30, 2004, at 5:41 p.m., but no message was left on his answering machine.

"Bill would always leave a voice message," he said. "There was no voice message."

Later, on cross-examination, Rice acknowledged telling Detective Ray Pickell in May 2004 that he couldn't remember if his friend had owned a set of weights.

"In 2004," said the defender, "your memory would have been better about 2003 than in 2007?" asked Tacopina.

"He had asked me the day before about the weights, and I couldn't remember," said Rice. "I tried to put myself back in time, and I saw the weights."

The final witness for the State was Frank Ruiz, a Dallas-based expert in the manufacture of plastic garbage bags. He testified that he had studied four of the black trash bags that had swathed Bill McGuire's remains in the suitcases, finding that they matched the six recovered with his clothes.

Ruiz said he had carried out four different kinds of tests, concluding that they had identical markings and were made on the same equipment. With the aid of charts and diagrams, he testified that the bags had all come from the same batch of raw plastic material, manufactured within several hours on the same production line.

In cross-examination, Steve Turano challenged his testing

methods, questioning one particular result showing differences in the chemical ingredients between the two sets of trash bags.

"The numbers didn't add up," said Turano, suggesting it was impossible to state whether the bags had been packed in the same box, or even handled by the same distributor.

Ruiz agreed, but later, on Chris Romanyshyn's re-direct, he maintained that when held up to the light, the bags displayed an unusual herringbone-type pattern.

"Those markings are very unique," he told the jury. "They show those bags had to come from a single line, a single manufacturer."

At 10:16 a.m. on Thursday, April 5, the state rested its case, after calling sixty witnesses over five weeks of testimony. Defender Steve Turano then filed a motion to dismiss the case. He argued that prosecutors had not provided proof enough to link his client to the murder, saying that there was not "a single stitch of evidence" of the involvement of an accomplice.

"[The State] failed to offer any proof that William McGuire was murdered in his apartment in Woodbridge, [or] anywhere in the State of New Jersey," he declared, outside the presence of the jury, who had been told to report back Monday morning for the start of the defense.

But Assistant Attorney General Patti Prezioso countered, saying, "there is an overwhelming abundance of evidence, clearly putting the defendant in the middle of the murder charge."

Judge DeVesa ruled against the motion, saying he felt the jury could reasonably conclude that the defendant had killed or dismembered her husband, either alone or with an accomplice.

But at the request of the State, he agreed to drop four of the lesser charges, of filing a false report and three charges of drug possession, to simplify things.

Earlier in the hearing, Joe Tacopina had dramatically announced that Melanie McGuire had taken and passed a polygraph test, asking the judge to admit those test results if his client decided to testify.

"We will submit Ms. McGuire to the State's polygraph examiner," said Tacopina, "and let the chips fall where they will. And we would ask the State to stipulate that the results be admitted into evidence."

Prosecutor Prezioso disagreed, saying that, while polygraphs may have some value as interrogation tools, they are not good evidence.

"The State has absolutely no interest in giving Miss McGuire a polygraph," she said. "There is a reason that it is not admissible in New Jersey."

To no one's real surprise, Judge DeVesa rejected the idea, saying it "would tend to undermine and interfere" with the jury's work to determine guilt.

But some cynics wondered if the polygraph question wasn't merely a defense ploy, one that ultimately generated a front-page story in the *Home News Tribune* that Friday, proclaiming that a lie detector had cleared Melanie McGuire. There was always the chance that a member of the jury might accidentally see it over the long Easter weekend.

FORTY-FIVE

The Defense

On Monday, April 9, Melanie McGuire arrived at Middlesex County Superior Court with a noticeable spring in her step. It was the first day of her defense, and she, her parents and supporters believed things were going their way.

The front-page story that the *Home News Tribune* had run on Friday, showing a large color photograph of Melanie McGuire, accompanied by a story announcing that she had passed a polygraph test, had certainly helped buoy her spirits. And over the weekend, Joe Tacopina was particularly upbeat, promising to call witnesses to speak of his client's character, with testimony that "will bring tears to your eyes."

But at 9:10 a.m., when Judge Frederick DeVesa came out of his chamber, he looked anxious. Before calling in the jury, he told the court he was concerned about the defense's polygraph motion on Thursday being widely reported in the local media, as well as by a prosecution witness appearing on Court TV, on Friday.

"There is at least a reasonable possibility," said the judge, "that some of the jurors might have inadvertently been exposed to mid-trial publicity. Therefore, the court feels it is necessary to interview jurors in chambers. This is a routine thing in any lengthy trial."

Two hours later, after the judge had questioned the jurors, he declared that they had not been contaminated, and the defense would proceed.

"A couple of jurors saw headlines, but nothing more," a smiling Steve Turano told reporters outside in the corridor. "There's no mistrial."

The defense began by calling Joanne Cascia, the speech therapist for Jack and Jason McGuire. She testified that the defendant had telephoned her the morning of April 29, 2004, cancelling an appointment, saying she and Bill had had a fight. Cascia said Melanie had told her he had walked out the night before.

The next day, Melanie phoned again.

"She was calling me on that day," said Cascia, "to see if Bill had come to the office looking for her or the kids."

In cross-examination, Patti Prezioso showed Cascia a report of an interview she'd allegedly given Investigator George Delgrosso, denying that Melanie McGuire had told her about obtaining a restraining order. Cascia said the report was wrong. Melanie had mentioned it the following week, when she had brought her sons to an appointment.

When the prosecutor questioned if she was changing her story because she was friends with the defendant, Cascia said no.

The next defense witness was George Lowery, one of Bill McGuire's NJIT clients, who testified about a conversation they had had about firearms, three months before his murder. Lowery, who works for Camden County Health Department as a computer programmer, testified that Bill McGuire had visited his office once or twice a month for a bio-terrorism project called "the Communicator," and they had become friends.

During one lunch together in early 2004, Lowery said, McGuire had discussed buying a gun. But that's all Judge De-Vesa would permit him to say, because earlier, outside the presence of the jury, Joe Tacopina had said his witness would testify that McGuire had told him he needed a gun, as his car headlights had been stolen several times. He'd said he planned to ask Melanie to buy the gun, as he couldn't get a permit.

But the judge ruled it unreliable hearsay, only allowing the witness to tell the jury they'd had a conversation, without elaborating.

On Tuesday, April 10—the twenty-second day of the trial—the defense called half-a-dozen character witnesses, who described Melanie McGuire as unusually caring and compassionate.

"She saved my life," declared her old Rutgers classmate Anthony Sciafani, after the mid-morning recess. "She is the best person I've ever known."

On cross-examination, Patti Prezioso asked if he was in love with Melanie McGuire.

"I feel a close bond with her," he replied. "Close like good friends."

Sciafani admitted only getting back in contact with the defendant after reading about her arrest in the newspapers. But he said he had been objective about her, "keeping an open mind."

The next witness was Alison LiCalsi, who had attended every day of the trial, making detailed notes in the public gallery for a possible book. The married mother of a 4-year-old adopted daughter told the court she had first met the defendant in 1987, when they'd worked together in a department store.

"She was in high school and I was in college," she said. "We became good friends. We speak every day."

LiCalsi burst into tears when Steve Turano asked about the defendant's character.

"I love her," she sobbed. "She's one of the sweetest people I know. I trust her."

In her cross-examination, Prezioso asked her about Melanie and Bill McGuire's wedding, which LiCalsi had attended in 1999, and whether the vows they had taken included a promise to be monogamous.

"If she cheated," said the prosecutor, "would that be a form of lying?"

"It depends on the marital relationship," said LiCalsi, who said she had been aware of the defendant's affair with Dr. Brad Miller.

Prezioso then asked if she knew that her friend had had a

second affair with another doctor, prompting Steve Turano to jump to his feet to object. Judge DeVesa sustained the objection, telling the prosecutor to move on.

The next character witness for the defense was Lorraine Blake, a neighbor of Michael and Linda Cappararo's. The retired teacher said she had known the defendant for about four years. Melanie had voluntarily come to Blake's home every Monday, Wednesday and Friday to give injections to her 28-year-old daughter Melissa, a multiple sclerosis sufferer.

"She's like family," she said. "Melanie is the sweetest, kindest, most generous, darling girl you'd ever want to meet."

Later, under Prezioso's questioning, Blake conceded that her conversations with McGuire were "light" and infrequent.

"I didn't know [Bill McGuire] had disappeared until it was in the papers," she said.

Her husband Richard Blake and wheelchair-bound daughter Melissa also took the stand to speak to McGuire's character.

"I was a complete vegetable," said Melissa. "Melanie came over and helped me get back into shape. She is a wonderful person [and] one of my best friends."

"The State has no questions," said Patti Prezioso, as the defendant wiped a tear from her eye.

After the jury was dismissed for the day at lunchtime, Judge DeVesa held a special afternoon hearing, to decide the scope of the evidence the remaining defense witnesses and experts would be allowed to give. One crucial witness for the defense was Bill McGuire's first wife Marci Paulk. She would testify about their unhappy marriage, and how he had walked out on her in 1994, in the same way he had done with Melanie, ten years later.

"The State has opened the door to the character of William McGuire," declared Joe Tacopina. "[There was] evidence of violence."

Prosecutor Chris Romanyshyn disagreed, arguing that what happened ten years ago was "totally irrelevant," and any testimony about his first marriage would be "inappropriate and inflammatory."

"The issue of the prior marriage is too remote," Judge DeVesa agreed, ruling that Paulk could not be questioned about her marriage to Bill McGuire, limiting her testimony to just an e-mail she'd received from him shortly before his death.

But the judge said he would allow a computer expert for the defense to address McGuire's incriminating Google searches.

Then Joe Tacopina stood up dramatically to announce that the defense had a possible eleventh-hour witness who could clear Melanie McGuire.

"The defense has been contacted by an individual," he told Judge DeVesa. "He's a truck driver who claims he may have relevant information regarding observations on April thirtieth on the Chesapeake Bay Bridge-Tunnel."

Tacopina said the man had made contact after seeing the trial on television, and had receipts and toll records proving that he had been on the bridge from late April 29 until early April 30.

"He's been trying to contact the state police," said the defender, adding that he would probably call the truck driver on Thursday, after having a chance to "vet" him.

"Do you have any other good ones?" asked the judge.

The next morning, the defense called Sharon Elizabeth LaBlue, a computer tech manager from Nashville, who had had a one-night stand with Bill McGuire, two years before his murder. The defense investigators had tracked her down through the address book in the victim's BlackBerry, flying her in the previous night.

But prosecutor Patti Prezioso tried to prevent her testifying, telling Judge DeVesa that anything LaBlue had to say was "irrelevant and a waste of time."

"What we're getting to specifically, is the character of the deceased," she said.

But Joe Tacopina argued, saying it spoke directly to the state of their marriage.

"Judge," he said, "the State has made Ms. McGuire's fidelity a big part of this case, with much fanfare. There was trouble in the marriage. It was not a one-way street and [he was] not a husband that was happy. I think it puts in proper context the state of the marriage."

Judge DeVesa said there was some relevance to the witness's testimony, in context of Cindy Ligosh's testimony that he had had a one-night stand with a colleague.

"It's more appropriate to a soap opera than a murder trial," said the judge. "We're not going to get into all the juicy details."

The attractive brunette in a dark trouser suit with a religious gold medallion around her neck, appeared nervous and upset as she testified about a two-day business trip to New Jersey in October 2002. She said McGuire had been her contact on a work project with NJIT, and it had been a strictly professional relationship until the final day of her visit, when he took her shopping and sightseeing.

In a breaking voice, LaBlue said they had later had dinner together and drunk margaritas.

"After dinner," said Tacopina, "where did you and Mr. McGuire go?"

"Back to my hotel," she replied in a barely audible whisper.

"Back at the hotel, did you have sexual relations with Mr. McGuire?" he asked.

"Yes, sir, I did," she replied, visibly embarrassed.

In early 2003, she testified, Bill McGuire had called, suggesting they get together again.

"I asked him not to contact me anymore," she said, "and I recommended that he and his wife seek marriage counseling."

On cross-examination, LaBlue said that during their time together, Bill McGuire had talked about his marriage, even showing her a picture of his two small sons. Under Prezioso's questions, she said he had even taken her to a jewelry store, showing her a ring he intended to buy for his wife.

"It was a large purple stone," she said.

On re-direct, Tacopina asked if he had taken her to the jewelry store before or after having sexual relations with her.

"It was before," she said.

"So he talked about his wife before, and then went back to your hotel room and had sex with you?"

"Yes," she replied.

"He was a *nice* man, you say?" said Tacopina sarcastically, as Prezioso jumped to her feet to object.

Then Judge DeVesa excused the witness, and she rushed straight to the restroom, breaking down in tears.

Later that day, the defense called its computer expert, Jesse Lindmar, to discredit the prosecution's contention that Melanie McGuire had made incriminating searches on the home computer. The defense contended that the searches were in fact made by Bill McGuire, as part of his NJIT assignment to develop a computer system to alert New Jersey's twenty-one county health departments in the event of a bio-terrorist attack.

Lindmar testified that he had studied a series of computer entries, finding that several searches for "undetectable poisons," "how to find chloroform," and "suicide" had been conducted at the same time connections had been made with the victim's NJIT website with visits to Internet gambling and real estate sites. The defense argued that it would have been impossible for Melanie McGuire to access her husband's NJIT website, as it was password-protected.

Under Patti Prezioso's cross-examination, Lindmar agreed he could not say for certain who had been at the keyboard when the searches were made.

On Thursday, April 12, the final day of defense testimony, a heavy storm shut off power to the court, delaying the start of proceedings by an hour. There was great anticipation as to whether Melanie McGuire would take the stand in her own defense. When reporters tackled Joe Tacopina on his client's intentions, he jokingly stuck his tongue out at them.

Finally, when power was restored, the defense called Sally Ginter, a polymer expert who owned her own consulting company in Dearborn, Michigan. Ginter had watched the prosecution's trash bag expert Frank Ruiz testifying on Court

TV, immediately calling the defense and offering her services free of charge.

"I was outraged," she explained.

The middle-aged woman told the jury that Ruiz had made a mistake.

"If these bags are the same," she said, "the chemistry has to be the same. The most key thing I see is that there are chemicals from the victim's bag that aren't in the bags that came from the apartment."

Then Frank Ruiz, the prosecution's garbage bag expert, returned to the stand as a rebuttal witness. He maintained that Ginter did not understand certain chemical variations in the bags, as the bags used recycled materials instead of the "virgin" plastics she was used to.

"In my expert opinion," he said, "the bags matched. Case closed."

The final defense witness was Marci Paulk, who would only be allowed to testify about one e-mail. She told the court that she was now living in Pennsylvania with her new husband and children.

The heavyset woman said she had met Bill McGuire in 1980/1981 when they were at Vernon Township High School together. They had married in 1986.

"Did you get divorced?" asked Joe Tacopina.

"Yes, I did," she said. "1994."

"Was that divorce a joint application," asked the defender, "or did you do that on your own?"

"Objection," snapped Patti Prezioso.

"The objection is sustained," said Judge DeVesa testily. "I've already indicated, Mr. Tacopina, that the details of the marriage between this witness and Mr. McGuire are not relevant in these proceedings."

"No," said Tacopina, "I wasn't going to list that, Your Honor. OK. After you got divorced in 1994, did you maintain contact with Mr. McGuire?"

Paulk said no, but in early 2004 she had suddenly received an e-mail from him through Classmates.com, saying he was sorry for what he had done, and asking her to please contact him.

Judge DeVesa then cut her off, telling Tacopina to only elicit testimony from his witness not involving "inadmissible and irrelevant hearsay."

"And Miss Paulk," he said, "don't volunteer information. Just answer the questions directly."

"Did you reply to his invitation?" asked Tacopina.

"No," she replied.

"No further questions."

Then finally the moment had come when Melanie McGuire would announce whether she would testify.

"Miss McGuire," said Judge DeVesa, as the defendant rose to her feet at the defense table. "Counsel have informed me that they do not intend to call any additional witnesses in these proceedings. So we now arrive at the point in these proceedings where you ultimately have to make a decision regarding whether you want to exercise your right to remain silent and not testify, or whether you want to exercise your right to testify.

"Have you made a decision regarding whether or not you wish to testify?"

"Yes, Your Honor," she said in a soft voice.

"And what is your decision?"

"I wish to remain silent."

FORTY-SIX

"They Tape to Kill"

On Monday, April 16, 2007—the morning of closing arguments in the Melanie McGuire trial—a violent nor'easter ploughed through New Jersey, with acting Governor Richard Codey declaring a state of emergency. By the time Melanie McGuire and her parents arrived at 8:40 a.m., water was dripping through the ceiling outside Courtroom 506.

Five minutes later, Judge Frederick DeVesa came out to the corridor, announcing that court proceedings would be delayed.

"It's going to be a long time," he sighed. "The attorneys can't get in because they're stuck in flooding, and only two jurors have arrived so far."

Soon afterwards Cindy Ligosh, her husband Bill and children Max and Laura arrived, and were ushered to a waiting room at the other side of the building, well away from where Melanie McGuire and her parents were sitting. The defendant, wearing a smart brown coat and yellow jacket, looked confident as she joked around with Selene Trevizas and Alison LiCalsi, as well as taking time to make small talk with the various TV producers milling around her.

Joe Tacopina was also in good humor and raring to go, after driving two-and-a-half hours from his home in Connecticut.

"It's the most fun part of my job," he told Rick Malwitz of the *Home News Tribune*. "I started putting it together a year ago . . . I'm chomping at the bit."

At 9:15 a.m., Judge DeVesa came out again to announce that Route 18 was closed due to flooding.

"We will try and get started as soon as possible," he said. "I apologize."

Just after 10:00 p.m., Patti Prezioso arrived, looking exhausted, after a grueling four-hour drive, her black corkscrew hair even more unruly than ever. Judge DeVesa had set a ninety-minute limit for the prosecution and defense's closing arguments, but each side would talk for twice that long.

At 10:38 a.m., despite Jurors #9 and #14 unable to make it because of the conditions, Judge DeVesa asked Joe Tacopina to begin his summation.

In the front row, directly behind the defense table, were the defendant's friends and family—Michael and Linda Cappararo, and Selene and Alex Trevizas. Behind them, in the third row, sat the Ligosh family, Nancy Taylor, Jon and Sue Rice, and Jim and Lisa Carmichael.

Sitting behind the prosecution's table were task force investigators Detective Sergeant David Dalrymple, Detective John Pizzuro, Detective Jeffrey Kronenfeld, and Investigators Don Macciocca, JJ Janowiak and George Delgrosso.

"Good morning, ladies and gentlemen," he began, walking up to the jury box. "When we began this process—the date was February nineteenth, 2007—you started by filling out those lengthy questionnaires to determine if you all qualified to be jurors in this case. But that was an important date, February nineteenth 2007, because on that date—aside from all of us sitting here getting ready to pick qualified jurors in the trial of Melanie McGuire—something else significant was going on.

"On February nineteenth, 2007, the head of the New Jersey State Police Major Crimes Unit—the head—Detective Investigator Scull made a very important phone call. When you were being asked if you could sit in judgment of Melanie McGuire, Detective Investigator Scull, the head of the New Jersey State Police Major Crimes Unit North, was calling Lieutenant Bruce DeShields—the head of the Major Crimes Unit for the Atlantic County region. And he asked him, in

February of 2007, if William McGuire's murder was connected to another murder in Atlantic City in 2004.

"If that doesn't send shivers up your spines . . . As we're sitting here getting ready to judge her, they're trying to determine if William McGuire's murder is tied to another Atlantic City murder.

"If they have a reasonable doubt, ladies and gentlemen, how could they not ask you to? Could you really blame them? The state of this evidence, the state of this case is in shambles. And we're going to go through it. There is no proof that Melanie McGuire murdered her husband. She did not murder her husband. There is no proof."

Getting into his stride, Tacopina said that even circumstantial evidence must be conclusive, telling the jury that "if you add up a lot of zeros, you still get zero."

Calling the case "a tragic rush to judgment," Tacopina said the State had never investigated anyone but Melanie McGuire, failing to follow up on any leads.

Investigators, he said, had invented the theory that Melanie McGuire had an accomplice, because otherwise it would have been impossible for such a slightly built woman to have accomplished the killing and disposal of her far larger husband's remains.

He accused detectives of trying to trap her for more than a year, when they should have been searching for clues that would have led them to the real killer.

"[Bill McGuire] was a big gambler," said Tacopina. "He gambled beyond his means for a man who made sixty-five thousand dollars a year, and had to scrape to make that closing."

Melanie McGuire, he told the jury, was an innocent woman betrayed by Dr. Brad Miller and Jim Finn, the two men who loved her.

"Brad Miller told you he was furious," declared Tacopina. "Furious when Melanie McGuire was closing on the house. That was his testimony. We know that he lies to the police, when they first go to interview him about any relationship with Melanie, about being angry. As we discovered here at this trial, we now know he perjured himself in the grand jury to conceal his involvement with Melanie, as he was tape-recording her. He was tape-recording her and carrying on a relationship with her at the same time."

But, he told the jury, all the wiretapping attempts by the New Jersey State Police to implicate her in the murder had failed miserably.

"You heard her in her most vulnerable moments with her most trusted friends," he said. "Law enforcement put the screws to them, and they did what they had to do. But those conversations with Jim Finn and with Miller were unrehearsed, without the benefit of counsel.

"They questioned her—the police, law enforcement, the attorney general. They used the voice[s] of Jim Finn and Brad Miller, but they were Trojan horses. It wasn't Jim Finn and Brad Miller. It was their voices asking the questions . . . and Melanie was remarkably consistent throughout all those conversations.

"And you know, when law enforcement does these things, they do it to kill. They tape to kill. It's the ultimate law enforcement technique. And the calls were staged and concocted to trap Melanie at her weakest moment, her most vulnerable moment, with people that she trusted."

He also attacked the prosecution's claim that Bill McGuire had been killed at the Woodbridge townhouse, saying there was not a shred of evidence any crime had been committed there.

He said Virginia Medical Examiner Dr. Wendy Gunther had testified that, although only two bullets were recovered, the victim had been shot three or four times.

"[Bullets] don't just evaporate," he said. "They go into a wall or floor. They searched. They looked for that. They pulled tiles, everything. There was absolutely no gunpowder residue found in that apartment. There were no holes or any damage from bullets anywhere in that apartment."

His voice rising with passion, Tacopina said there had been five searches of the McGuires' apartment, with absolutely no evidence being found.

"There was no blood," he said. "There was no DNA evidence in this crime at all. There was no tissue at all—not in the drains, not in the pipes, not in the vents. Nothing. Not in the grout, not in the tracts. They pulled that place apart. They moved a family out of that house to search it again."

The fact that there were no saw marks in the bathroom tub or shower stall, he argued, demolished the state's contention that the victim had been cut up there with a reciprocating saw.

"It would be impossible not to have any marks on the tub," he said.

He also attacked the state's theory that the plastic trash bags found with the body parts had come from the Wood-bridge apartment. He said the chemical composition of the two sets of bags did not match, arguing that even if they were similar, they could have been in Bill McGuire's possession anyway, as he was in the process of moving house.

He also ridiculed the state's contention that his client had Googled topics like "undetectable poisons" and "how to commit—murder."

"The State cannot have it both ways," he declared. "They want you to believe that in one instance, Melanie was a master criminal—she got all the hard things right, the simple things she was just messing up. And on the other hand, she was stupid enough to leave a trail of breadcrumbs that a Boy Scout could follow. She gets a gun two days before her husband goes missing, in her name, but not a stitch of evidence of a murder or an accomplice. Why? Because she's a really good planner?"

He pleaded with the jury to make the right decision and free Melanie McGuire, and let her go home to her children.

"For two years her life has been on my shoulders," he said, turning around to point at his client, who was dabbing her eyes at the defense table, "and I'm about to turn it over to you. I'm going to ask you to deal with it well. Michael and Linda—Melanie's parents—have asked me to take care of their daughter in this time of need. And I've tried to do my best, and I hope I haven't worn your patience at all, but it's an important responsibility, and I want you to just please stop the injustice.

"Please let her go on with her life, get back with her family, kids, and move on. She's not guilty of this crime. She didn't commit these crimes—that is why the case is in the state it's in today. Thank you."

Joe Tacopina sat down at 1:38 p.m.—two hours and fifty-nine minutes after starting his speech.

Then Judge DeVesa asked Patti Prezioso how long her closing speech would take.

"I suggest I'll be just as long as Joe," she told him.

"It's an equal time issue?" asked the judge.

He then announced that the courthouse would close at 2:00 p.m. because of the storm, telling the jury to come back at 9:00 a.m. Tuesday morning for the State's closing argument.

At 9:50 the next morning, the fourteen remaining members of the jury entered the courtroom, filing past Melanie McGuire to take their places in the jury box. Straight in front of them, next to the court reporter's desk, the largest of the Kenneth Cole suitcases had been placed on the floor, a grim reminder of what had befallen Bill McGuire.

Assistant Attorney General Patti Prezioso began her closing argument a minute later. It would last exactly three hours, one minute longer than Joe Tacopina's.

"Good morning, ladies and gentlemen," she said. "If a stranger breaks into a house and efficiently kills the occupant, there's no reason to move the body. The murderer can leave it right there. The murderer doesn't have to move the body, because the murderer wasn't supposed to be in the house. The murderer need only to leave and the murderer's identity remains a secret.

"Not the case when the murderer is the wife of the victim. She must move the body so that the illusion is created that the murderer is someone else. She needs to put the body in a place where it would open up speculation that it could be someone else and that he could have conceivably gone there.

"She must also create the illusion that he is still alive, and she was behaving as if she believed he was still alive. This defendant did all of that. However the overwhelming evidence dispels all illusion. The evidence presented to you in this case presents an absolutely crystal clear picture of this defendant's participation in her husband's death."

She told the jury that McGuire had killed her husband at 2902 Plaza Drive so she could collect his assets, while avoiding losing custody of her two young children in a messy divorce.

"She knew her husband well," said the prosecutor. "She knew a divorce from him would not be easy. She wanted him dead . . . and she wanted to be the next Mrs. Miller."

Prezioso said that the defendant had decided murdering her husband was a better option than simply getting a divorce.

"The circumstantial evidence in this case overwhelmingly proves Melanie McGuire murdered her husband," she told the jury. "This was a complex plan executed by a very smart and meticulous woman. It's amazing we know as much as we do."

Prezioso said there was "a mountain of evidence" against her, asking the nine women and three men of the jury to convict.

She reminded the jury how the defendant was nine months pregnant, when she had oral sex with Dr. Miller in an office, embarking on a three-year relationship with him.

By the beginning of 2004, she wanted out of her marriage to Bill McGuire.

"She wanted to keep her children," said the prosecutor. "And she wanted the money out of the marriage, so she could have a life of her own."

Prezioso told the jury that Melanie McGuire had killed her husband before abandoning his car in Atlantic City. She had wanted to create the impression that he had fled the house, and then been murdered by someone else. The plastic garbage bags, she said, containing the victim's remains, matched ones from their townhouse. And, she told the jury, at least thirty-five minuscule pieces of his flesh had been trodden into his car by the defendant.

Then she used a PowerPoint presentation, showing jurors a detailed timeline of how the State believed the murder was committed.

Two days before the murder, she said, Melanie McGuire had

driven to Pennsylvania to purchase a gun and bullets, consistent with the ones found in Bill's body, after soliciting advice from her friend Jim Finn.

Then, on April 28, 2004, she had dropped her children off at day care, before stopping off at a nearby Walgreens, using a forged prescription to buy the date-rape drug chloral hydrate.

A few hours later, after the closing, Prezioso suggested, Bill McGuire was in a celebratory mood.

"I submit to you [he very] likely [had] a glass of wine," she said. "And it's very likely that his had an extra kick to it. And when he passed out that night and his eyes closed, he had no idea that his eyes would never see his children again."

She told the jury that they didn't have to believe that the "killing and cutting" took place in the townhouse in order to convict.

She attacked as unreasonable Melanie's story about finding Bill's car in Atlantic City but then forgetting where she parked her own car, taking a taxi to the Woodbridge train station and then remembering where she parked and taking a second taxi back to Atlantic City. First Prezioso explained that it made no sense for Melanie to have taken a cab from Atlantic City all the way up to Woodbridge when her mother and stepfather lived far closer, in Barnagat, and she reminded the jury that there was no record of her alleged cab ride back from Woodbridge to Atlantic City.

She then concluded that Melanie must have had an accomplice: "There were no cab rides," she declared, "and if there were no cab rides, then there was an accomplice. Because otherwise how did she get back to her own car?"

For the first time during the trial, she suggested the defendant's mother and stepfather had played roles in the homicide: "And does the State think that this defendant had help? Yes. Exactly how much help or what part she had assistance with remains unknown. We know that her father went with her to Atlantic City on those trips that were later disputed. She disputed them because she had to hide them. He was with her."

Michael Cappararo appeared shaken and started whispering to his wife. And Linda Cappararo started shaking her head in a pronounced manner when Prezioso suggested that she might have babysat her grandsons while Melanie drove to Virginia Beach: "The defendant picked up the kids. The grandmother of the children came up north. She went south. The children went into the grandmother's car and then the defendant goes through Raritan North, which all of us New Jerseyans know would put her right near the entrance to the N.J. Turnpike off the Garden State Parkway, where you could head straight out to Delaware Memorial Bridge and take Route 13 right down to the Chesapeake Bay Bridge."

Throughout the trial the State contended that the defendant had an accomplice, and this was the first time Prezioso had suggested who they might have been, although no one had been charged.

"Please follow the evidence," Prezioso said in closing. "Apply the law and let justice be done. Melanie McGuire participated in killing her husband. She possessed a gun for an unlawful purpose, she committed perjury and she is guilty of every count that she stands charged [of] before you. Thank you."

FORTY-SEVEN

Verdict

On Wednesday morning, after receiving final instructions from Judge DeVesa, who advised using "common sense," the nine women and three men of the jury filed out of the courtroom to begin deliberations. And though her fate lay in their hands, Melanie McGuire appeared coolly confident of the outcome.

Just an hour into deliberations, the jury requested the defendant's e-mails to Jim Finn regarding the purchase of the gun, as well as a complete list of all trial exhibits. Judge De-Vesa complied, sending the e-mails and exhibit list into the jury room.

For the rest of the day, McGuire, her parents, Alison Li-Calsi and Selene Trevizas waited patiently in the hallway outside Courtroom 506. Linda Cappararo passed the time reading her Barbara DeAngelis book while Joe Tacopina studied league soccer results in a daily Italian sports newspaper he subscribed to.

"This is the hardest part," he remarked.

At 4:00 p.m., when the judge dismissed the jurors for the day, McGuire, who remained free on $2.1 million bail, hugged her attorneys and left, looking upbeat as she and her parents breezed past the TV news crews and photographers, refusing to comment.

At 9:00 a.m. Thursday morning, the jury began a second day of deliberations. Ninety minutes later, they requested a second look at the grainy video, allegedly showing Melanie McGuire walking into the Passaic Rite Aid to buy the $50 American Express gift card used to mail the FedEx package to prosecutor Prezioso.

The jurors were then brought back into the courtroom to view the video. After watching it, the panel asked that it be paused on the shadowy female figure. Then several members of the jury got out of their seats, approaching the screen for a better look.

The panelists then returned to the jury room, and for the rest of the day, McGuire huddled with her attorneys in a conference room at the other end of the court. Then at 3:30 p.m. Judge DeVesa dismissed the jury, giving them the afternoon off, as he had other court business.

Later, Patti Prezioso would admit being anxious during the jury deliberations.

"When you have a circumstantial case," she said, "and you have a very physically beautiful defendant, who was becoming the media darling . . . There's a reason it's hard to convict celebrities, because jurors tend to give extra benefit to certain people, that I don't think the run-of-the-mill defendant gets."

At 1:00 p.m. on Friday, Judge Frederick DeVesa abruptly halted deliberations amidst concerns that certain jurors might have been exposed to "extensive media coverage" of the case. He announced that he would be interviewing each juror, as a result of unspecified reports he had received.

For the next several hours, the jurors came into his chambers one by one, to be questioned in the presence of all four attorneys. It would later emerge that some of the jurors had been reading an online Court TV blog of the trial by a woman named SummerMadness, who had been attending the trial daily, and giving her personal impressions of it. There had been some debate among the jurors about who the panel member with "hard eyes" was.

During Judge DeVesa's questioning, it was also revealed that Luann Bachetti, one of two jurors excused on Monday because of the bad weather, had left a note on the vehicle windshield of another female juror, who lived nearby:

I am praying for all of you today, that you will have the wisdom to do what is right.

Later the juror telephoned to thank her, promising to "be in touch" when everything was over.

"I'm just a very religious person," said Bachetti in a phone interview with the judge. "I prayed for help in making the right decision. I wasn't trying to get a message to her."

While the closed-door interviews were taking place, there was speculation that Judge DeVesa might declare a mistrial.

But at 4.30 p.m., DeVesa brought the jury back into the courtroom, apparently satisfied that the panel had not been contaminated. He then warned them to avoid any further conversations about the case, ordering them to tell friends and relatives not to discuss it.

He then dismissed them for the weekend. "I'm told the weather outside is beautiful," he said, "so I'll see you on Monday morning."

While the jury was weighing her fate, Melanie McGuire secretly recorded her first exclusive interview with ABC's *Primetime* for a special entitled "Sex, Lies and Secret Lives." It had long been rumored among reporters covering the trial that ABC would win the battle of the ratings, as Joe Tacopina had ties with the network. But, unknown to everyone, McGuire—who had refused to testify in court, apparently fearing cross-examination by Patti Prezioso—was still recording her nightly video diary for CBS's *48 Hours*.

There were also plans for her to write a book, once she was found innocent by the jury.

"It's indescribable," she told *Primetime* correspondent Cynthia McFadden. "This is the definition of terror. Absolute mortal terror."

"Did you murder your husband?" asked McFadden.

"No," she replied, staring straight at the camera without emotion.

"Did you shoot your husband?"

"No. No."

"Did you dismember your husband?"

"No," she said, suddenly bursting into tears. "Nor do I know who did. No matter how I felt about my husband, I could never have done this to my sons."

Then McFadden asked about Dr. Miller's testimony that they had first had oral sex when she was nine months pregnant.

"I'm so not proud of that," she admitted. "[It was] hard for me to hear it. Hard for me to think, 'Oh my God, my parents are hearing this. My eighty-four-year-old grandmother is hearing this.'"

Asked how she felt, watching her former lover on the stand, testifying against her, McGuire said she had thought, "How could you? How could you?"

"If you could go back in time," asked McFadden, "would you still have an affair with him?"

"I want to sit here and say no," said McGuire. "But I'm not going to be a hypocrite. The answer is yes. What he did to me wounded me mortally, but one thing that I am is candid and blunt. And the answer is yes."

McGuire said her decision not to take the stand in her own defense had been a hard one.

"If I were a juror," she said, "I would want to hear it from me. I would absolutely want to hear it from me, and I think that's human nature. If you don't have anything to hide, why aren't you getting up there and talking about it?

"But I hope that after being present in that courtroom for a number of weeks and hearing all of the testimony, that they would understand, perhaps, why I chose not to."

Finally, McFadden asked how she felt now, as the jury deliberated, her life hanging in the balance.

"It's frightening and it's terrifying," she replied. "And what I just keep clinging to is proof beyond a reasonable doubt, and that they have to be firmly convinced that I planned this and I did this."

Monday, April 23, was an unseasonably hot spring day, with temperatures expected to hit the mid-80s. During the seven-week trial, the weather had run the full gamut from snow and sub-zero conditions, to heavy storms and now an early summer.

When Melanie McGuire and her parents arrived at superior court for the fourth day of deliberations, she appeared cheerfully optimistic.

At 9:30 a.m. the jurors resumed their deliberations, but two hours later they asked the judge to define the word "purposefully." This led to some speculation among reporters that they were close to a verdict.

The jurors were brought back into court to be given a simple legal definition before breaking for lunch.

It was a beautiful day and Melanie McGuire, wearing a low-cut powder blue sweater, chatted with her parents and Selene Trevizas on a couple of benches, just a few yards from the white Court TV satellite van. She had a big smile on her face, and looked nothing like a murder defendant on trial for her life.

Soon after 1:00 p.m., deliberations resumed, and the waiting began again.

Then, twenty minutes later, there was a knock on the jury room door, and foreman Donald Adams handed Sheriff's Officer Willie Hernandez a handwritten note. After thirteen hours, fifty-seven minutes of deliberation, they had finally reached a verdict.

Hernandez took the note straight into the courtroom, handing it to Clerk of the Court Denise Hacker, who first informed Judge DeVesa before alerting the attorneys.

A few minutes later, as news of the verdict spread, Courtroom 506 began to fill up. There was a palpable change in the relaxed atmosphere, as a visibly emotional Melanie McGuire was brought into the defense conference room with her family and friends, to prepare for the verdict.

Court TV technicians positioned cameras and the two pool photographers took their places alongside the jury box. The interest in the trial was so high, the courtroom next door would relay the verdict on closed circuit television to the overflow.

Then the defendant was escorted in by Joe Tacopina and Steve Turano. She looked apprehensive, as if the full gravity of the situation had finally hit her. Her parents, half brother Christopher and several aunts and uncles sat directly behind her at the front row of the public gallery.

Sitting between her two attorneys, Melanie McGuire wept uncontrollably, and was comforted by Joe Tacopina, as she clutched a tissue.

Cindy, Bill, Laura and Max Ligosh, together with Nancy Taylor, then took their places in the third row next to victims' advocate Gail Faille, who had been at their side every inch of the way.

At 2:04 p.m., Judge DeVesa entered the court.

"I'm told the jury has reached a verdict," he said. "I'll ask you please not to express feelings of agreement or disagreement with the verdict. I know many of you have very strong feelings about this, but I'll just ask the jury to do its job."

One minute later, the jury entered the courtroom, solemnly filing past Melanie McGuire for the last time, avoiding her gaze. Judge DeVesa confirmed that they had reached a unanimous verdict, and the court clerk read each charge to the foreman, Donald Adams.

"Mr. Foreman," said Clerk Hacker, as Melanie McGuire stared helplessly at the jury box. "How do you find as to the count of the indictment charging the possession of a firearm for an unlawful purpose on or about April twenty-sixth, 2004, and on or about May fifth, 2004, in the township of Woodbridge, Middlesex County, New Jersey, elsewhere or within the jurisdiction of this court?"

"Guilty," said the foreman, as Melanie McGuire's eyes shut tightly, her shoulders sagged and Tacopina shook his head in disbelief.

"How to do you find as to the count of the indictment charging Melanie McGuire with the murder of William McGuire between, on or about April twenty-eighth, 2004, and on or about May fifth, 2004, in the township of Woodbridge, Middlesex County, New Jersey?"

"Guilty."

At the word "Guilty," McGuire fell apart. Her face crumpled as she began shaking, her head dropping onto Tacopina's shoulder.

"How do you find," continued Hacker, "as to the count of the indictment charging Melanie McGuire with desecrating human remains on or about April twenty-eighth, 2004, and on or about May fifth, 2004, in the township of Woodbridge, Middlesex County, New Jersey?"

"Guilty," said the foreman, as McGuire buried her head in her hands, sobbing uncontrollably into her tissue.

"How too do you find as to the count of the indictment charging Melanie McGuire with perjury on or about April thirtieth, 2004, in the City of New Brunswick in the County of New Jersey?"

"Guilty."

Then came the lesser charges.

"How do you find as to the count of the indictment charging Melanie McGuire with hindering prosecution on or about August eleventh, 2005, in the City of Trenton, Mercer County, New Jersey?"

"Not guilty."

"How do you find as to the count of the indictment, charging Melanie McGuire with hindering prosecution on or about October ninth, 2005, in the City of Passaic and in the City of Clifton, Passaic County, New Jersey, and in the City of Trenton, Mercer County, New Jersey?"

"Not guilty."

"How do you find as to the count of the indictment charging Melanie McGuire with tampering with or fabricating physical evidence, on or about October eleventh, 2005, in the City of Passaic in the County of Passaic, New Jersey, and in the City of Trenton, Mercer County, New Jersey?"

"Not guilty."

"How do you find as to the count of the indictment charging

Melanie McGuire with the possession of a controlled dangerous substance, that is Xanax, on or about October ninth, 2005, in the City of Clifton and the County of Clifton, New Jersey?"

"Not guilty."

Then after Hacker individually polled each juror, Judge DeVesa thanked them for their service and dismissed them. He then set sentencing for July 13, 2007, and, ignoring Joe Tacopina's pleas to allow her a couple of days' grace to say good-bye to her children, revoked bail, saying she was no longer entitled to the presumption of innocence.

"She stands convicted of a very horrible and brutal murder, that was carried out with a level of complexity and methodical detail," he said.

As she was helped up, Joe Tacopina cradled her in his arms, stroking her hair to reassure her. She looked at him blankly in stunned bewilderment, like a trapped wild animal.

Then, after one last lingering look at her mother and stepfather, two sheriff's officers led Melanie McGuire out of a side entrance, where she was handcuffed out of the view of photographers and taken away.

In the third row of the public gallery, Bill McGuire's two sisters clasped each other's hands tightly, holding back tears. Across the courtroom, Linda Cappararo sunk her head on her husband's shoulder, remaining there without visibly moving for the next thirty minutes, until Tacopino and Turano emerged visibly shaken from an emotionally charged meeting with their client. Then, after spending twenty minutes with their attorneys, the Cappararos and Selene Trevizas left through a back door to avoid the television cameras.

Later, Joe Tacopina gave an impromptu press conference to Court TV and reporters in the corridor outside the courtroom.

"This is round one," he declared defiantly. "Certainly she plans on fighting on."

Asked how his client was taking the verdict, he said not well.

"I told her to stay strong," he said. "There's a lot ahead of us and . . . it's tough. I'm not pretending she's not distraught and broken-hearted. She has two kids, who she fears she'll never see again. So she's very very crestfallen and distraught."

There were "real issues" for appeal, he continued. The defense had not been aware that Dr. Brad Miller had lied under oath to a grand jury—calling it a clear Brady violation. And he said the defense also wanted to know if the jury had been contaminated during the trial.

"The fight is a long one," he declared. "This really is the first leg of that fight, and I'm not going to be deterred. We will continue to fight for her exoneration. Period."

An hour later, at a press conference two blocks away at the Middlesex County Prosecutors Office, an emotional Cindy Ligosh addressed the media, noting that next Sunday would mark the third anniversary of her brother's murder.

"Today is a happy day for us," she said. "At the same time, it's a very sad day, because Melanie has left two children without a father or a mother."

Then Patti Prezioso walked up to the microphone.

"I'm very relieved," she said. "I do think the verdict does speak loudly. I feel justice was served."

But she refused to discuss whether there would be any further arrests in the case, merely saying that the investigation continued.

After leaving Middlesex County Superior Court, Melanie McGuire was transported to Middlesex County jail in North Brunswick, arriving at 4:00 p.m. Then, after undergoing a psychological evaluation, she was taken to a secret medical facility and placed on suicide watch. On Tuesday morning she was admitted to a state psychiatric hospital for observation and counseling.

"Right now they want to make sure she is not a threat to herself," explained Steve Turano. "It's not unusual when someone is looking at the sentence she is looking at."

And on Tuesday, Michael Cappararo had a brief telephone conversation with his daughter.

"I love you," he told her. "And we believe in you."

Then, after she whispered that she loved him too, the telephone call was cut off.

Later that day, Cappararo told *Home News Tribune* staff reporter Rick Malwitz that he and his wife were "outraged" by the guilty verdict.

"This is the worst moment of my life," Linda Cappararo told *48 Hours* several days later. "It was like a death hearing those words and seeing her face, and just knowing that these twelve people could think she killed her husband."

McGuire's friends and former RMA patients were also shocked at the verdict, many believing her to be a victim of a tragic miscarriage of justice.

"We all went into that courtroom believing she was going home," said her best friend Selene Trevizas. "So when the verdict came out, it was a complete shock."

Selene believes that Melanie's supporters may have underestimated prosecutor Patti Prezioso's powers of persuading a jury.

"She's an excellent speaker," said Selene. "She captivates. But we know the facts are there. I mean, they can't prove anything at all."

On a sunny Sunday, April 29—six days after the verdict—Cindy, Bill Ligosh and their children brought little Jack and Jason McGuire to their father's grave at the Brigadier General William C. Doyle Veterans Memorial Cemetery in Wrightstown. They brought colored balloons to the graveside, symbolically letting them soar into the afternoon sky in memory of Bill McGuire.

Cindy announced plans to exhume her brother's remains and give him a proper funeral, instead of the abbreviated one Melanie McGuire had insisted on. She said she felt "tortured" every time she visited his grave, looking down at the inscription, which still read "Beloved father and husband."

"We want to rip it out with our bare hands," she declared, saying she had contemplated placing masking tape over the offending word, but thought it disrespectful to the cemetery.

Her daughter Laura, who had sat in the public gallery for

the entire trial, said the defense had assassinated her uncle's character.

"Seven weeks of lies, lies, lies," she sobbed. "It was horrible, frustrating, to have to listen to that day after day, and not to be able to say anything."

FORTY-EIGHT

Who Is the Real Melanie McGuire?

On Tuesday, May 8, Melanie McGuire was discharged from
the Ann Klein psychiatric center to Middlesex County Adult
Correction Center in North Brunswick, where she would remain until sentencing. Five weeks later, she was back in Judge
Frederick DeVesa's courtroom, after her attorney had filed
motions to have her conviction overturned.

The hearing came the day after Father's Day, and Michael
Cappararo was complaining about visiting his stepdaughter in
jail. He now had to talk to her via telephone through a heavy
Perspex glass screen.

"She's looking down, I'm looking up," he said sadly outside
the courtroom before the hearing. "She's just missing her children."

Regina Knowles, who had visited her several times since
the verdict, said McGuire was not doing well.

"She was a skeleton of the Melanie that I knew at that
point," she said. "Emotionally, there was so much missing.
There was so much gone. Having lost her children I think was
the hardest hit of all."

When McGuire, in handcuffs, wearing a regulation green
jumpsuit and no makeup, was brought into the courtroom by
two armed guards, she looked a pale, haunted shadow of herself. But she managed to smile weakly at her parents, and
friends Selene Trevizas and Alison LiCalsi, who were in the
first row behind the defense bench.

"There were extraneous influences in the jury [and] it denied Miss McGuire a fair trial," said a tanned Joe Tacopina. "I objected to live coverage . . . as I was concerned about people seeing things on television."

Tacopina cited SummerMadness and other Internet blogs, saying they had given a "scathing analysis" of his client, and were highly prejudicial.

He also expressed concern that an excused juror had left a note on another juror's car before deliberations, saying it could have influenced the verdict.

Judge DeVesa ruled that after his interviews with each juror on the Friday of deliberations, he was satisfied none of them was influenced by any of the media coverage.

Then Steve Turano argued for a new trial, saying the State had not proved beyond a reasonable doubt that Bill McGuire had been murdered and dismembered in the Woodbridge townhouse. He said the State's case lacked motive, and, despite five searches of the apartment, no blood, DNA or tool mark evidence had been produced.

Judge DeVesa rejected his argument, saying he believed the jury had been able to make the inferences they needed to make.

"This was a well-planned and well-executed criminal episode," he said, as the defendant looked on blankly, "with volumes of concealment that had no direct evidence where it took place. This episode spanned almost four states and involved poison and surgically made cuts to William McGuire's body."

Later, during the lunch break outside the court, a playful Joe Tacopina joked around with reporters.

"We'll be filing a motion at the end of the day," he teased, without elaborating. "And getting ready to duck."

And true to his word, at the end of the hearing, Steve Turano stood up and dropped a bombshell. He announced that a witness had come forward, claiming to have "crucial" evidence that Bill McGuire had owed the mob $90,000.

Turano said the witness, a prison inmate serving a 7-year-sentence, could provide testimony supporting the defense theory that mobsters had executed and disposed of Bill McGuire's body.

"He was working for known members of crime families in Philadelphia and south Jersey," said Turano.

He said the mystery witness, a bookkeeper who had worked for several organized crime families, had seen Bill McGuire arrive for a meeting with a loan shark in April 2004. At the end of the meeting, the capo had told him to put McGuire down for $90,000.

Turano told the judge that the witness had picked Bill McGuire's photo out of a lineup at a jailhouse meeting. He had also taken a sworn statement, which would be filed with a sealed motion for a new trial.

Joe Tacopina then addressed the judge, saying that inmates offering the authorities information usually do it in exchange for a lesser sentence.

"What can we offer him?" said the attorney, adding that the witness should remain anonymous, as he would be in "serious jeopardy" if his name became public.

Visibly angry, Patti Prezioso stood up.

"Judge," she snapped, "can we talk in your chambers?"

On Tuesday, June 26, ABC broadcast its one-hour *Primetime* special on the Melanie McGuire case. As she sat alone in a jail cell, contemplating her fate, millions of viewers heard her protest her innocence.

"I know why I'm sitting here," she told Cynthia McFadden. "It doesn't mean that I did it though."

Filmed just days before the verdict, at her parents' home in Barnegat while she was out on bail, McGuire claimed that if she were going to "fabricate a story," she would have done a far better job.

"The bottom line is, 'Am I an angel? Am I a perfect person?' Absolutely not. But does that make me a sociopath, or a liar?"

Two days later, McGuire's defense team filed a motion demanding a new trial, in light of the new witness who claimed to have witnessed Bill McGuire borrowing $90,000 from the mob.

"The State will be opposing this motion," said Patti Prezioso. "We remain confident in the jury's verdict."

On Tuesday, July 17—a week before sentencing—Melanie McGuire's hopes for a new trial were dashed when the bombshell defense witness turned out to be a fraud. An investigation by the New Jersey State Police had discovered that 27-year-old Christopher Thieme, who had been convicted of beating a young woman with a pool cue, had a long history of telling fanciful lies to anyone who would listen.

In the past he had claimed to have been related to King Charlemagne and eighteen American presidents, as well as boasting of connections with the Irish Republican Army.

"The state's investigation revealed that Thieme is entirely incredible," read a twenty-four-page prosecution reply to the defense motion.

After detectives interviewed Thieme in jail, he recanted his story, now claiming that attorney Steve Turano had promised him McGuire's parents would help him with his appeal and financially compensate him if he falsely testified on her behalf.

"It's laughable," said Turano, confirming that the defense had withdrawn its new trial motion. "It's absolutely false."

Joe Tacopina said he'd had a duty to file the motion after hearing Thieme's claim.

"It seemed to be graphic and detailed information," he said. "What this guy did was despicable."

The afternoon before she was due to be sentenced for the murder and dismemberment of her husband, Melanie McGuire gave a dramatic interview to CBS's *48 Hours* from the Middlesex County Adult Correction Center. Wearing a pink blouse with no make-up, she looked tortured, now facing the rest of her life in prison.

"It's absolutely indescribable," she sobbed. "The hell for me, the hell for my family. This is my life now. This is what I have to deal with. I can't make anybody believe, who's convinced that I've done this, that I didn't. All I can continue to do is tell the truth, and it's not the most flattering truth. But it's the truth."

At 8:00 a.m. Thursday, July 19, 2007, the line outside Courtroom 506 started forming. An hour later, when the court officers opened the doors, they first allowed family members, press representatives and investigators who had worked on the case to come in. But eventually more than one hundred spectators, including three members of the jury, packed the public gallery to witness the spectacle. Members of the press, including blogger SummerMadness, were seated in the jury box.

When assistant prosecutor Patti Prezioso walked in sporting a smart new pageboy haircut, she caused quite a stir.

"I just decided to do it," she announced.

At 9:25 a.m. Michael Cappararo walked into the courtroom with his son Christopher, and Selene and Alex Trevizas. Melanie McGuire's mother Linda had stayed at home to look after her two little grandchildren Jack and Jason, as she had a visitation.

A few minutes later, victims' advocate Gail Faille brought in Bill and Cindy Ligosh and their children Laura and Max, followed by Jon and Sue Rice, and Jim and Lisa Carmichael, taking their seats in the third row behind the prosecution bench.

At 9:50 a.m., two armed female guards brought in a manacled Melanie McGuire, wearing a loose-fitting green jail uniform. Her eyes were red from crying, and she looked pale and lethargic, making several reporters wonder if she was sedated.

After first officially withdrawing the motion for a new trial, Joe Tacopina asked Judge DeVesa to give his 34-year-old client a minimum 30-year prison term, saying that she would be appealing the conviction.

"The best we can walk out with today is a sentence of thirty years without the possibility of parole. That's an enormous sentence and I find myself asking for a sentence like that for Melanie McGuire.

"We in no way, shape or form agree with this verdict. We in no way, shape or form apologize for her conduct. She did not commit this crime. We all sympathize with the family of William McGuire. And make no mistake about that. He is a victim and they are victims, but Melanie McGuire and her family are victims as well."

Previously the defense had given Judge DeVesa a "realm of

literature" from friends and family, all pleading for the most lenient sentence. But the only one to address the judge was her friend Alison LiCalsi.

"I can honestly say she's not the woman depicted by the prosecution, the media and the Internet blogs," she told Judge DeVesa, as McGuire sobbed into a tissue. "That creation, that fiction, bears no resemblance to Melanie."

LiCalsi said that Melanie had chosen the nursing profession to help others, and that even in jail, she had tutored a high school dropout, as well as helping a woman kick heroin addiction.

"I stand here today profoundly sad," she said, "but also deeply proud and honored to call Melanie McGuire my friend."

Judge DeVesa thanked her, saying he had read all the letters from her supporters and would consider "their comments and remarks."

Prosecutor Patti Prezioso then rose to her feet to deliver her final address to the court, arguing that Melanie McGuire should get the maximum sentence.

She told Judge DeVesa that even after seven weeks of the trial, the court had still not heard everything about the defendant.

"Your Honor," she said, "the evidence showed that Melanie McGuire is someone who kept secrets from her family and friends. A secret affair that Your Honor is aware [of], not with just one man, but with two, during her short marriage to Bill McGuire.

"This is a defendant who puts on a face and shows persons before her whatever it is she wants to show. And as I stand here today, as a prosecutor who has investigated the case for three years, I don't know who the *real* Melanie McGuire is."

Then Bill McGuire's niece, Laura Ligosh, got up and walked over to a podium in front of the jury box, to give the first of three victim impact statements.

"When I remember my uncle," she began, her soft voice breaking with tearful emotion, "the first thing I see is a water-logged suitcase. The suitcase is open, filled with black plastic trash bags. The bags are pushed aside and I see two long pale objects. These objects are a man's legs. No body, no face. Just parts. And I recognize these legs. These are my Uncle Billy's legs. And we used to tease him endlessly about the silly shorts he loved to wear, proudly parading the vast majority of his chubby, pasty, white Irish legs for all the world to see.

"When I remember my uncle's wedding, I don't see a handsome, happy man in his natty black tuxedo, a spring in his step. I see a diagram of a body that has been horribly desecrated and carved up into parts small enough to fit in three little suitcases.

"The family and friends of Billy McGuire will suffer his loss for the rest of our days, while his heartless murderer stands only to suffer the loss of her freedom. All we can ask is that you take her freedom, as she took our Billy's."

Then Jon Rice stood up, telling the judge how he would never be able to forget viewing "gruesome pictures" of his friend's bloated face to identify him.

"Those hideous images will forever be burned in our memory," he said. "I will never have another best friend like the one I found in Bill."

And he urged the judge to sentence Melanie McGuire to the maximum sentence possible for her crimes.

Cindy Ligosh then stood up to deliver the eulogy to her brother that she had never been allowed to make at his funeral. She lamented the military-type burial service, saying there was no Mass, no casket and not even a priest in a church. Unfortunately, she told the judge, the setting for his eulogy will be a "courtroom with his killer present."

"I would like to ask Your Honor to let her sentence reflect the gravity of the crime she has committed," she said. "She's a cold-blooded killer who has taken a valuable life. She has no soul, and she cannot be rehabilitated.

"Please don't make her children suffer anymore, knowing that someday the woman who took their father from them may be free and want to reenter their lives. Don't give her the opportunity to harm these children again. Make that decision for them.

"This woman has displayed an inappropriate haughty arrogance for three years. And since she has committed this crime, she has not shown one ounce of remorse, shame or compassion.

"Give a sentence that will wipe that arrogance off of her face. Never let her have hope. We have no hope. She had no pity, show her no pity. She showed no mercy, give her no mercy. She alone passed sentence on her husband and her sons. And she chose for them a life sentence, and I ask you, on behalf of our family, to give her a life sentence in return."

Then Judge DeVesa asked Joe Tacopina if the defendant wished to make a statement before he imposed sentence.

"No, Your Honor," said the attorney.

Imposing sentence, Judge DeVesa said the "depravity" of her crimes simply shocked the conscience of this court.

"The nature and the complexity and the scope of this criminal episode," he said, as the defendant sat weeping at the defense table, "involved many, many overt actions committed over a three-week period, spanning four different states, and reflected a willfulness and a malice that goes far beyond the elements of the crime of murder in our law.

"The desecration of William McGuire's remains was particularly heinous and depraved. His body was treated as trash. It was cut and sawed apart and then packaged in garbage bags. His remains were left to decompose in the waters of another state without identification, so that his family and friends might always be deprived of a dignified funeral service and burial.

"The depravity of the murder was further manifested by the efforts on the part of the defendant to portray William McGuire as an abusive husband and a chronic gambler who was indebted to organized crime figures, as part of her attempt to shift the blame for his murder to others.

"History is replete with evildoers who have done some good deeds, and they also have their supporters. She callously murdered her husband, and even joked about his death in intercepted phone calls.

"In this case, the crime was so heinous, so cruel and so depraved, that the court finds that the maximum sentence should be imposed."

And he sentenced her to a term of life imprisonment for the first count of murdering her husband, meaning she will be almost 101 years old when she is eligible for parole under New Jersey law. On count two, for illegally possessing a firearm, he sentenced her to 10 years, to run concurrently with the life sentence. And on the third count of the desecration of human remains, she was sentenced to another 10 years, also to run concurrently. She also received 5 years for perjury, which he merged with the first two counts.

As Melanie McGuire was led out of the courtroom, to spend the rest of her life behind bars, her cousin John Moran angrily shouted, "The lies that you created will not stand," at prosecutor Patti Prezioso.

Outside the courtroom, Joe Tacopina said he was looking ahead to the appeal.

"This marks the end of phase one," he declared. "Phase two starts now . . . We're ready to roll."

Epilogue

After sentencing, Melanie McGuire was taken to the Edna Mahan Correctional Facility in Clinton, New Jersey, and placed in a high security cell. Prisoner #000319833C joined eighty other female inmates in the maximum security wing of the prison, known as the "max max" section.

Her new home would be a six-by-nine-foot cell with a bed secured to the floor, a sink and toilet and a standing locker. She is allowed a television, and may make collect calls that are automatically cut off after twenty minutes.

She can have visitors three times a week, and Selene Trevizas is a regular.

"She's really OK," Selene said three months after sentencing. "Her biggest fear is her kids. She's supposed to speak to them every single week . . . she hasn't spoken to them once. She's written letters to them, but she doesn't know if they are being read."

Cindy Ligosh is still fighting in Family Court for full custody of Jack and Jason McGuire, who have both been examined by doctors and found not to be autistic. They have now settled into their new lives with the Ligosh family, and have moved on.

"They don't ask about their mother, thankfully," said Cindy. "They continue to see their grandparents."

In September 2007, Patti Prezioso resigned from the New Jersey Office of the Attorney General to become a partner in the private practice of McCusker, Anselmi, Rosen & Carvelli. Detective Sergeant First Class David Dalrymple was awarded the prestigious New Jersey Trooper of the Year award for his work on the Melanie McGuire case.

In March 2008, Jamie Kilberg of the Washington D.C.–based legal firm Baker Botts, who is handling the appeal, said everything was presently in a "holding pattern," while the trial transcripts were being prepared. Once he received them, he said, he would start drafting the appellant brief.

"I speak with her on the phone," he said. "She seems to be adjusting well."

In the American legal system, a criminal defendant is presumed innocent until proven guilty beyond a reasonable doubt by a jury of his peers. In this case, a jury rendered its verdict of guilty, ultimately accepting the prosecution's theory that Melanie McGuire killed her husband, Bill.

A convicted defendant is entitled under American law to appeal his conviction in an effort to overturn the jury's finding of guilt. As of going to press, Melanie McGuire's appeal has not yet been resolved.

CPSIA information can be obtained
at www.ICGtesting.com
Printed in the USA
LVHW050913250821
696066LV00002B/180

9 781250 025876